THE SHAPE OF
BRITISH HOUSING

E. R. Scoffham

GEORGE GODWIN London and New York

George Godwin
an imprint of:
Longman Group Limited
Longman House, Burnt Mill, Harlow
Essex CM20 2JE, England
Associated companies throughout the world

*Published in the United States of America
by Longman Inc., New York*

First published 1984

British Library Cataloguing in Publication Data
Scoffham, E. R.
 The shape of British housing.
 1. Architecture, Domestic – Great Britain
 – History
 I. Title
 728.3'0941   NA7328

 ISBN 0-7114-5797-2

Library of Congress Cataloging in Publication Data
Scoffham, E. R. (Ernest Rowland), 1939–
 The shape of British housing.
 Bibliography: p.
 Includes index.
 1. Housing – Great Britain. 2. Architecture,
Domestic – Great Britain. I. Title.
HD7333.A3S32   1984   363.5'0941   83-8892
ISBN 0-7114-5797-2 (pbk.)

Set in 10/12pt Linotron 202 Bembo
Printed in the United Kingdom by
The Pitman Press Ltd, Bath

CONTENTS

Acknowledgements   iv

Introduction   1

1 Ample gardens and tree-lined roads   4

2 Prairie planning   17

3 Neighbours and cars   27

4 Brave new world   51

5 City of towers   59

6 Streets in the air   79

7 The alien casbah   99

8 Trojan horse   129

9 Intervention   142

10 Compromise   163

11 Basic shapes   195

12 Xenophobia   218

References   233

Bibliography   239

Index   242

ACKNOWLEDGEMENTS

Many people have contributed in different ways to the outcome of this work; but had it not been for the intervention of the late Professor Jack Napper at the end of my final year at King's College, Newcastle, in inviting me to become involved in the expanding housing work of his practice, none of it would have happened. It is to him that my first thanks must be addressed. His integrity, however, would not allow that acknowledgement to pass without the inclusion of Alec Collerton and Bill Barnett, during what were heroic and formative years. Professor John Tarn encouraged the initial research upon which this work is based and to him go my thanks alongside those to the Royal Institute of British Architects who granted me a Research Award which helped finance this venture. The work would have remained unrealised had it not been for the further intervention of George Godwin and the Longman Group Ltd, in particular the patient editing of Stuart Macfarlane and Bobbi Gouge, and without the valued contributions of Lynne Bellamy, assisted by Renata Loj and Sue Pinkett, who typed the manuscript; and Liz Haynes, assisted by David Young, who prepared the list of References; all of them of the University of Nottingham. Glyn Halls of the Department of Architecture must be given a special mention for photographing and processing the diverse array of illustrative material under trying conditions. Credits for original photographs are given throughout where applicable.

Ernest R. Scoffham,
Department of Architecture
University of Nottingham

22 February 1983.

PUBLISHER'S NOTE

We have been unable to trace the copyright holders of Figs 1.2, 3.3, 12.8, 10.22, 10.23 and 10.25 but would be grateful for any information which will enable us to do so.

For Charles and Emma, so that the circle might be complete.

When Pentagruel sailed thither from France and had got into the main ocean, he doubled the Cape of Good Hope and made for the shores of Melinda. Parting from Me'damoth, he sailed with a northerly wind, passed Me'dam, Gelasem, and the Fairy Isles; and keeping Uti to the left and Uden to the right, ran into the port of Utopia, distant about three and a half leagues from the city of the Amaurots.

From *Utopia*, by Sir Thomas More, 1516.

Me'damoth	—	from no place
Me'dam	—	nowhere
Gelasem	—	hidden land
Uti	—	nothing at all
Uden	—	nothing
Utopia	—	no place
Amaurots	—	the vanishing point (all from the Greek)

INTRODUCTION

A number of studies has been made of housing finance, housing politics, the government of housing and so forth, while others have supported the advantages of a particular approach, either sociological, administrational, financial or architectural. In the main, architectural studies have been concerned with images of a world that might be attained if only the world would catch up with their thought processes, or, alternatively, they have been a laudatory record of past achievements. None of them have appeared to be concerned with the development of housing design solutions over a period of time so that motives might be related to achievements in an evolutionary manner – for what appeared to be appropriate in one year might not have been so a couple of years later. In retrospect it seems that a number of alternatives have been continually available, when in fact they have only been relevant to a particular stage in time when events were such as to make them attractive.

This study then is historical. It is about a period since the end of the Second World War that has seen considerable changes in social customs and has witnessed complex technological advances, both being inextricably linked, and which in turn have influenced thinking about the provision of appropriate housing. It is a study about the architecture of housing, but limited to the manner in which the dwelling has been viewed in a town-making context; that is, the built form, or shape, of housing. It is not concerned to give an exhaustive coverage of social or political aspects nor is it concerned with individual house planning, aesthetics or architectural detailing except where these have affected built-form solutions. It is also a study about mass housing – about the provision and assembly of dwelling units, by others, for an anonymous population, and does not deal with the individual one-off dwelling where the occupant has a far greater control over the outcome of his habitat. It is particularly concerned with the lessons to be learned from achievements in Britain, but embraces, as it must, both public and private sectors of housing provision.

Hence what will be discussed is the manner in which those responsible for the shape of housing have seen their role in providing a setting for the lives of ordinary people – people who have had, until very recently in post-war affairs, little say in the creation of their environment. In this ordained position of townmaker and organiser of human settlements the environmental professions have sought and devised patterns – frameworks within which society would follow a civilised way of life. That they have so often failed in this task will also be discussed.

Much of post-war housing thinking by architects originates from two distinct Utopian views of the town by Ebenezer Howard and Le Corbusier. Both strove to provide that civilised framework, but whereas Howard's was a social argument Le Corbusier's was an architectural one. Events since the Second World War demonstrate that, at least in the public sector, housing is predominantly a social service; and that Howard's Utopia is, for Britain, nearer the mark than Le Corbusier's ever was – for Le Corbusier provided visual images (after all he was an architect) and images are more convenient tools to grasp than are social theories. They are particularly convenient for architects who have to translate idea into reality; and here lies the dilemma of post-war housing architecture. The translation into reality of Howard's view, by many after Raymond Unwin, provided an image that architecture found lacking and consequently it hung its hat on the more exciting visual images of Le Corbusier. Howard's social Utopia became submerged under the highly visual Utopia of Le Corbusier. Social meaning was lost, and ever more complex technical imagery was devised to correct the balance, until society itself seemed to say enough: enough of these social disasters, these technological wonders so prone to failure, these Utopian dreams, this one-sided visual perversity. Those who had the ability, through greater affluence, to choose their own housing, plumped for the speculative products of Howard's Utopia. Those for whom housing was a service, who could not so exercise their choice, found instead their voice, and architecture was left out in the cold.

In this situation it is argued that further Utopias are useless, that evidence indicates an historical regression, a pushing back of the clock to times when built form was representative of the hopes and aspirations of individuals, to a time when architecture provided a service to society rather than a package for it. It will be shown that three distinct trends in built form indicate this regression: the evolution of a kind of domestic vernacular, possibilities for greater individual choice, and a realisation that most of the fundamental criteria upon which post-war land use and built form have been based are false. This reshuffling of values could bring about the reintroduction of built forms that traditionally answered the problem of urban growth before the population and industrial explosions of the nineteeth century caused a desire to control size. But for architecture to have a part in this it too must change, it must be seen to solve basic problems, not provide glossy envelopes for other more serious ones, become less concerned with images and more with realities, and above all, respect society, as an accumulation of individuals, for all its banal and distasteful views, for society will in the end judge, just as it has done in the aftermath of Corbusian hysteria.

In including projects to demonstrate the evolution of built form one is wary of providing merely a catalogue; schemes are chosen because they appear, as far as can be traced, to provide a significant influence in architectural thinking. There are undoubtedly many more projects in similar vein or have similar objectives to those chosen. But before analysing in some detail the development of built form since the Second World War a necessarily brief review must be made of events leading up to, and during, the war, in order to, as it were, set the scene – a scene that provided, as a backdrop, a pattern of housing that has survived criticism and time to be looked at today as something more desirable, familiar and British.

1 AMPLE GARDENS AND TREE-LINED ROADS

By the beginning of this century the industrial towns of Britain had become accretions of chaos superimposed on an existing pattern of country lanes; they were choked by repetitive gridiron streets of terraced workers' houses, skewered by the lines of clanking railways and asphyxiated by the belching industry which was both their cause and their effect. The town was in an appallingly noxious, noisy, insanitary and unhappy state.

A few industrialists had been notable for their concern not to add to this scene of urban squalor. Robert Owen had attempted model industrial villages in Scotland in 1816, while Titus Salt had built Saltaire in the 1850s to embody his view of urban morality and J. S. Buckingham's idealistic Victoria of 1848 was never realised. At Cadbury's Bourneville in 1878 and at Lever's Port Sunlight in 1888 these ideals were developed into a theme of workers' cottages around village greens, which evoked something of the rural manufacturing and marketing town tradition that had been the urban framework for generations before the population explosions of the industrial revolution had destroyed an innate ability to comprehend growth and size.[1]

Opportunities for social progress in the face of this oppression were developed by writers such as John Ruskin, Henry George and Edward Bellamy, who appeared more influential than either Cadbury or Lever in stirring Ebenezer Howard to document his own ideas for a route out of the prevailing inhumanity in 1898.[2] *Tomorrow, A Peaceful Path to Real Reform* made no attempt to adapt the existing conurbations; instead it proposed a fresh start on comparatively virgin land to produce a city in a garden, an amalgam of the advantages of both town and country, and in 1902 it was renamed *Garden Cities of Tomorrow*. 'Each generation should build to suit its own needs, and it is no more in the nature of things that man should continue to live in old areas because their ancestors lived in them, than it is that they should cherish the old beliefs which a wider faith and a more enlarged understanding have out-grown.'[3]

In his book Howard painted a picture of boulevards leading to a central park around which were public buildings, of a 145-acre (58.6 ha) public park containing recreation grounds, of a glazed-over shopping arcade and, above all, of tree-lined streets of houses with ample gardens.[4] It was an image that had a far-reaching effect on future housing and planning in Britain, and indeed elsewhere in the world.

The route to its realisation was far from easy. Both sides of the political fence ridiculed it on publication – 'merely fantastic', 'futile and impractical'.[5]

However, there was enough support around for Howard to form the Garden City Association in 1899, and in 1901 he managed to attract the influential Ralph Nevill, later Mr Justice Nevill, as its chairman and Thomas Adams as its secretary, together with other people from industry and public life who were to increase its influence, and among whom were George Cadbury and W. H. Lever.[6] The determination of the Association resulted in the registration of a pioneer company and to the eventual purchase, in 1903, of a 3,818 acre (1,545 ha) site in Hertfordshire, about 35 miles (56 km) from central London, which was to become the first garden city – Letchworth.[7] The Association needed plans in order to start building; Howard needed someone to translate his images into realities. Two architectural firms were asked by the pioneer company to compete in the preparation of sketch plans: Hasley Ricardo and Professor W. R. Lethaby who were well established, and Barry Parker and Raymond Unwin of Buxton who were then relatively unknown,[8] but who in 1901 had published a book on the layout of building estates[9] which illustrated in practical terms something of Ebenezer Howard's vision. In the event the plans of Parker and Unwin were selected for implementation. Interestingly the competition was financed by Rowntrees who in 1902 had asked Parker and Unwin to design their model village at New Earswick. In his book Howard had in mind a municipal authority which would control the overall pattern of building, one which would guide development according to a set of rules and permit harmonious variation from them in order to allow ample opportunity for 'individual taste and preference'.[10] Parker and Unwin, on the other hand, sought a compromise between rows of houses and detached villas, and wished to prevent 'discordant colours or style of building' by giving an appointed architect controlling powers similar to those of an estate landlord.[11] This discrepancy of outlook was to account for much of what followed. Parker and Unwin were concerned with architectural control of the parts of the town, rather than on Howard's social concern for the working of the town as a whole. It is from this divergence of views that the garden suburb movement arose, a movement which succeeded in submerging Howard's argument for planned new towns until it surfaced, of necessity, during the grim years of the Second World War.[12]

Raymond Unwin did not remain involved for long at Letchworth. By 1907 he had become committed to his own suburban creation at Hampstead and in 1914 he retired from architectural practice, but certainly not from influence. The firm's architectural work at Letchworth was continued by Barry Parker until he in turn retired in 1943.[13] Letchworth became a focus of attention for those concerned with urban reform from many parts of the world. Quite naturally their attention was diverted by what was to be seen in terms of layouts and housing standards rather than by the less tangible social advances of the town's origins.[14] Thus Unwin became influential despite his short period of involvement at Letchworth. His arguments were persuasive in the face of less well informed, non-technical and instinctive opponents. They were concerned with matters of detail and not of content, of 'picturesque gables and hand-made tiles'.[15] The result of this was that

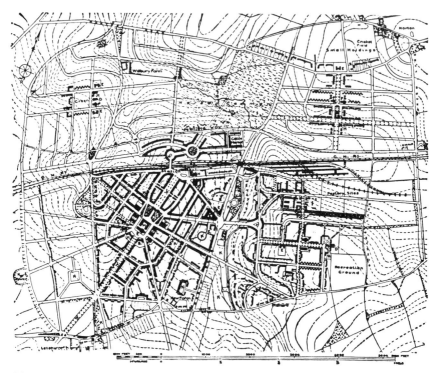

Fig. 1.1 Parker and Unwin's original 1903 plan of Letchworth (*from The Letchworth Achievement by C. B. Purdom, J. M. Dent and Sons*)

Letchworth grew without a controlling plan, by a process of accretion that had typified the nineteenth-century town it had been the intention to remedy. Nevertheless the physical contrast between the resultant environment and the pervading reality of the existing conurbations was Letchworth's achievement. The individuality of most of the houses, however variable the quality, their gardens, and the grass verges and trees lining the surrounding roads, were undoubted advances and welcome pleasures.[16]

In 1901, while Howard was publicising his ideas to gain support for his garden cities, Unwin had published a pamphlet advocating that there was 'nothing gained by overcrowding'.[17] This was an economic argument to show that through the building of unnecessary roads money had been wasted and had taken away much of the land that could otherwise have been used for garden space, because of a false premiss that the close proximity of houses reduced cost. To counter this he advocated no more than 12 houses to the acre (30/ha), a standard which he introduced at Letchworth and which he was later to see enshrined in public housing legislation in 1918, when he was Chief Architect to the Ministry of Health. Howard, on the other hand, had no such limitation of density in mind. He wrote that the average size of a plot should be 20 ft by 130 ft (6 × 39.5 m), and the minimum 20 ft by 100 ft (6 × 30.5 m).[18] When roads were allowed for this gave a density of 17–18 houses to the acre (42–45/ha), which Lewis Mumford has maintained was the density of the traditional town before overbuilding caused overcrowding.[19]

Unwin's apparent incomprehension of the nature of planning is to be found again in his famous *Town Planning in Practice*,[20] which appears as an expansion of the influential theories of Camillo Sitte for the establishment of a system of 'organic town building',[21] and which has been criticised as being 'intellectually incomplete' in its lack of appreciation of the perennial dilemma to control, yet to permit, individual choice.[22] Thus through a series of misunderstandings Letchworth led to the proliferation of the garden suburb and not to further garden cities as had been the Garden City Association's intention.

Simultaneous with Howard's campaign, developments were taking place in transportation through technical advances in electric power and the internal combustion engine, and the resultant mass transportation systems aided and abetted the fungoid sprawl of suburbs in ever-widening circles around the existing conurbations.[23] It was natural, therefore, that a garden suburb movement should come into existence with the intention of promoting the development of suburban estates on 'garden city lines'. Indeed in 1914 the then Secretary of the Garden City Association was moved to comment that these suburbs had nothing in common with the movement except the name which had been 'dishonestly appropriated', and that they were schemes of 'speculation, exploitation and jerry-building' promoted from a false premiss.[24]

Unwin's Hampstead was one of these suburbs, and an influential one. For Londoners it was easier to go to Hampstead, described as the second project on garden city lines, to see what Letchworth was like, than it was to go to Letchworth itself. Consequently Hampstead gained a higher place in the public mind than the real garden city.[25] In fact Hampstead's houses were much better, and were more consistently laid out, than those at Letchworth. Building lines were maintained and groups of houses arranged around culs-de-sac as architectural and social groups, and in short terraces, to improved standards of design and detailing. The social objectives of Dame Henrietta Barnett and the co-partnership methods of Hampstead's tenants considerably facilitated this outcome, and visitors at the time saw something far better in terms of design and management than the parent garden city movement had so far been able to achieve. Indeed, if they did appreciate this, it is doubtful whether they would have done so without the undeniable attraction and reputation of Raymond Unwin.

Unwin's reputation made him one of the most influential members of the Tudor–Walters Committee,[26] established in 1917, which reported on 24 October 1918, for in the Committee's report were to be found many of the standards he had already advocated for densities, for layouts and for the design of houses – standards which had been partly implemented at Letchworth and more rigorously at Hampstead.

The Tudor–Walters Committee had been established to find out the housing requirements of ordinary people and how these might be achieved, and it was implemented through the tremendous publicity given to 'Homes Fit for Heroes' at the end of the First World War. Its recommendations were

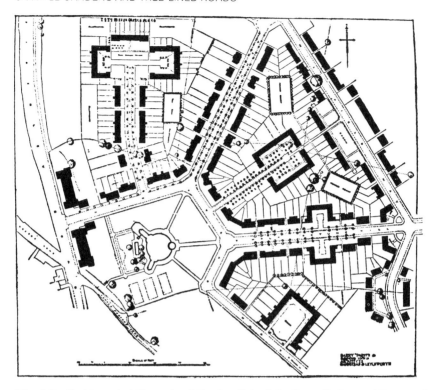

Fig. 1.2 Part layout of Hampstead Garden Suburb by Barry Parker and Raymond
Unwin (*from Town Planning in Practice by R. Unwin, Benjamin Blom Inc*)

those which are, in the main, readily accepted today: among them a third
living-room, a separate bathroom and three bedrooms, a maximum of 12
houses to the acre (30/ha) and a minimum spacing between facing houses of
70 feet (21 m). These were undoubted improvements on nineteenth-century
working-class housing standards and they became, at the same time, both the
image and the reality of social aspirations for the ordinary person.

These standards were written into legislation through the 1919 Housing
Act which provided subsidies for speculative housing built in accordance with
them.[27] The Act remained as the basis for all municipal and speculative
housing during the inter-war years. It provided for an environment and an
aspiration in contrast with the two-roomed slum that had been impossible
of attainment a few years earlier.[28]

From the point of view of the Garden City Association, the 1919 Act was
about the worst thing that could have happened,[29] for in popular eyes it had
been imagined to be a measure in favour of garden cities, none of which it
produced. The Act's intention was to produce, to tremendously improved
standards, as many houses as could be built in a short space of time. Its
legislators had resisted all suggestions that the garden city might provide the
basis for a national housing policy. Howard had mounted a propaganda
campaign for the building of fifty garden cities, and a National Garden Cities

Committee was formed. In an attempt to gain support for its ideas the Committee published in 1918 and 1919 to no avail.[30]

Yet mainly as a result of personal initiative by Howard the year 1919 saw the foundation of Welwyn Garden City.[31] This was the only other town besides Letchworth to be established in accordance with the motives of Howard and the Garden City Association until after the end of the Second World War. During the inter-war years a few measures that recognised the existence of the garden city movement did find expression in legislation due to pressure from the National Garden Cities Committee. A section of the Housing (Additional Powers) Act of 1919 gave the Minister powers to acquire land for the building of a garden city project that met with his approval,[32] and in 1921 power was granted for the advancement of loans to develop garden cities.[33] This latter measure proved to have some benefit to Welwyn Garden City but nowhere else. Welwyn's achievement during the inter-war period was that it carried on and developed techniques of house groupings, street and cul-de-sac layouts and architectural detailing from Letchworth and Hampstead, in what was to become a familiar and consistent idiom of pitched roof, rough cast walls, green paint and water butts, amid ample gardens and tree-lined roads.[34]

Yet the boost to house-building that had been given by the 1919 Act saw huge new projects. The confusion that resulted from the Act in the meaning of 'garden city' and 'garden suburb' meant that it was only with difficulty that the title of garden city was prevented from being attached to the London County Council's vast Becontree Estate.[35] Started in 1919 Becontree covered 2,770 acres (1,121 ha) and by 1941 it had become the largest public housing estate anywhere in the world. Manchester City Council, under the chairmanship of E. D. Simon (later Lord Simon of Wythenshawe) commenced, in 1926, the building of what it called a town on 2,568 acres (1,039 ha) just outside the city boundary in Cheshire.[36] Yet the Wythenshawe estate was a suburb of Manchester despite the inclusion of local industry and social facilities. Liverpool City, too, appropriated the name 'garden city' and used the title 'satellite town' for its suburban extension at Speke. Recognition of these misunderstandings came in 1946 when the Minister was compelled to refer to them all as 'suburbs of their respective cities' when he introduced the New Towns Bill to Parliament.[37]

In 1931 the then Minister of Health, Arthur Greenwood, acting upon a report to the London Regional Planning Committee by Raymond Unwin which advocated with some urgency the setting up of satellite towns, established a departmental committee under the chairmanship of Lord Marley to examine experience to date about garden cities, villages and satellite towns and to make recommendations.[38] While this committee was deliberating, the Comprehensive Town and Country Planning Act was passed in 1932, and this remained in force until the 1947 Town and Country Planning Act. It established planning on an entirely new basis and was the first serious attempt to be constructive about town planning problems.[39] Meanwhile events were further accelerated by Trystan Edwards' suggestions for new towns

42

Fig. 1.3 Layout of Sherwood Estate; City of Nottingham housing built 1921–27
(*Cecil Howitt and Partners*)

throughout Britain in 1933.[40] The Marley Committee reported in December
1934 in somewhat schizophrenic manner. It advocated adoption of the type
of development usually associated with the idea of a garden city, yet went
on to say that once a town reaches a certain size further growth should take
the form of complete and separate planned units. Interestingly enough it also
rejected ideas for higher building and increased densities. Gradual realisation
of the benefits of new towns, of decentralisation, and of a national planning
and housing policy was dawning. In 1936 the London County Council
considered a proposal for building satellite towns, a policy which the Labour
Party had officially adopted since 1918, and in 1934 had again advocated as
part of an attack on slums.[41] In the event the proposal was not pursued.

   The continuation of policies for massive house-building programmes, so
relevant at the end of the war, throughout the 1920s and 1930s had disastrous
effects. The insistence on large gardens and low densities had increased
residential land consumption unbelievably. The new suburbs were immense,
one-class housing estates – municipal estates for the working classes and specu-

Fig. 1.4 City of Nottingham housing of 1926–28; Lenton Abbey Estate by Cecil Howitt (*E. R. Scoffham*)

Fig. 1.5 Speculative housing at Uplands Estate, Southampton, by Herbert Collins in 1921 (*John Ford*)

lative estates for the lower middle classes. Results in architectural terms were appalling, and in totality as monotonous and repetitious as the nineteenth century by-law streets they were intended to improve upon.[42] Yet almost 4 million families had been rehoused between the end of the First World War and the end of March 1939 and this represented about one-third of the total population of England and Wales at the time.[43]

Increasing concern about the expanding growth of London caused the Prime Minister, Neville Chamberlain, to appoint a Royal Commission in 1937 under the chairmanship of Sir Montague Barlow.[44] Among its members were Professor Patrick Abercrombie, and Mr G. Parker-Morris. The Committee was instructed to investigate the distribution of the working population. It reported unanimously in December 1939 that national action was necessary in order to decongest urban areas and advocated a policy of decentralisation in which garden cities were to be included. Patrick Abercrombie pointed out the deficiencies of planning legislation in order to bring some of the proposals to fruition, in a dissentient memorandum. This report was a source of information on the whole problem of town planning and housing and was published on the 31 January 1940, by which time Britain was at war, and on the 7 September 1940, London received the first impact of the blitz.

In October 1940 Lord Reith was appointed Minister of Works and Buildings, with the optimistic instruction to study the problems of post-war reconstruction. He assembled a group of advisers from government, academic life, industry and the professions whose task was to plan the future. The outbreak of war had caused wholesale decentralisation of population, schools and industry. The bombs had finally put away any lingering arguments there might have been against decentralisation. 'Not since the Great Fire of London has there been such an instant desire to see a new London, more spacious, more beautiful, more worthy of the heroic people who inhabit it rise from the desolation'.[45] Little attempt had been made between the wars to relate housing to other aspects of living. The Garden City vision had degenerated into a sprawling housing estate movement, while in the town centres sanitary but inhuman high-density flatted blocks had increased urban concentration.

Despite this misfortune, the influence, persistence and pressure of those who had understood Ebenezer Howard's principles had at last made their mark in the publication of the Barlow Report. Its contents had to be regarded seriously by Lord Reith and his advisers for the errors it had exposed could now no longer be disputed.[46] In January 1941 Lord Reith took action by appointing a committee on compensation and betterment as recommended by Barlow, and chaired by Mr Justice Uthwatt. This committee reported in August 1942, recommending the nationalisation of development rights in land to facilitate reconstruction,[47] but no action was to come of it until the post-war Labour Government dealt with land betterment as part of a general policy.[48]

In 1941 Lord Reith appointed another committee under the chairmanship of Lord Justice Scott to look at the problems of building in rural areas. The committee recommended acceptance of the original ideas of the garden city movement, and made an attempt to define green belts as a means of permanently separating these new self-contained towns from their parent conurbations.[49] Earlier, between 1935 and 1938, the LCC had made proposals for a green belt round the city but this nominal attempt was made irrelevant by the wartime halt on house-building. Only later did Patrick Abercrombie make more practical proposals in conjunction with a general plan for the location of new towns.[50] This plan was contained in two reports which were prompted by the desolation of London by German bombs. The influence of the garden city movement was recognised in the 1943 County of London Plan[51] which was prepared for the LCC by its then Chief Architect J. R. Forshaw and Professor Patrick Abercrombie. Abercrombie had been appointed by Lord Reith in August 1942 to prepare a plan for the London region and this was published as the Greater London Plan in 1944.[52] Here was a comprehensive survey of an area of 2,599 square miles (6,731 km²) and an argument for the development of satellite towns was one of its major themes.

The official mind had at last grasped the importance of decentralisation and of its realisation by way of garden cities. Abercrombie's intention was to discourage further growth within the London region and to redistribute what was already in existence to improved standards, in general following the Barlow Report's recommendations.[53] Four concentric rings of land use were proposed: the inner suburban ring of nineteenth-century building from which there was to be decentralisation, the suburban ring which was to be regarded as fully built-up, the encircling green belt of about 5 miles (8 km) in width, and the outer ring in which the decentralised population would be accommodated in eight new towns.[54] Abercrombie instanced Letchworth and Welwyn as models for these new towns, and praised the foresight of Ebenezer Howard. As an example he prepared a detailed study of one of his proposed new town sites for comparison with what he suggested was the success at Welwyn Garden City.[55] No action on this report was taken by the wartime Coalition Government except that it asked local authorities to consider the contents. The Government did, however, reject the idea of a central planning authority as Abercrombie had advocated, but in the event town planning was detached from the Ministry of Health as a separate Ministry of Town and Country Planning.[56]

The end of the war saw an end, too, to the wartime Coalition Government. A general election brought the Labour Party to power with an absolute majority over all other parties for the first time ever in Britain. Under Clement Attlee it pledged to realise the visions and the dreams for a future society that had spurred the nation forward during the dark years just ended.[57] One of its first tasks was to reorganise the planning system. The existing planning Acts of between 1909 and 1932 were deemed to be ineffective for the task ahead, but the Coalition Government's Act of 1944 which included a 'ceiling price' for land at 1939 levels was felt to be adequate to control the danger of immediate speculative profiteering.[58]

However, new legislation was needed to deal with the overspill problem. The Greater London Plan recommendations of Patrick Abercrombie were accepted in principle as the basis for this new legislation. In October 1945 the Minister of Town and Country Planning, Lewis Silkin, appointed an advisory committee chaired by Lord Reith to consider the establishment and administration of new towns as balanced communities, following a policy of planned decentralisation. For although the idea of new towns was now well established no firm decisions had been reached as to how they might be financed and administered. The urgency of the task resulted in the committee producing three reports in quick succession: in January, April and July 1946.[59] Practically the entire contents of these reports were based on studies of Letchworth and Welwyn. Entirely new towns were favoured but the extension of older towns was not excluded. A target population was established of from 30,000 to 50,000, and a development corporation was recommended to be established for each site. Among its tasks was the provision of houses.

The New Towns Committee found that the Government had taken action before its final report had been signed. Indeed, Lewis Silkin had introduced the New Towns Bill to Parliament eleven weeks before. It became law one week after the date of the committee's final report, on the 1 August 1946,[60] and only a week after the Act received royal assent the Minister announced the proposal for the first new town at Stevenage.[61]

The Government then proceeded to review the entire town planning machinery which was necessary to deal with the problems of compensation that were holding up rebuilding. Previous legislation was repealed by the Town and Country Planning Act of 1947,[62] and the nationalisation of development rights in land was adopted, though modified from the manner Uthwatt had proposed in his report.[63]

The war years of 1939 to 1945 saw unprecedented, unhappy and unimaginable changes. Socially as well as technically it was a watershed. The desire now was for a 'new society', a fresh basis for a better future.[64] A mould had now been cast which could provide for the construction of that future. Lord Reith's committee had set out the task ahead 'to avoid the mistakes and omissions of the past. Our responsibility . . . is rather to conduct an essay in civilisation, by seizing the opportunity to design, solve and carry into execution for the benefit of coming generations the means for a happy and gracious way of life'.[65] Nevertheless on its route through Parliament the New Towns Bill attracted the lone prophetically critical voice of Viscount Hinchingbrooke in a statement that encapsulated the mistakes and omissions of the future in that it would, 'lead us into gigantic schemes of construction which are impossible of attainment in a free society' and he went on to pity 'the men, women and children who will be enticed into chromium-plated soulless homes'.[66]

REFERENCES

1. C. and R. Bell, *City Fathers*, 1969.
2. C. B. Purdom, *The Building of Satellite Towns*, 1949 edn p. 27.
3. E. Howard, *Garden Cities of Tomorrow*, 1945 edn, p. 146.
4. Ibid., p. 54.
5. F. J. Osborn, in Preface to E. Howard, op. cit., p. 11; *Fabian News*, Dec. 1898.
6. Ibid., p. 12.
7. Ibid., p. 12.
8. C. B. Purdom, op. cit., p. 86.
9. R. Unwin and B. Parker, *The Art of Building a Home*, 1901.
10. E. Howard, op. cit., p. 54.
11. R. Unwin and B. Parker, op. cit.
12. C. B. Purdom, op. cit., p. 88.
13. Ibid., p. 91.
14. F. J. Osborn, op. cit., p. 13.
15. C. B. Purdom, op. cit., p. 102.
16. Ibid., p. 103.
17. R. Unwin, *Nothing Gained by Overcrowding*, 1901, (repr. 1912).
18. E. Howard, op. cit., p. 54.
19. L. Mumford, in *Introductory Essay* to E. Howard, op. cit., p. 32.
20. R. Unwin, *Town Planning in Practice*, 1909.
21. Camillo Sitte, *Der stadte-bau nach seinen künstlerischen Grundsätzen*, 1889.
22. C. B. Purdom, op. cit., p. 102.
23. F. J. Osborn, op. cit., p. 15.
24. E. G. Culpin, *The Garden City Movement Up to Date*, 1914 edn.
25. C. B. Purdom, op. cit., p. 41–2.
26. Sir J. T. Walters, *The Provision of Dwellings for the Working Classes*, 1918.
27. Housing Act 1919 (Addison Act).
28. G. and E. G. McAllister, *Town and Country Planning*, 1941, p. 66.
29. C. B. Purdom, op. cit., p. 181.
30. F. J. Osborn, W. G. Taylor and C. B. Purdom, *New Towns After the War*, 1918; National Garden Cities Committee, *A National Housing Policy*, 1919.
31. F. J. Osborn, *New Towns After the War*, 1942 edn.
32. C. B. Purdom, op. cit., p. 363–4.
33. Housing Act 1921.
34. F. J. Osborn, *New Towns After the War*, p. 14; C. B. Purdom, op. cit., p. 59.
35. C. B. Purdom, op. cit., p. 43; G. and E. G. McAllister, op. cit., p. 115.
36. C. B. Purdom, op. cit., p. 46.
37. Ibid., p. 47.
38. Ibid., p. 366; *Report of the Departmental Committee on Garden Cities and Satellite Towns* (Marley Report), 1935.
39. C. B. Purdom, op. cit., p. 43.
40. A. T. Edwards, *A Hundred New Towns for Britain*, 1934.
41. C. B. Purdom, op. cit., p. 47.
42. J. Tetlow and A. Goss, *Homes, Towns and Traffic*, 1965, p. 28.
43. G. and E. G. McAllister, op. cit., p. 114.
44. *Royal Commission on the Geographical Distribution of the Industrial Population* (Barlow Report), Cmnd 6153, 1940.

45. G. and E. G. McAllister, op. cit., pp. 168–9.

46. C. B. Purdom, op. cit., p. 368.

47. Lord Justice Uthwatt (chairman), *Report of the Expert Committee on Compensation and Betterment* (Uthwatt Report), Cmnd 6386, 1942.

48. C. B. Purdom, op. cit., p. 369.

49. *Report of the Committee on Land Utilisation in Rural Areas* (Scott Report), Cmnd 6378, 1942.

50. C. B. Purdom, op. cit., pp. 369–70.

51. J. R. Forshaw and P. Abercrombie, *County of London Plan*, 1943.

52. P. Abercrombie, *Greater London Plan*, 1944.

53. C. B. Purdom, op. cit., p. 370.

54. P. Abercrombie, op. cit.

55. C. B. Purdom, op. cit., pp. 372–3.

56. Ibid., p. 374.

57. F. Schaffer, *The New Town Story*, 1972, p. 31.

58. Ibid., p. 33.

59. Lord Reith, *First Interim Report of the New Towns Committee*, Cmnd 6759, 1946; *Second Interim Report of the New Towns Committee*, Cmnd 6794, 1946; *Final Report of the New Towns Committee*, Cmnd 6878, 1946.

60. New Towns Act 1946.

61. F. Schaffer, op. cit., p. 38.

62. Town and Country Planning Act 1947.

63. Uthwatt, op. cit.

64. H. Bruckmann and D. L. Lewis, *New Housing in Great Britain*, 1960, pp. 9–10.

65. Lord Reith, *First Interim Report of the New Towns Committee*, op. cit., p. 4.

66. Quoted by F. Schaffer, op. cit., p. 37.

2 PRAIRIE PLANNING

Lord Reith's intentions 'to avoid the mistakes and omissions of the past'[1] were spelled out in the New Towns Act.[2] A major objective was the desire to prevent the atmosphere of the housing estate despite it being obvious that large housing schemes would be required both in the new towns and in existing cities to deal with the now urgent housing shortage. Even in Letchworth and Welwyn Garden City, certain parts of these towns had been recognisable as housing schemes while others were seen as the product of 'middle class' or private enterprise building.[3] The monotony of these vast schemes was properly objected to, but in addition, and with an enviable logic, the Act saw a solution to the differences between 'working-class' and 'middle-class' areas in the building of what it called 'middle-class houses'.

The New Towns Act said that approximately 340 acres (137.5 ha) should be the land area for a unit of 10,000 people. This was a density of 29.4 persons to each residential acre (72.6/ha) including roads and small open spaces, and was just over Unwin's rural area limit of 8 dwellings to the acre (20/ha) on the basis of 3.5 people per dwelling. Thus, the Act went on, in apparent ignorance of the relativity of density and urbanity, 'compact development is envisaged'.[4]

Yet as if to counter this, the adverse effects of taking averages when designing houses were recognised in that a variety of house sizes was seen to be necessary for 'there are no average people'. Research was admitted to be necessary on the subject of dwelling sizes, but in establishing standards the Act felt that each new town should devise its own, to which all those building in the town should conform. Then it added a word of warning, that standardisation, 'should not be tolerated for its own sake' as it could easily 'become a substitute for work and thought'.[5] Individuality and personal feelings should be allowed expression, with standardisation being practised only when it was relevant. Sameness and monotony were seen as the dangers.

The Act sought a more scientific basis for housing, and pursued this in looking for the intellectual reasoning for each town's plan throughout the town, from its master plan, through its neighbourhood plan, to the plan of the individual house. It was here that it directed the most constructive critical attention be given, so that the architectural and planning results would be consistent.

As these were broad general intentions, something more practical was required to bring them to reality. In 1944 the Burt Committee had established seven basic constructional requirements for the individual house.[6] These were: strength and stability, resistance to fire, resistance to vermin infestation, durability and ease of maintenance, freedom from damp, adequate thermal insulation and adequate sound insulation.

This was rapidly followed by recommendations on standards of space and equipment, and on aspects of house layout, in the Dudley Report of 1944.[7] Lord Dudley's findings were based on the defects of the kind of inter-war housing that had resulted from the Tudor-Walters Report of 1918.[8] A greater variety of house size and type was of prime importance. Space standards should be increased, particularly in the kitchen areas to accommodate extra equipment, and a better provision of outbuildings for cycles, tools and fuel was required. Changes in internal planning arrangements were advocated, which in general were functional ones designed to offer better-shaped rooms for the activities and kind of furniture that had to be accommodated. They included the provision of access from all main rooms to the hall and landing areas, the desirability for stairs with direct light and ventilation and an upstairs bathroom which was not to be located above living-rooms for reasons of sound transmission.

In the 1930s domestic standards had been increasing rapidly due to the development and subsequent acquisition of items of specialist equipment and fittings. Central heating was a topic of debate yet solid fuel for the traditional open fire was often inadequately stored. Water was now heated by a space heating appliance or by the cooking stove, and the greater availability of gas and electricity for domestic consumption had led to a decline in the use of solid fuel for cooking. Kitchen fittings were on the increase and equipment had been developed for home laundry. Lord Dudley made recommendations to deal with the space required for this new-found affluence.[9]

Methods of meeting the Dudley Report's recommendations were described and illustrated in the *Housing Manuals* of 1944 and 1949.[10] Three basic house types, as distinct from house sizes, were proposed in both Manuals: the kitchen–living-room house, the working-kitchen house and the dining-kitchen house.

In dealing with questions of housing layout Dudley commented that, 'too often in the past the most that was hoped for of a council housing estate was that it should be unobtrusive'.[11] The inter-war years had seen concentration on standards of amenity and equipment. Aspects of appearance and of the overall environment had in general been secondary considerations despite the efforts of the garden city and suburb enthusiasts. Houses were a tremendous advance on previous working-class standards. The 'home of one's own', levels of comfort and the creation of some 4 million new gardens were the major achievements in popular eyes.[12] However, neither the Dudley Report, nor the 1944 *Housing Manual*, made any constructive suggestions regarding layout techniques. Dudley attributed bad planning to a reluctance to employ architects. The same kind of idealism for increases in space standards that had followed the First World War seemed to be occurring again.[13]

Nevertheless the problem of improving the visual aspects of housing estates was given some attention by a subcommittee of the Central Housing

Advisory Committee in 1948. This report[14] dealt particularly with ways of improving the appearance of already existing housing estates but most of the advice it contained was also relevant to the design and layout of new estates. Its major preoccupation was the creation of openness in the layout. The defects of the majority of older terrace housing: darkness, noise and lack of privacy, were of prime concern to the Committee and this reflected a universal view at the end of the war. In extremely low key it recommended that high front fencing be removed and replaced with a low type backed with flowering shrubs, and that rear gardens should be given improved privacy by a hedge division and a stub-wall or fence, about 8–10 feet (2.4–3.0 m), long, on the line of the party wall.

In the following year the 1949 *Housing Manual*[15] took up this openness theme and related it to new housing. A greater degree of openness in layout could be achieved by including bungalows and a few three- or four-storey blocks in a predominantly two-storey family house estate, the *Manual* recommended. It also advocated the introduction of these different housing units to provide incident, emphasis and focus both architecturally and socially.[16]

The 1949 *Manual* increased space standards for the average three-bedroomed house to 900–950 square feet (83.6–88.3 m²) and was more specific about the sizing of different rooms than was the 1944 *Manual*. But it was in the manner in which different house types could be grouped that the *Manual* was progressive. To give continuity of building form the linking of pairs of houses by means of their outbuildings was recommended, as was the use of gable ends rather than the more usual hipped roof. Access to the rear of houses was thought best through a covered passage preferably serving a pair of houses, or alternatively a way through the dwelling itself, in which case special refuse disposal arrangements would have to be made.[17]

Broad-frontage houses, both terraced and semi-detached, were recommended to give 'greater architectural continuity' than narrow- frontage houses. In an attempt to avoid the claustrophobia of inter-war flatted estates daylighting was dealt with at some length, particularly at higher densities where it was felt that blocks might get so close as to obstruct one another. Terraced houses were advocated particularly for housing in urban areas and it was here, in retrospect, that the 1949 *Manual* was remarkable in making a special effort to commend the three-storey terrace house for areas of higher density 'such as in the 100–120 zones', because it 'enables an urban character to be given to the development'.[18] Yet on the question of density generally, a gross density for the new towns and other outer areas was stated as 30–40 people to the acre (74–99/ha): only in the existing congested areas would it be higher, in which case 60 per acre (148/ha) should be the maximum.[19]

In reality, however, things were very different. The first task at the end of the war was to deal with an extreme shortage of houses. A temporary house programme was initiated[20] to take advantage of mass-production techniques that had been developed during the war, particularly in the aircraft industry, and to overcome the sad fact that the labour force of the country was depleted. The result was a series of standardised prefabricated single-storey houses that were erected on available sites, often those created by bombs, as temporary accommodation until more permanent homes were made available. Little opportunity was seen in using the potential of industrial production for permanent houses at this time. Lord Reith's comments on standardisation, referred to earlier, seemed to be at the root of this apparent blind spot. The temporary house-building programme lasted until 1948 by which time the permanent house-building programme was felt to be sufficiently advanced. Nevertheless there are still a few towns in Britain with an area of 'prefabs' awaiting replacement almost forty years after the end of the war.[21]

Immediate housing needs were the first priority and it was the local authorities that were authorised by the Labour Government to take the major responsibility. Subsidised houses were made available for all incomes and these were to be allocated according to priority on an authority's waiting list.[22] In 1945 only 3,000 permanent dwellings were completed, by comparison with the average rate between 1934–39 of 350,000 per year, and by 1947 the programme had expanded to 140,000.[23] The private developer was severely restricted in this programme by the Government. A licence had to be obtained for private building and the granting of this was controlled until the end of 1949 by a fixed selling price, and after this date by a 1,500 square foot (140 m^2) maximum space limit. Consequently, between 1948 and 1952 80 per cent of all house-building was by local authorities.[24] As a way of recognising the need for subsidised housing for all incomes the Labour Government omitted the term 'working class' from the 1949 Housing Act. The public authority advance into post-war housing was reinforced in the 1946 and 1949 Housing Acts and the 1944 and 1947 Planning Acts as well as by the 1946 New Towns Act.[25]

Consequently for a period of some 10 years after the war houses were built by local authorities to satisfy the general shortage and they were built as quickly as possible on almost any available site. The appalling slum clearance and bomb-damaged areas of the inner cities were put aside while the more urgent task of creating homes was tackled.[26] Most of these houses and their layout were poor. Little design work had of necessity been done since 1939 and many authorities as well as most private builders resumed operations where they had finished. The system of building licensing meant that throughout the country individual permissions were sought for thousands of individual houses, predominantly bungalows, to designs of the 1930s, and where inevitably there was little consideration for site or for context.[27] The semi-detached house, in layouts little changed from those of the 1930s, became the product of local authority housing and, indeed, it has remained so for many of them. Despite the pressure of the *Housing Manuals* it was inadequate in architectural terms, and it provoked Gordon Cullen to coin the term 'Prairie Planning' in 1953, to describe the result.[28] 'Prairie' sprawl was countered in London by early high-density post-war LCC housing under J. H. Forshaw's direction as chief architect, but this was a relatively small proportion, and in a different context, when compared with the amount of low-rise suburban housing elsewhere.

A census in 1951 revealed the same deficit of homes to households as in 1931. The housing situation continued to be desperate and a balance of payments crisis, an aftermath of the war, was a main political issue. An economy drive was necessary. The, by then, Conservative Government, for the nation had been somewhat disillusioned by Labour's inability to produce their far-reaching and radical promises quickly enough, had to do something. Harold Macmillan, as Minister of Housing, advocated adoption of a 'People's House', of no more than 900 square feet (84 m²) for a three-bedroom house equipped only with essentials.[29] Despite the earlier example of the 1949 *Housing Manual* for a wider use of terraced houses little had been done except in a few higher-density schemes. A by-product of this crisis was the more general adoption of the terrace, and its substitution for the ubiquitous 'semi'. Two publications in 1952 and 1953[30] provided the example, and as a result local authorities were compelled to take advantage of the economies inherent in the terraced house.

One of these publications, *Houses 1952*, indicated wider use of the through living-room thereby giving a greater degree of flexibility in orientation. There were problems in the adoption of terrace houses particularly regarding fuel and refuse, and a greater circulation area was needed when a deep plan was used on a narrow frontage. But the density advantages, and the reduction in costs of drainage, roadworks and services were of more importance to the economy drive. Tunnel access to rear gardens decreased in popularity as it was unsuitable to a narrow-frontage house and alternative front servicing arrangements became necessary.[31] In a bulletin issued by the Ministry of Housing in 1952[32] methods were illustrated of achieving a 30 per cent increase in density by using narrow-frontage houses, especially in terraces. It was realised that for reasons of spacing according to sunlight, daylight and privacy criteria, variations in block depth made little difference, whereas frontage variations increased densities considerably.

Harold Macmillan's objective was 300,000 houses per year. In 1952 the figure was 240,000, in 1953, 320,000 and in 1954 it was 350,000. Thus in 15 years house-building rates were back to the levels of the late 1930s.[33]

The return of a Conservative Government was important in another direction. As was predictable, the system of building licensing was gradually relaxed. Subsidies for local authority housing were reduced and encouragement was given to dwellings for owner occupation. This change of policy from almost wholly local authority housing to a greater involvement of private enterprise started in 1952 and proceeded gradually until the 1954 and 1956 Acts.[34] In November 1956 the general housing needs subsidy was abolished altogether except for its continuation for one-bedroomed dwellings.[35]

In the first eight new towns it was not until 1951 before their housing programmes got under way. The balance of payments crisis had meant that a start had been permitted only on preliminary works such as roads and sewers. By 1954 just over 1,000 houses had been completed in the new towns while a further 3,000 were under construction. New-town houses also had to comply with the Macmillan economy drive, and when these restrictions were eased some much more basic and fundamental questions were being asked.[36]

Layouts and house groupings had, since the war, been a general repetition of those of the inter-war years. House standards had been improved but the basic shape had remained the same. It was planted in layouts that demonstrated the same violent reactions to the overcrowding of the conurbations, the nineteenth-century industrial town in particular, as after the First World War. Openness, air and light made up the theme. As the Conservative economy drive began to be felt in a demand for higher densities, more intensive land use and tighter house groupings, fears began to be expressed of a return to nineteenth century slum conditions.

Yet in 1953, on the other hand, when only a few houses had been built in the new towns, disappointment was being expressed with the results by both the architectural and planning professions. Some basic philosophies were questioned by J. M. Richards and by Gordon Cullen.[37] The new towns had been intended to provide self-contained conditions for all aspects of life, a key to their success being that rapid and parallel development of all aspects of this self-containment was essential. But in the economic circumstances of the time they were started, and because of untold administrative difficulties, this proved to be a greater problem than could have been foreseen.[38]

Political motivation was to build as many houses as possible, and the green belt was under continuous threat from dormitory housing estates on the fringes of the city. In the eight designated new towns houses were rapidly being built without the necessary industries, shopping and social amenities that would guarantee their self-containment. Indeed Bracknell, the nearest of the new towns to the London conurbation, became almost another suburb, so defeating the main purpose of decentralisation.[39] The design and planning professions had fallen for the general demand for openness and continued the same sprawling dispersal that typified the 1930s.

The result of this was low densities; the houses becoming cottages, both in name and in nature. While Howard's followers had achieved densities of 18.6 persons to the residential acre (46/ha) at Letchworth and 21.8 (54/ha) at Welwyn, the London new towns were much lower. In 1953 Stevenage was 13.0 to the acre (32/ha), Crawley 12.5 (31/ha), Hemel Hempstead 12.0 (30/ha) and the highest, Hatfield, was 17.4 to the acre (43/ha).[40]

In addition to this the houses were mediocre in planning and dull in appearance, while their rents were higher than elsewhere. The lack of local industry in the early stages of development meant that the first housing estates became dormitories for workers in the city. Subsequent industrial development did not succeed in capturing all the working population.[41]

It was loneliness and separateness that were the most serious problems. New town immigrants were from the cities, and they were ingrained with a deeper more meaningful neighbourliness than was being offered to them.

This neighbourliness was a product of compactness, of urbanity, and open-ness was an unfamiliar phenomenon. The dilemma was exposed in sociologi-cal studies by Willmott and Young,[42] and also by Margaret Willis who supported this view in that 'many of the people . . . prefer to live near a scene of activity'. She found criticism of the cul-de-sac too, for its residents expressed feelings of being 'cut-off' and preferred to live where there was 'something going on'.[43]

However, the 'home of one's own', the individual garden and the much improved schools, viewed against the two-roomed slum many families had moved from became the overriding advantages. The number who actually returned to the bustle of London was small, between 2–5 per cent of the total.[44]

Comparisons were inevitably made between new town housing estates and suburbia. The low densities advocated for the new towns at their conception and the relative cheapness of their land had encouraged the similarity. Decentralisation as an idea was not condemned by this similarity[45] but the prevailing architectural and planning criticisms[46] did put a halt to the creation of more new towns for some time.

The effect of decentralisation by these first new towns was minimal. Of the 200,000 resettled inhabitants in 1958, 140,000 were from the London area, but the population of the Greater London area had diminished by only 500,000 between 1939 and 1957. Movement of population to the South-East of England was continuing as never before. Just over 3 million new dwellings had been completed between the end of the war and 1959 but of these only 76,000, or 2.5 per cent, were to be found in the new towns.[47]

Urbanity and compactness were the qualities so far most lacking in post-war housing. They were attributed to the persistent introduction of regu-lations since the early years of the century, and were accentuated by a mis-understanding and hence misapplication of garden city principles from Unwin onwards. Elizabeth Denby made comparisons with the urbanity of Georgian and early Victorian squares in London and some surprising density calcu-lations were the result.[48] Little heed was taken of them for it was by now impossible to turn the tide of regulations. Density zoning, road widths and sight lines, the space required for underground services, street by-laws and daylighting angles were all blamed for pushing buildings further and further apart. It seemed as if it was rapidly becoming impossible to build compact towns.[49]

The horrors of nineteenth-century slum life at the beginning of the century had led to the creation of density controls. Dispersal had eventually followed, but this was no cure for slums, for as J. M. Richards expressed in 1946, 'the real cause of slums is not congestion but poverty' and the corollary of decentralisation in this situation was 'to perpetuate the same conditions whilst depriving their victims of the consolation that company provides'. He concluded that 'the wide spacing of buildings as such therefore brings no benefit to anyone'.[50]

In terms of numbers the bulk of the housing shortage had been overcome

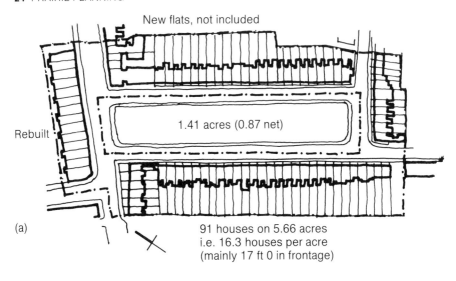

New flats, not included

1.41 acres (0.87 net)

Rebuilt

(a)

91 houses on 5.66 acres
i.e. 16.3 houses per acre
(mainly 17 ft 0 in frontage)

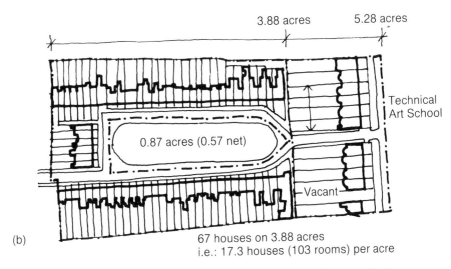

3.88 acres   5.28 acres

Technical
Art School

0.87 acres (0.57 net)

Vacant

(b)

67 houses on 3.88 acres
i.e.: 17.3 houses (103 rooms) per acre

Fig. 2.1 Density studies by Elizabeth Denby, (a) Paultons Square, Chelsea, and
(b) Cleaver Square, Lambeth (*E. R. Scoffham – adapted from studies by
Elizabeth Denby in Architectural Review, December 1956*)

by 1956. Coupled with the declining overall rate of growth of the population,
this caused a shift in emphasis to the qualitative rather than quantitative
aspects of housing policy.[51] The more complex and appalling slum clearance
and redevelopment areas of the cities had been kept virtually in storage; but
in 1954 the Housing Repairs and Rents Act, and in 1956 changes in subsidies,
shifted the emphasis in their favour.[52] A more general recognition of shortcomings in the new towns, not least of which was their statistical record,
meant that decentralization could no longer be the main objective of housing

and planning. This series of events resulted in concentration on problems of the cities where a mode of building developed that was to have far greater implications than those of the new towns.[53]

The dilemma of the period was, in a sense, prophesied by J. M. Richards from his observations of inter-war society.

It may be that our bored housewife, watching the passing traffic from the scullery window or half listening to the radio as she moves from room to room, would be happier in the hum of the city, if her standard of life there were raised and if she had clean air to breathe and a playground for the children. But maybe her proper milieu is suburbia, with its offering of a fuller life through fantasy as well as fellowship.[54]

But before considering the inner redevelopment sites it is necessary to trace developments in two areas where the new towns in particular made their most significant contribution to post-war built form.

REFERENCES

1. Lord Reith, *First Interim Report of the New Towns Committee*, Cmnd 6759, 1946, p. 4.
2. *New Towns Act.* 1946.
3. Ibid.
4. Ibid.
5. Ibid.
6. *Post-War Building Studies, No. 1*: House Construction (Burt Report), 1944.
7. W. H. E. Dudley, *The Design of Dwellings* (Dudley Report), 1944.
8. J. T. Walters, *The Provision of Dwellings for the Working Classes* (Tudor-Walters Report), 1918.
9. W. H. E. Dudley, op. cit.
10. *Housing Manual*, 1944, and 1949.
11. W. H. E. Dudley, op. cit.
12. H. Ashworth, *Housing in Great Britain*, 1957, p. 113.
13. A. W. C. Barr, *Public Authority Housing*, 1958, p. 20.
14. *The Appearance of Housing Estates*, 1948.
15. *Housing Manual*, 1949.
16. Ibid, p. 24.
17. Ibid, p. 23.
18. Ibid, p. 47.
19. Ibid, p. 19.
20. Housing (Temporary Provisions) Act 1944.
21. R. Sheppard, *Prefabrication in Building*, 1946.
22. Housing (Temporary Provisions) Act 1944.
23. H. Ashworth, op. cit., p. 40.
24. Ibid., pp. 40–1.
25. A. W. C. Barr, op. cit., p. 19.
26. Ibid., p. 21.
27. F. Schaffer, *The New Town Story*, 1972, p. 102.
28. G. Cullen, 'Prairie planning', *Architectural Review*, July 1953.
29. Circular 38/51, 1951.

30. *Houses 1952*, Second Supplement to the *Housing Manual*, 1949, and *Houses 1953*, Third Supplement to the *Housing Manual*, 1949.
31. A. W. C. Barr, op. cit., p. 63.
32. *The Density of Residential Areas*, 1952.
33. H. Ashworth, op. cit., p. 44.
34. *Houses, the Next Step*, 1953; Housing Repairs and Rents Act 1954; Housing Subsidies Act 1956.
35. H. Ashworth, op. cit., p. 152.
36. F. Schaffer, op. cit., pp. 103–5.
37. J. M. Richards, 'Failure of the New Towns', *Architectural Review*, July 1953, pp. 29–32; G. Cullen, 'Prairie planning', *Architectural Review*, July 1953, p. 33 ff.
38. H. Bruckmann and D. L. Lewis, *New Housing in Great Britain*, 1960, p. 10.
39. J. M. Richards, op. cit., pp. 29–32.
40. Ibid., pp. 29–32.
41. M. Bruckmann and D. L. Lewis, op. cit., p. 17.
42. P. Willmott and M. Young, *Family and Class in a London Suburb*, 1957.
43. M. Willis, *Environment and the Home*, 1954, p. 15.
44. J. B. Duff, *British New Towns*, 1963, p. 71.
45. I. Nairn, 'Counter attack', *Architectural Review*, Dec. 1956. p. 415.
46. T. Mellor, 'The persistent suburb', *Town Planning Review*, Jan. 1955, pp. 251–4; I. Nairn, 'Subtopia' *Architectural Review*, June 1955.
47. Quoted by H. Bruckmann and D. L. Lewis, op. cit., p. 31.
48. Elizabeth Denby, 'Oversprawl', *Architectural Review*, Dec. 1956, pp. 424 – 30.
49. W. Manthorpe, 'The machinery of sprawl', *Architectural Review*, Dec. 1956, pp. 409 – 25.
50. J. M. Richards, *The Castles on the Ground*, 1946, pp. 74–5.
51. H. Ashworth, op. cit., p. 56.
52. A. W. C. Barr, op. cit., p. 21.
53. H. Bruckmann and D.L. Lewis, op. cit., p. 60.
54. J. M. Richards, *The Castles on the Ground*. p. 75.

3 NEIGHBOURS AND CARS

Ebenezer Howard had seen the necessity for dividing his garden city into sections. Each of these so-called 'wards' was intended to be more-or-less self-contained with a full range of social amenities, shops, schools, industry and housing. He proposed six wards, each with a population of 5,000 people, to be separated from one another by wide boulevards.[1]

In this subdivision of the town into sections, for reasons he had described in sociological terms, Howard had provided the germ of a favourite preoccupation of planners in post-war town-building. That preoccupation was the idea of the neighbourhood unit.[2]

First use of the term 'neighbourhood unit' appears to have been in connection with a planning competition in Chicago in 1916.[3] But it was not until 1929 that a classification of the idea was made by Clarence Perry.[4] Subsequently development of the neighbourhood concept took place in America, notably by Perry, and it returned to Britain after the war, with greater credibility, so that it appeared to be American in origin.[5]

Unwin's architectural translation of Howard's vision had crossed the Atlantic where it had joined forces, in the early years of the century, with the 'community centre movement'. Here the motivating idea was the use of the school for communal activities, so providing a common local meeting place in order to encourage social activity.[6]

The neighbourhood theme embodied this community focus, its basic principle being that the neighbourhood was a unit of a larger whole and a distinct entity in itself. Perry established the regulating elements of a neighbourhood: size, boundaries, open spaces, institutional uses, local shops and an internal road system.[7] The population ordinarily required for one primary school was Perry's basis in the determination of size. Density was important but more so was distance. The school was centrally placed and the maximum walking distance for a child established at half to three-quarters of a mile (0.8 to 1.2 km).

Perry also saw busy traffic routes forming the most obvious boundaries to residential areas. The central school would act as a community centre for the neighbourhood and it would be surrounded by a system of small parks and recreation areas, the area of which would be 10 per cent of the total unit area. Smaller children's playgrounds would be provided throughout residential areas so that no child was more than a quarter of a mile (0.4 km) from one. Regarding shops Perry was far-seeing. They would be located at the edges of the unit adjacent to the shops of the next adjoining neighbourhood.

He saw a greater concentration of shops at traffic junctions as being able to offer wider choice and competition.

Clear influence from Howard was apparent in Perry's writing. Their sociological ideas had much in common, yet Perry went further in definitions, and in extending the idea to already built-up areas in addition to new residential districts.[8]

Perry's general planning principles were soon applied in a development of the neighbourhood unit at Radburn, New Jersey. The plan of the town was prepared by Clarence Stein and Henry Wright, and documented by Stein in his *Towards New Towns for America*.[9] The school was the focus, generating the size of the neighbourhood at 7,500–10,000 people, and was used as the community centre. Through traffic was restricted to the edges of the unit and on these the shopping centres were located. It was the detailed planning of the residential sections that made Radburn remarkable, in that proposals for pedestrian and traffic segregation were introduced to link detailed design with broader concepts. The neighbourhood unit idea became closely interwoven with detailed solutions to traffic and pedestrian movement. It formed the roots of a dilemma that was to mount in significance alongside the rising graph of car ownership in post-war years.[10]

In Britain neither Letchworth nor Welwyn were carried out in accordance with Howard's intentions for subdividing the town into wards. They do,

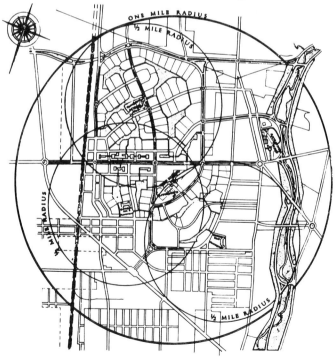

Fig. 3.1 General plan of Radburn, New Jersey, indicating neighbourhoods (*from Towards New Towns for America by C. S. Stein, MIT Press. Copyright 1957 by Clarence Stein*)

however, demonstrate the need for neighbourhood units in retrospect. It was their slow rate of growth from inception that had disguised this need.[11] Yet Barry Parker had adopted a neighbourhood pattern from the beginning in his design of the Manchester Wythenshawe estate in 1930. By 1938 something over 30,000 people were housed in Wythenshawe alongside light industries and social amenities. But this and one or two other exceptions went unnoticed amid the sprawl of inter-war suburbia.[12]

In 1940, C. B. Fawcett, Professor of Geography at London University, suggested his own ideas for residential units which were very similar to those of Perry but did not appear to originate from them. He was concerned about the anonymity of the individual and gave the name of 'vill' to a unit based on social factors, the most important of which was the primary school. He was most concerned that a residential unit should not derive from economic, administrative or architectural considerations.[13]

But the first discusssions of the neighbourhood unit that had more immediate relevance for post-war housing, were contained in a comprehensive survey of the needs of residential areas by the National Council of Social Service in 1943.[14] Its recommendations were based on experience of the defects of inter-war housing, the rigidity of working-class and middle-class housing areas and the inadequacy of social facilities. It was concluded that neighbourhood units should be the basis of town enlargement or new town planning projects. Each neighbourhood, the report recommended, should contain a maximum of 2,000 dwellings for a population of from 7,000 to 10,000 people; each should be a comprehensive part of the town to which it belonged and contain a 'socially balanced population'. The size of these units, it was reported, should depend on walking time, distance and population density taken as a whole.

The Dudley Report of 1944[15] reinforced these recommendations. A 10,000-person maximum population was suggested, with all houses within 10 minutes walk of the neighbourhood centre. Neighbourhoods would vary in size according to density, and would be between 168 (68 ha) and 482 acres (195 ha) for this population, with full provision of all facilities for communal life. Dudley recommended what within this unit smaller groups of a homogeneous character, providing for 100–300 families, offered better hopes for success. Open space should be closely related to dwellings and a continuous pattern of open space could provide a system of safe pedestrian routes. The 1944 Housing Manual[16] went even further regarding size of neighbourhoods, and suggested they might be as small as 5,000 people, but gave a warning, subsequently unheeded, that schools and other communal facilities should be completed for use at the same time as the houses.

Lord Reith, however, was more flexible, perhaps even non-committal, in suggesting that his recommendations did not imply any one standardised pattern of physical or social structure. In towns of 30,000–50,000 people all dwellings could be within walking distance of the town centre, work places and countryside, so enabling attainment of a 'sense of unity and local pride'.[17] Perhaps Lord Reith's committee had doubts that the neighbourhood unit was not, as generally advocated at the time, the universal panacea for earlier failings in housing areas. Perhaps they realised, as did others much later[18] that the idea could not be applied, without modification, to the kind of life that it was envisaged might follow in post-war Britain.

In spite of this reservation, the neighbourhood unit came to be applied in the planning of the first new towns. It was to dominate town planning thinking for many years. As might be expected each neighbourhood was planned to have its own small shopping centre within walking distance of houses – Perry's grouping of centres was not taken up seriously until the later new towns were planned. Each was to have a primary school and meeting hall, pub and church as a focus for communal life. Often a historical local or traditional name was adopted to give each area an identity.[19]

Nevertheless many of the values held sacred to the neighbourhood concept were subsequently demolished. The emphasis on social unity came to be dismissed as a pious hope when much more practical aspects such as a child's walking distance, and the commercial viability of a small shopping centre, were the realities.[20] Nor did the success of a neighbourhood unit seem to depend on size or on density. The sociological cries of loneliness in low-density suburban, and later garden city, sprawl, and the perennial pleas for a more compact urban huddle to give a sense of community had not yet been satisfactorily resolved.[21] Community life was beginning to be something other than could be provided by adoption of the neighbourhood concept alone.

A breakdown in the concept of the neighbourhood as defined by Perry, came as a result of the Dudley Report's recommendation of the 10,000-person unit. This provided more children than could be catered for by one primary school and consequently two were provided. Perry's idea of the school as the focus of community life weakened as both schools could not serve that function. One perhaps was chosen, but more often than not the neighbourhood centre became a parade of shops, near to one of the schools, with the other school much further away.[22] The neighbourhood unit of 10,000 people proved to be unsatisfactory.

That community life depended on more complex factors than had been envisaged was dawning. Identity of interest, and a desire to take part with others in that interest, was a prime factor. The by now increasing level of car ownership meant that people could travel to pursue their interests, and were not limited to immediate neighbours for friends. People could now support activities of a communal nature anywhere in the town.[23]

As a result a break with the neighbourhood idea came in 1955 when Cumbernauld new town was designated as the fifteenth of the post-war creations. On a spectacular site, and under Chief Architect Hugh Wilson's directions the town was planned as one unit, with a multi-level town centre along the top of the predominant ridge. The surrounding houses were at a higher density than in the earlier new towns and none were more than a few minutes walk away from the centre upon which the whole life of the town was focused. Skelmersdale, by the same Hugh Wilson as consultant, was based on Cumbernauld's premiss of the town centre as a strong and imaginative focus for its inhabitants.[24]

Of the earlier new towns, Harlow in particular, was to come closest to Perry's original ideas. A variation of the neighbourhood unit, the 'neighbourhood cluster', was adopted for residential area subdivisions. At Harlow there were four clusters grouped around three major subcentres, while the town centre acted as centre for the fourth cluster. Each neighbourhood unit had its own primary school and a few local shops but the neighbourhood centre was at the junction of units, and so served a larger number of people – from 17,000 to 25,000. This variation has been found to be much more successful than the plantation of standard 10,000-people units.[25]

In 1961 the LCC published the fruits of its frustrated efforts to build its own new town at Hook in Hampshire.[26] Here the subdivision of residential areas was by 'superblocks'; their size determined by a reconciliation of several factors: statistical, social and visual. Superblocks varied according to the density and household structure of different parts of the town. In the inner town a walking distance of 10 minutes, or half a mile (0.8 km), governed the length of the blocks, and if the primary school was centrally located each child had a quarter of a mile (0.4 km) to walk, a two-form entry school being required for every 4,000–5,000 people. Thus, as at Cumbernauld, the areas nearer the centre orientate themselves towards it, and only in the outer town were there to be separate neighbourhoods with their own facilities.

Later, at Runcorn, there was a return to the grouping of neighbourhoods as at Harlow. A separate public transport route, presently single-deck buses, circulates in a figure-of-eight throughout the town linking each local centre with the others and to the town centre. Each local centre serves a community of 8,000 people, and this is divided into four neighbourhoods, each of 2,000 people.[27] Perry's grouping was very closely followed, yet organised in a manner which recognised the necessity for public and private transportation. The design of one of these communities was the subject of a significant architectural competition in 1967.[28]

An acceptance of the growth of private car ownership was made at Washington in the north-east and at Milton Keynes.[29] Both plans were by Llewellyn-Davies, Weeks, Forestier-Walker and Bor and were very similar. They adopted a grid-pattern of roads at 1 km (0.6 mile) intervals; within each square was a 'place' at Washington, and a 'village' at Milton Keynes. Recognition was made of the need for identity and grouping at all levels. The neighbourhood became a framework for the town rather than a formula for its organisation. Criticism was made in the Washington Report of the idea of breaking a town up into separate residential areas with fixed boundaries and an inbuilt range of services. The consultants maintained that this was no longer valid, as each family or individual would have contacts at a whole range of scales from small groups round the home, upwards to facilities in the region outside the new town boundaries. The town was seen as a more complex overlapping structure.[30]

Despite this apparent negation of the neighbourhood idea, its survival as

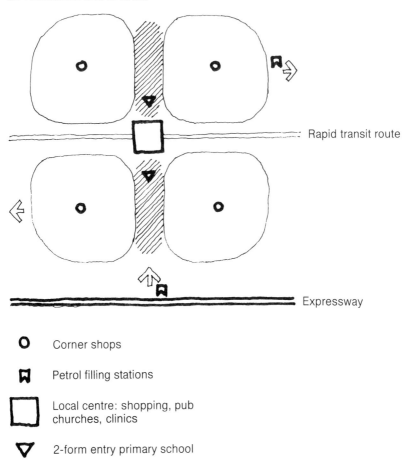

Rapid transit route

Expressway

O   Corner shops

R   Petrol filling stations

☐   Local centre: shopping, pub
churches, clinics

▽   2-form entry primary school

Fig. 3.2 Neighbourhood cluster diagram, Runcorn (*E. R. Scoffham – adapted
from Runcorn New Town Master Plan by Runcorn Development
Corporation*)

a means of subdividing residential areas, in all manner of names and forms
would appear to support its validity. The primary school is still a basic factor
in deciding population limits, although the social and community focus upon
the school, advocated by Perry, is no longer absolutely justified as a result
of increasing mobility, affluence and different social customs.[31] Mobility, the
unprecedented growth of private transportation, proved to be one of the first
post-war initiators of changes in built form. It was a factor that altered
traditional concepts of the neighbourhood unit, and altered, too, traditional
concepts of house groupings and street patterns.

Car ownership and the growth of road traffic was, in the 1920s,
increasing far more rapidly in the United States than elsewhere in the world,
and it was here that the idea of separating traffic from pedestrians originated
in a form that proved to be acceptable in post-war Britain. By 1895 five cars

had been registered in America, yet 33 years later, in 1928, the number had grown to over 21 million; the existing gridiron pattern of city roads had become unsafe, noisy and noxious and traffic was almost at a standstill.[32]

The growth of the garden city movement in Britain, and its debasement as a result of policies at the end of the First World War, came to influence American thinking, both on the neighbourhood unit, and on the idea of vehicular segregation. Camillo Sitte has been shown to have considered the classification of roads according to traffic upon them, and the identification of separate bicycle, bridle and pedestrian ways.[33] Raymond Unwin had been much influenced by Sitte's writing and had demonstrated this in his own *Town Planning in Practice*.[34] These reactions against nineteenth-century bylaw housing and gridiron street patterns had been reinforced in the Tudor-Walters Report,[35] where it was urged that road widths should be apportioned according to the amount of traffic upon them by planning main streets to be direct routes for through traffic, while minor roads should be arranged to benefit their building frontages and be without through traffic.

Raymond Unwin had favoured the cul-de-sac in his layout for Hampstead garden suburb in 1905, and for New Earswick. Frequently recurring geometrical layouts demonstrated a reaction against gridiron bylaw street planning, and these came to include the cul-de-sac, with variations such as hollow squares and loop roads. These minor roads did not need the same heavy construction as did main thoroughfares in view of the lightness and volume of the traffic upon them. Culs-de-sac and squares offered a reduction in road length per house, as houses meeting at internal angles shared a common frontage.[36] Economies were particularly important at this time as the cost of roads and services was increasing in relation to the cost of land.

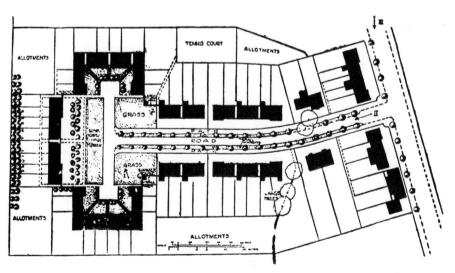

Fig. 3.3 Cul-de-sac arrangement by Raymond Unwin for utilising a greater depth of land (*from Town Planning in Practice by R. Unwin, Benjamin Blom Inc*)

The Tudor-Walters recommendation of 12 houses to the acre (30/ha), reducing to 8 (20/ha) in rural areas, had enacted Unwin's earlier economic argument that there was *Nothing Gained by Overcrowding.*[37] Events were now beginning to wear the basis of his argument thin, for the layouts being developed were irregular in pattern, and left a variety of different land shapes between roads to be allocated to houses. This resulted in corresponding increases in road frontage per house by comparison with the earlier rectangular nineteenth-century patterns.

In this context the virtue of the cul-de-sac was that it enabled some of these awkward pockets of land to be utilised economically as the cul-de-sac could be of a light construction and it allowed an increased number of houses along road frontages.[38] Between the wars the cul-de-sac became a predominant layout theme. At Welwyn Garden City there were variations in which the extent to which the vehicle penetrates alters, so giving a range of options from immediate road access, to the detachment of the house from the road with access off a pedestrian footpath through a landscaped green.[39]

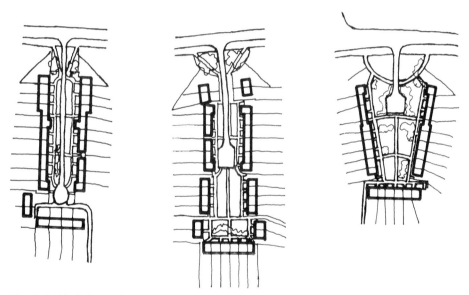

Fig. 3.4 Variations of culs-de-sac at Welwyn Garden City indicating variable road penetration and greens (*E. R. Scoffham*)

Landscaped greens as a device for separating road from house were essentially English in their nature being analogous to country village greens and town squares. A common London analogy, in Notting Hill and South Kensington, has a private green for the residents of surrounding houses, each house having access to the green through a small back yard, with the front of the house facing the roadway.[40] This traffic-free green, with private access from surrounding houses, has been seen as the 'precursor of Radburn' by Gordon Stephenson.[41]

A development of this dual access to houses had originated in the late nineteenth century in mining districts. The dumping of concessionary coal meant that a solution was devised which turned the houses round so that their backs faced the roadway thus enabling easy delivery of coal to stores without passing through the house. House fronts thus faced an open space and had footpath access by way of private gardens.[42]

When Clarence Stein was appointed Chairman of the Commission of Housing and Regional Planning in America at the end of the First World War he looked abroad for inspiration. In 1923 he came to Britain to study the two garden cities and Hampstead garden suburb, and returned to America 'a disciple of Ebenezer Howard and Raymond Unwin'.[43] In 1924 Stein persuaded Alexander Bing, a successful property developer, to establish an association for the purpose of building an American garden city, in which the English garden city philosophy of the 1920's would be modified to accommodate American car ownership.[44] But before starting development the company decided to build a small prototype scheme at Sunnyside Gardens, New York. Between 1924 and 1928, 1,202 homes were built on 55.82 acres (22.6 ha) of the 77 acre (31.2 ha) site.[45] Stein was planner jointly with Henry Wright, and chief architect of the Regional Planning Commission. It was this liaison that formulated the basic ideas of what has become known as 'Radburn Planning'.[46]

Sunnyside Gardens was never planned as a whole for the local engineer's office would not allow modification of the existing gridiron street pattern. Street blocks were 600–900 feet (183–274 m) in length by 190–200 feet (58–61 m) wide and the design was for buildings to surround the perimeter of each block, with the interior space giving about 120 feet (37 m) between buildings. Each house had a private garden about 30 feet (9 m) long leaving a central communal area about 60 feet (18 m) across for the use of all residents in the surrounding houses.[47] It was a commercial success, and in 1928 the City Housing Corporation was sufficiently convinced to allow a start on the American garden city. A site was purchased at Fairlawn, New Jersey, of about 2 square miles (5.18 km^2) in area, where it was possible for Stein and Wright to develop their ideas without any existing restrictions. Stein tabulated their objectives in modifying garden city concepts to the motor car in these terms: use of the 'superblock' in place of the gridiron block, use of specialised roads planned and built for one instead of for all uses, complete separation of pedestrian and car, houses turned around to have living-rooms and bedrooms facing gardens and service rooms towards access roads, and the use of a park as the backbone of the neighbourhood joining open areas within each superblock.[48] The neighbourhood unit concept was thus linked to detailed design considerations and in part realised in the form that it became generally applied in post-war Britain.

At Radburn, as the Fairlawn site was named, the separation of pedestrians and wheeled traffic was achieved by using a superblock of 30–50 acres (12–20 ha). This was penetrated around the edges by culs-de-sac, and had a central core of parkland containing schools, playgrounds, swimming pools

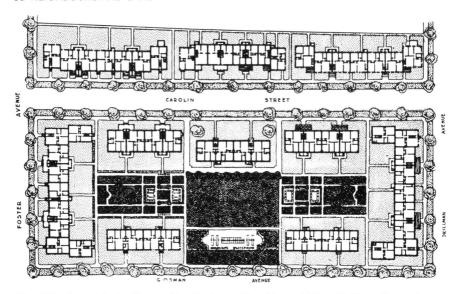

Fig. 3.5 Superblock, Sunnyside Gardens, New York, 1924–28 (*from Towards New Towns for America by C. S. Stein, MIT Press. Copyright 1957 by Clarence Stein*)

and so on. Several superblocks grouped together formed a neighbourhood and the footpaths formed a connected system, with underpasses or overpasses where they crossed roads. Each house fronted a road or a cul-de-sac on one side where there was a garage, and had an entrance from the footpath system on the other. Thus full accessibility by car was achieved while children could walk to the various amenities and to neighbours in safety. Houses were mainly detached or semi-detached and they had their main entrances located so that they could be reached from either road or path side. The private garden was on the path side overlooked by the living-rooms and as many bedrooms as possible, while the kitchen and garage faced the cul-de-sac. Placing the kitchen on the service side was done because Stein felt that this would be the side on which most events would happen – deliveries, visitors, and so on. But it was soon found to be the side most attractive for children's play; the reasons being that mothers wanted to keep them in sight from the kitchen, and that hard surfaces were attractive to children with wheeled toys. Stein suggested a future through kitchen–dining room to avoid the former problem and the provision of larger hard surfaces on the park side to counter the latter. On the general question of separating vehicles and people he did, however, admit that 'we never will do so completely, nor do I think we should attempt to'.[49]

Building started in 1929 and by 1931 two superblocks of the first neighbourhood and one of the second were complete. The depression followed soon after and building ceased in 1933. Only one school was built and many other facilities were never realised. Radburn never became a garden city, it never had a green belt to detach it from the conurbation and it never secured

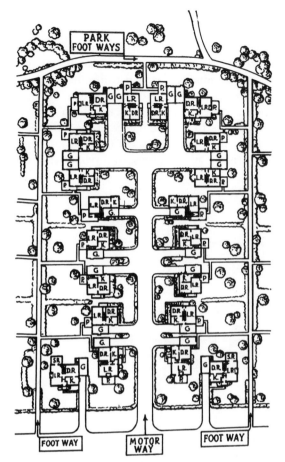

Fig. 3.6 Layout of Burnham Place, Radburn, New Jersey, 1929–33 (*from Towards New Towns for America by C. S. Stein, MIT Press. Copyright 1957 by Clarence Stein*)

industry. Yet people lived happily and safely in the completed superblocks so demonstrating the principles of a new form of layout that became increasingly accepted in residential areas in both America and Europe.[50]

Subsequent developments in America used some of the ideas of Radburn and they were: Chatham Village on a 45 acre (18 ha) site in Pittsburgh between 1930 and 1935 which contained 197 dwellings; Phipps Garden Apartments near the Sunnyside Gardens site; Hillside Homes in New York built between 1933 and 1935; Greenbelt, Maryland some 13 miles (21 km) from Washington which contained 1,885 dwellings and was carried out between 1937 and 1943; Greendale, Wisconsin; Green Hills, Ohio; and Baldwin Hills Village, Los Angeles, built in 1941, which contained 627 dwellings.[51]

Baldwin Hills Village was the most interesting of these as it developed further some of the ideas of Radburn. Within one superblock of 80 acres (32 ha) it eliminated internal through roads, provided vehicle access to dwellings by culs-de-sac, separated circulation for pedestrians from that for vehicles by footpaths through green spaces, and introduced a more efficient and spacious arrangement of garage courts.[52] Baldwin Hills introduced terraces rather than detached and semi-detached houses. The garages for these were grouped in courts instead of being individually attached to houses, and the houses themselves did not open directly on to the courts. Instead a small enclosed private garden, and then a belt of planting backed by a row of garages, screened their entrances. Access to the garages was by a footpath parallel to the terrace with connecting links to the garage court at intervals. The backs of houses had increased privacy and less noise and risk of children

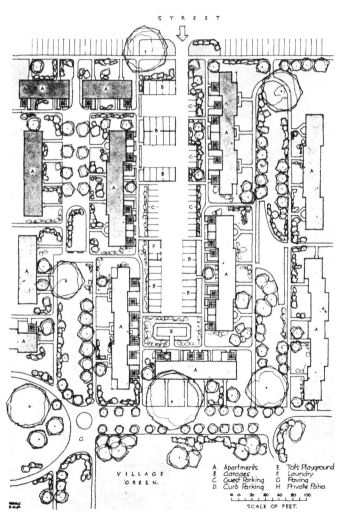

Fig. 3.7 Layout of garage court and pedestrian areas at Baldwin Hills Village, Los Angeles, 1941 (*from Towards New Towns for America by C. S. Stein, MIT Press. Copyright 1957 by Clarence Stein*)

rushing out on to roads was reduced. A clubhouse, tennis courts, child centre and play area were located within the superblock, yet surprisingly there was no school or shopping centre.[53]

Gordon Stephenson visited Radburn under construction in 1929 when he was studying town planning as a Commonwealth Fellow at Massachussetts Institute of Technology, and Arthur Ling made Stein's government-sponsored schemes the subject of his town planning diploma thesis at London University.[54] Lewis Mumford brought the Radburn idea to a wider audience when his *Culture of Cities* was published in 1938.[55]

Official recognition came to Britain in 1944 when the Dudley Report[56] drew attention to the difference between the cul-de-sac as used before the war as an occasional element in layouts, and its use as part of a total system of planning as had been done at Radburn. The Report contained work done by a group in the then Ministry of Town and Country Planning, among whom were Gordon Stephenson and Thomas Sharp. Soon after Stephenson left the Ministry to occupy the Chair of Civic Design at Liverpool University he invited Stein to England to write up an account of the 'New Towns of America' for the *Town Planning Review* in 1949.[57]

Independently of this in 1942 the then Assistant Commissioner of the Metropolitan Police, Sir Alker Tripp, had proposed a clear definition of roads for different priorities, from national down to residential levels. He established a theory of 'precinct planning' – areas which would be without through traffic and be in themselves a centre of life and activity. Thus a traffic expert arrived at more-or-less the same definition of a Radburn superblock, and pre-dated Buchanan's 'environmental areas' by some 20 years.[58]

The 1949 *Housing Manual* reinforced Dudley on an economic front. It suggested the use of footpath access with maximum 150 feet (46 m) walking distance, particularly at the ends of culs-de-sac and around small greens. It advocated terraced instead of semi-detached houses, and the use of narrow carriageways for quadrangles and short culs-de-sac. The *Manual* went on to suggest that it should seldom be necessary to provide groups of more than ten garages in any one location because of the noise and nuisance they created, yet on the question of provision of garages it urged authorities to under-estimate needs but to reserve space for them in the future.[59]

In Britain the principles demonstrated at Radburn were slow to start after the war. The first example was not to appear until 1950–52 when Gordon Stephenson collaborated with the Borough Engineer of Wrexham, J. M. Davis, to plan the layout of an estate at Queen's Park, Wrexham. The building of the estate was let as separate contracts and the superblock idea as a result became confused when the boundaries between contract areas did not coin-cide with them – all, that is, except the first section where the superblocks have an internal footpath system interrupted by one over-long cul-de-sac. There is a children's playground and the central footpath provides a safe and short route to bus stops at the southern end. But for access to schools, shops and so on, roads must be crossed. Two-storey houses were adopted with a few two-storey flat blocks. They have their main entrances on the footpath

0   50 100 150 200 250 300
Feet

Fig. 3.8   Layout of Section 6, Queen's Park, Wrexham, 1950–52 (*E. R. Scoffham – adapted from drawing by Gordon Stephenson and Wrexham Borough Council*)

side, sometimes opening directly into the living-room, and the dining kitchen occupies the other side opening into the garden from which a gate gives on to the cul-de-sac.[60] A reversal of the Radburn road–house–garden situation thus appeared at Wrexham.

The provision of garages was in fact very low – only one in five houses had one. The main emphasis at the time was to see what economies came out of this new form of layout in terms of house costs, not on new ways of accommodating the car with safety. The 1949 *Manual* provided the clue in that car provision should be underestimated with economic aspects emphasised. Stephenson referred to the evident need for garages but the Ministry would not allow their provision until a list of signatures of those requiring them had been presented.[61]

Despite the efforts of Lewis Womersley, at Northampton in 1952 and at Sheffield from 1953 onwards, and of Arthur Ling at Coventry in 1951–56, full attainment of Radburn principles was elusive.[62] At the Greenhill-Bradway estate in Sheffield Lewis Womersley introduced part-Radburn ideas to a large scheme of 3,250 dwellings. Sections 2 and 6 were laid out on a system of double access to dwellings and section 7 was a self-contained superblock. The remainder of the estate was conventionally laid out. Section 7 was planned with a shopping centre, pub, bus terminus, central grassed spaces – but no school, and no children's playground. Dwellings are in two-storey houses, and four-storey maisonette blocks. Houses have the main entrance on the footpath side and this opens into a central hall leading to a through living-room at one side, and a dining-kitchen on the other. The kitchen overlooks the footpath and hence the place where children are

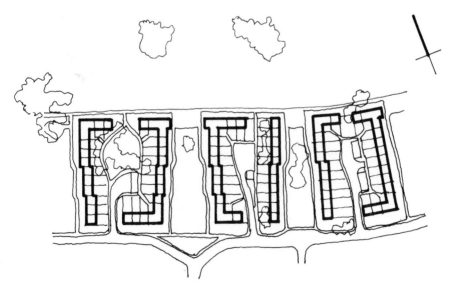

Fig. 3.9 Part layout of Eastfields, Northampton, 1952 (*E. R. Scoffham – adapted from drawing by Lewis Womersley and Northampton Borough Council*)

expected to play. Private gardens are on the service side through gates from the culs-de-sac, and so the same relationship prevails as at Wrexham. Garage provision was even lower than at Wrexham; originally only 15 per cent.[63]

Willenhall Wood in Coventry was built between 1957 and 1959 when Arthur Ling was Chief Architect. It was in two parts, one being the main superblock surrounded by a loop road, and the other an extension across this road. Both parts had the, by now, usual system of culs-de-sac penetrating into the housing areas, and widening out to form garage courts with rear access to the houses. What was significant at Willenhall Wood was that the gardens were much more private than at Wrexham and Sheffield because the garages were arranged to screen them from the road, and high fences were adopted. The houses came nearer to Stein's objective of a through dining-kitchen to give adequate supervision of children playing at either side of the house. Unfortunately about half the houses have living-rooms facing north

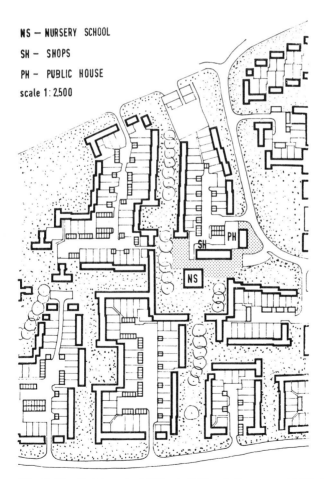

Fig. 3.10 Part layout of Willenhall Wood, Coventry, 1957–59 (*from Homes, Towns and Traffic by J. Tetlow and A. Goss, Faber & Faber*)

or east thus posing a problem of orientation that was not present at Sheffield due to the use of through living-rooms. Garage provision was 51 per cent and it was generally understood that car-owners could have a garage in the court nearest their house.[64]

Similar hybrid and often half-hearted efforts at so-called Radburn layouts were taking place in the new towns, at Harlow, Basildon, Stevenage and Hemel Hempstead during the 1950s. Too often it was the rear gardens that faced into the garage courts, the front doors facing pedestrian routes. Confusion occurred where houses were situated alongside main culs-de-sac or access loops, as the desire to have the front of the house facing the road was an overriding one. Thus some houses had vehicle access from the front, some from the back. Even those houses with rear access from a garage court faced a dilemma as to which entrance was, in fact, the front. An assumption that everyone would walk to amenities had led to the placing of front doors on the pedestrian side. Once visitors arrived by way of the garage court there was immediate confusion: either a lengthy walk to the intended front entrance or a short cut up the garden to the back door. Studies of early examples suggested two solutions to this problem: either place the private gardens on the footpath side and reverse the front–back situation, or place the rows of houses at right angles to access roads rather than in the orthodox position of a corridor street.[65] This situation had never occurred in Stein and Wright's schemes. Radburn had provided gardens on the footpath side and Baldwin Hills had detached the houses from the garage court thereby allowing solely pedestrian access to the front door.

The confusion in Britain was attributed to the fact that examples here started off on a different basis, with attention paid more to amenity with economy than to a proper means of dealing with the motor car.[66] Thus Radburn in Britain had many versions, none of which were to Stein's stated principles in entirety. Britain was slow to recognise the increase in car ownership, and for the first 6 or 7 years after the war the Ministry would not approve layouts which allocated more than one garage to every four houses. According to Tetlow and Goss, 'after a war in which mobility played a decisive part we were unprepared for mobility in times of peace'.[67]

Schemes such as Willenhall Wood, where garage provision was 51 per cent, had provided some timely warnings. The grouping of large numbers of garages had resulted in dreary and monotonous areas of tarmac, fences and low buildings that were visually unacceptable. The contrast of this with neat and landscaped fronts was marked. Rising car ownership predictions made it apparent that more radical changes would be required if a satisfactory solution to the accommodation of the car was to be found.[68]

This more radical approach was incorporated into the planning of Cumbernauld, which was started in 1956. It was the intention that foot and motor traffic should be separated to the maximum extent possible. This meant two separate circulation systems which would cross by means of an underpass or an overpass, and at these points bus stops would be located.[69] The assumption was for a car ownership of 0.7 cars per family, and this in itself was an exception, for it was only in 1956 that the Ministry allowed New Town Development Corporations to increase their provision to one in eight, and to leave space for one in four. Later this was increased to one in three, and to one per dwelling for the most expensive houses.[70]

The visual problems inherent at Willenhall Wood and earlier new town schemes had been aggravated by the Ministry's 1952 economy drive which had resulted in an increasing use of narrow-frontage houses. Dual access layout situations using a narrow-frontage house brought serious internal planning deficiencies: entry direct to living-room, long passages from front to back and so on. To overcome these weaknesses wide-frontage houses were developed, especially at Cumbernauld. It became possible to provide entrances from both sides, front or back, without passing through one of the rooms, and a more square garden resulted which was easier to screen at the sides for privacy. It was also evident to Cumbernauld planners that a more satisfactory house to garden relationship came about by reversing the earlier situation – by combining the private garden with the pedestrian routes and landscaped open spaces. By detaching house blocks from the garage courts or culs-de-sac it was possible to regain the traditional front door situation to

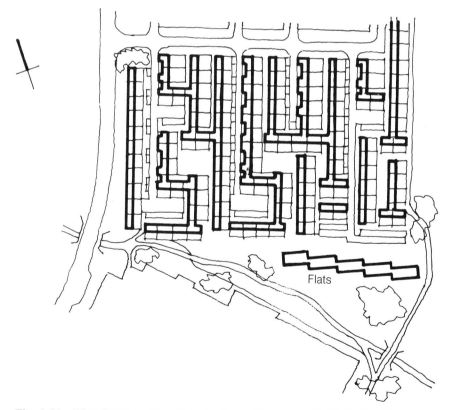

Fig. 3.11 Wide frontage houses at Carbrain, Cumbernauld (*E. R. Scoffham – adapted from drawing by Cumbernauld Development Corporation*)

which everyone came on foot.[71] Cumbernauld's influence as a town designed both for the motor car and the pedestrian has been widespread. Many projects in this country followed its lead in the derivation of new house types, of fresh house–garden–car relationships and in the design of landscaped pedestrian ways leading to a vertically segregated town centre.

In 1958 the Ministry of Housing and Local Government, as it had become, tabulated the amount of land which would be required to achieve certain levels of car provision.[72] It was established that 220 square feet (20 m²) of space was required for each car, not counting access roads. Thus one car to every 1.5 dwellings used 23 per cent of the minimum net space about buildings; one car to every two dwellings used 17.3 per cent, one to three used 11.5 per cent, one to four used 8.6 per cent and one to five used 6.9 per cent. One-third of dwellings, it was suggested, should have parking spaces initially, with provision for doubling this eventually. The Ministry also noted that there were five well-known methods of providing parking: off-street in the open, single storey lock-up garages, garages in underbuildings, integral garages with houses, and multi-storey garages. It went on to state that garages in underbuildings or multi-storey garages would be necessary in order to provide garaging at the ratio of one car to three dwellings.[73] While the Ministry was here mainly concerned about urban renewal schemes, it was indicating that some dual use of land would be required, surface provision alone being too greedy.

By 1961 the same Ministry admitted that one family in three now owned a car, and called for new arrangements in view of the use of residential streets by delivery and services vehicles.[74] But on the question of these new arrangements it was retrograde. While stating the need for segregation and for car storage, it predicted that 'much future terrace housing will probably have access to both sides of the house, so meeting most of the requirements'.[75] It predicted one car per household in Great Britain by 1980 and stated that it was a necessity to design at the outset for this provision.[76]

Like Cumbernauld, Hook, the LCC's abortive new town in Hampshire, did not follow the Mark I new town lead of neighbourhoods around a town centre. It did, however, provide a theoretical statement of town planning objectives and practice in relation to the motor vehicle. A definitive system of areas for children's play was established giving their location and size, and this included the private garden. The car standard was one per dwelling plus one visitor's space for every two dwellings. A rationalisation of cul-de-sac length, walking distance and car location was made, and the term 'cul-de-sac' extended so as not to preclude occasional loop roads as service access. Garage courts were given attention, and a conclusion reached that reversed the front and back situation of early Radburn schemes to that proposed at Cumbernauld, or in the Hook Report's words, 'just as they do in some of the later nineteenth century London squares and gardens in the Ladbroke Grove area of London'.[77]

The need to keep house to garage walking distances short was stressed and this suggested that car groups should be small and visually manageable.

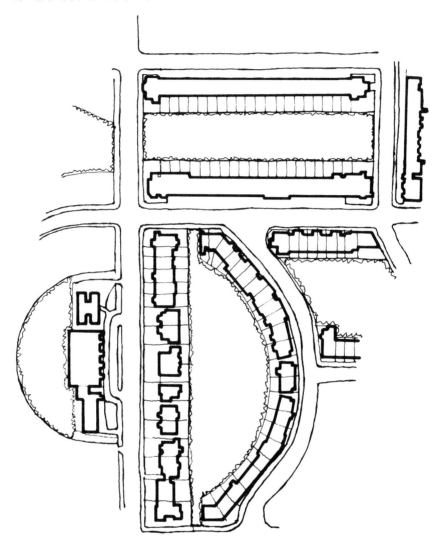

Fig. 3.12 Part of Ladbroke Grove area, London, showing open space at the rear of houses (*E. R. Scoffham – adapted from Architect and Building News, March 1969*)

Long distances, the LCC maintained, encouraged owners with a road frontage to leave their cars on the road and not in the garage court. A variety of solutions for this court was sought and here the LCC found experiment was needed.[78]

Yet it was not until the publication of *Traffic in Towns* that a full awakening to the problems of coping with the motor car, and road traffic in general, took place.[79] *Traffic in Towns* contained the technical report of a team led by Colin Buchanan and a report by the Crowther Steering Group which recommended acceptance of Buchanan's conclusions. It was published in

November 1963 and welcomed by Parliament on the 10 February 1964 in a debate which carried the motion, '. . . accepts the need for a balance to be struck between the growth of traffic and the quality of urban life, and accepts that the modernizing and reshaping of our towns should proceed within the framework of the main planning concepts embodied in the reports'.[80]

This framework established that traffic could be quantitatively assessed in relation to the density and pattern of land use and that the amount generated should be related to the capacity of the streets which in turn depended on the standard of environment desired. A balance between the quality of urban life and the volume of traffic was admitted to be essentially a design problem in the arrangement of buildings and access ways. The working theory between the three examples cited relied on a network of primary distributors independent of a network of 'environmental areas'. Such areas had only limited vehicle penetration and the pedestrian was dominant – similar to the 'precincts' of Sir Alker Tripp and the 'superblocks' of Clarence Stein. The achievement of worthwhile results could only be obtained, according to Buchanan, if investment in the motor vehicle was matched by spending on town redevelopment – on the roads to accommodate it.

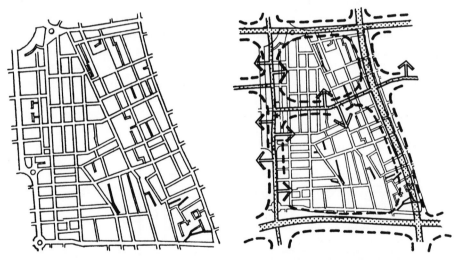

Figs. 3.13 and 3.14 Environmental areas proposed by Colin Buchanan for an area of London; before and after diagram (*from Homes, Towns and Traffic by J. Tetlow and A. Goss, Faber and Faber*)

Unfortunately, the Buchanan Report was translated too naively as a road-building programme, the environmental areas he advocated were rarely created as envisaged. The achievement of a quality of life compatible with the motor car was all too frequently missed. It was the 'rules'[81] for the creation of new roads that largely contributed to this missed opportunity. Carriageway widths, sight lines, gradients and speed curves were all, in part, responsible for destroying much of the urban quality that the Hook Report stood for, and which Buchanan reinforced. A desire for speed and safety, readily calculated by mathematics, has often submerged Buchanan's corollary for a quality of urban life which has to be seen and experienced to be appreciated.

Largely as a result of Buchanan's forecasting, new developments in 1972 were generally planned to accommodate 1.3 cars per family with additional space for parking visitors' cars. Increasing ownership of touring caravans and boats was creating an additional storage problem. The pre-war Whitehall philosophy that tenants of subsidised houses should not own cars had passed, yet it lingered for too long after the end of the war.[82] The space requirements for this level of provision were vast. The separation of car from house created large garage and parking areas that became increasingly difficult to manage visually, and a greater degree of convenience than this separation provided was now required. The opposing factors of safety and convenience that Stein so adequately solved at Radburn are being seen today in a different light.

At Milton Keynes a car-orientated society is accepted, as it had been at Radburn in 1929. Low densities were advocated by the consultants – for a car-orientated town did not need to crowd its occupants together.[83] A lowering of density to 30 people to the acre (74/ha) reduced the incidence of traffic on residential streets and hence accidents. Safety and convenience were related to density, and as a result the car was re-attached to the house. The Bean Hill estate by Foster Associates demonstrated this progression of thought.[84] Culs-de-sac were adopted, along each side of which single-storey houses were arranged in terraces, each with space for two cars immediately adjacent to the front door. A wide-frontage house provided access to the enclosed garden through a dining-kitchen, but the single-storey plan involved bedrooms facing the roadway, albeit with an open grassed front in garden city style to act as a privacy space. The essence of inter-war suburbia lingers in a new form in this latest of our new towns.

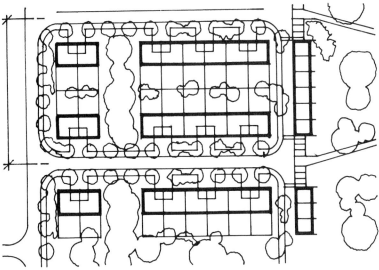

Fig. 3.15 Part layout of Bean Hill Milton Keynes (*E. R. Scoffham – adapted from drawing by Foster Associates*)

REFERENCES

1. E. Howard, *Garden Cities of Tomorrow*, 1945 edn., p. 51.
2. C. B. Purdom, *The Building of Satellite Towns*, 1949, p. 33.
3. J. Tetlow and A. Goss, *Homes, Towns and Traffic*, 1965, p. 38.
4. C. S. Perry, *Neighbourhood and Community Planning*, Regional Survey of New York, vol. 7, 129.
5. C. B. Purdom, op. cit., p. 33.
6. J. Tetlow and A. Goss, op. cit., p. 38.
7. C. S. Perry, op. cit.
8. J. Tetlow and A. Goss, op. cit., p. 41.
9. C. S. Stein, *Towards New Towns for America*, 1958 edn.
10. See later in this chapter.
11. C. B. Purdom, op. cit., p. 408.
12. J. Tetlow and A. Goss, op. cit., p. 48.
13. Ibid., p. 55.
14. National Council of Social Service, *The Size and Social Structure of a Town*, 1943.
15. W. H. E. Dudley, *The Design of Dwellings* (Dudley Report), 1944.
16. *Housing Manual*, 1944.
17. Lord Reith, *Final Report of the New Towns Committee*, Cmnd 6878, 1946.
18. J. Tetlow and A. Goss, op. cit., p. 65.
19. F. Schaffer, *The New Town Story*, 1972, p. 71.
20. Ibid., p. 72.
21. I. de Wolfe, 'Civilia', *Architectural Review*, June 1971, pp. 326–408; I. de Wolfe, 'Sociable housing', *Architectural Review*, Oct. 1973, pp. 203–18.
22. J. Tetlow and A. Goss, op. cit., p. 92.
23. F. Schaffer, op. cit., p. 72.
24. Ibid., p. 73.
25. J. Tetlow and A. Goss, op. cit., p. 93.
26. London County Council *The Planning of a New Town* (Hook Report), 1961.
27. A. Ling, *Runcorn New Town Master Plan*, 1967.
28. See Chapters 7 and 8.
29. Llewellyn-Davies, Weeks, Forestier-Walker and Bor, *Washington New Town Master Plan and Report*, 1966; *Milton Keynes Interim Report*, 1969.
30. J. Tetlow and A. Goss, op. cit., p. 129.
31. Ibid., op. cit., p. 251.
32. C. S. Stein, op. cit.
33. G. R. and C. C. Collins, *Camillo Sitte and the Birth of Planning*, 1965.
34. R. Unwin, *Town Planning in Practice*, 1909.
35. *The Provision of Dwellings for the Working Classes* (Tudor-Walters Report), Cmnd 9191, 1918.
36. A. Miller, 'Radburn, its validity today: Part 1', *Architect and Building News*, 13 Mar. 1969, pp. 40–6.
37. R. Unwin, *Nothing Gained by Overcrowding*, 1912.
38. A. Miller, op. cit.
39. C. B. Purdom, *The Building of Satellite Towns*, 1949 edn.
40. A. Miller, op. cit.
41. G. Stephenson, 'The planning of residential areas', *RIBA Journal*, Feb. 1946.
42. R. Longstreth Thompson, *Site Planning in Practice*, 1923.
43. C. S. Stein, op. cit.

44. A. Miller, 'Radburn planning, an American experiment', *Official Architecture and Planning*, Mar. 1966, pp. 370–82.
45. C. S. Stein, op. cit.
46. A. Miller, 'Radburn Planning, an American experiment', op. cit.
47. C. S. Stein, op. cit.
48. Ibid.
49. C. S. Stein, op. cit.
50. A. Miller, 'Radburn Planning, an American experiment', op. cit.
51. Ibid.
52. A. Miller 'Radburn, its validity today: Part 2', *Architect and Building News*, 27 Mar. 1969, pp. 30–4.
53. Ibid.
54. G. A. Atkinson, 'Radburn layouts in Britain, a user study', *Official Architecture and Planning*, Mar. 1966, pp. 380–2.
55. L. Mumford, *Culture of Cities*, 1938.
56. W. H. E. Dudley *The Design of Dwellings* (Dudley Report), 1944.
57. G. A. Atkinson, op. cit.
58. J. Tetlow and A. Goss, op. cit., p. 53.
59. *Housing Manual*, 1949.
60. G. Stephenson, 'The Wrexham experiment', *Town Planning Review*, Jan. 1954, pp. 271–95.
61. Ibid.
62. J. Tetlow and A. Goss, op. cit., p. 152.
63. J. L. Womersley, 'Some housing experiments on Radburn principles', *Town Planning Review*, Oct. 1954.
64. A. Miller, 'Radburn planning, an American experiment', op. cit.
65. A. Miller and J. A. Cook, 'Radburn estates revisited', *Architects' Journal*, 1 Nov. 1967, pp. 1075–82.
66. Ibid.
67. J. Tetlow and A. Goss, op. cit., p. 67.
68. Ibid, p. 105.
69. Ibid, p. 98–9.
70. F. Schaffer, op. cit., p. 114.
71. J. Tetlow and A. Goss, op. cit., pp. 105–6.
72. *Flats and Houses*, 1958, pp. 78–9.
73. Ibid, pp. 80–1.
74. Sir G. Parker-Morris, *Homes for Today and Tomorrow* (Parker-Morris Report), 1961, p. 36.
75. Ibid, p. 39.
76. Ibid, p. 45.
77. London County Council, op. cit.
78. Ibid.
79. C. Buchanan, *Traffic in Towns* (Buchanan and Crowther Reports), 1963.
80. Quoted by R. Spurrier, 'The architectural implications of the Buchanan Report', *Architectural Review*, May 1964, pp. 355–7.
81. *Roads in Urban Areas*, 1966.
82. F. Schaffer, op. cit., pp. 114–15.
83. Llewellyn-Davies, Weeks, Forestier-Walker and Bor, *Milton Keynes–Interim Report*, op. cit.
84. 'Homes for tomorrow', *Architects' Journal*, 9 May 1973, p. 1136.

4 BRAVE NEW WORLD

José Luis Sert, writing in America during the war about the outcome of studies by architects involved in the Congrès Internationaux d'Architecture Moderne (CIAM), observed that the cities of the world cannot survive unless they are made to serve their functional ends by a new architecture; an architecture in which it is recognised that our cities are 'not streets and buildings merely, not aggregations of people merely, but equally the heart and content of society'.[1]

Expression of this 'new architecture' was to come in the large post-war urban renewal schemes of slum clearance, and of rebuilding on blitzed sites. It is interesting to note that urban developments are historically older in Britain than Ebenezer Howard's concept of garden cities.[2] Earliest attempts at redevelopment date from the 1860s in London where tenements were built by charitable trusts to provide improved conditions for nineteenth-century slum-dwellers.[3] The background of post-war urban redevelopments was formed by these early trusts and thus by tradition urban redevelopment in Britain was associated with slum clearance and its replacement by relatively high-density housing.

This tradition was continued in a new architecture which originated during the beginning of the modern movement in England, and for which Le Corbusier was almost entirely responsible. His *Ville Contemporaire* was published in 1922,[4] his *Plan Voisin* in 1925,[5] and 1927 saw the publication in English of *Vers une Architecture*.[6] *Ville Contemporaire* established a vision of twenty-four identical skyscrapers rising above uniform lower blocks, in a layout which was rigidly formal and symmetrical – a city for 3 million people. *Plan Voisin* was in the same vein but with more attention paid to parks and gardens between buildings. The general rigidity remained despite this being a plan for superimposition on the centre of Paris. No merging of existing and proposed features took place – it was an absolute pattern.

Sweden, however, had started from just this point. A co-operative estate on the island of Kvarnholm near Stockholm was planned by Olaf Thunström in 1927. It was informal and recognised existence of the rock and pine forest landscape. It combined mill, elevators and different block forms of housing in a planned mix.[7] Subsequently Baudouin and Lods had built a bleak estate of fifteen-storey point blocks and three-storey blocks at La Muette, Drancy, comprising 1,200 dwellings. In Holland, J. F. Staal built a single point block at Daniel Willink Plein, Amsterdam, in 1931, and van Tijen, Brinkmann and van der Flugt built a single high slab, the Bergpolder Flats in Rotterdam, in

Fig. 4.1 Vision of a city of towers by Le Corbusier from *Vers une Architecture* (*Architectural Press*)

1934.[8] High slabs, his Siemensstädt project of 1929, were also Walter Gropius's recommendation to the 1930 Congrès Internationaux d'Architecture Moderne.[9]

Britain became a refuge for emigré architects, artists and intellectuals during the 1930s. Among them were Walter Gropius who went into partnership with Maxwell Fry, Marcel Breuer who entered a partnership with F. R. S. Yorke, and Eric Mendelsohn who formed a partnership with Serge Chermayeff.[10]

Opportunities to build produced unornamented, industrial forms reminiscent of Le Corbusier's Villa Savoie and Gropius's Bauhaus buildings at Ulm. Among these isolated examples of the new architecture, albeit not mass housing, were Welles Coates' block of Isokon flats in 1933–34 and the Tecton–Lubetkin blocks, Highpoint 1 of 1934–35 and Highpoint 2 of 1936–38 in Hampstead. But from the point of view of what was to follow perhaps the most important step was Gropius and Fry's 1935 plan for a group of three slab blocks set in an English parkland setting on St Leonard's Hill, Windsor. This estate continued the individual English desire for parkland and open space, evident in garden city and suburbia alike – a tradition following the London Square, village green and country house in a landscape, a tradition Gropius had quickly assimilated.[11] In terms of working-class housing the most significant was Kensal House in Ladbroke Grove built in 1936 on the site of an old gasworks. It was designed by Maxwell Fry in conjunction with a committee of architects which included Robert Atkinson, C. H. James, Grey Wornum and Elizabeth Denby.[12]

Fig. 4.2   Kensal House, Ladbroke Grove (*Department of Architecture Slide Library, University of Nottingham*)

The design of local authority flats, particularly in the London area, began to be influenced by this modern movement from the mid-1930s. Oaklands, a LCC scheme, contained horizontal balcony lines, rounded corners and flat roofs, yet its large White City high-density project was predominantly Georgian in inspiration. Subsidies were directed towards slum clearance, as private house-building was again profitable, and the LCC continued a policy of building flats in the inner area. Densities rose to avoid excessive overspill and ill-afforded commuting expenses and the Pembury and South Lambeth estates demonstrated that high standards of design could still be maintained.[13]

Yet in the main these inner redevelopment areas were drab and unimaginative geometric layouts. The general policy was to provide, on the same area as that from which old buildings had been cleared, new accommodation for as many persons as were there before clearance took place, while at the same time leaving ample space between buildings for light and air. Regarding standards for this space the LCC maintained that reasonable privacy was obtained by means of a grass forecourt of not less than 15 feet (4.6 m) and that the arrangement of blocks to provide light and air usually provided adequate communication and playground space between buildings. Practically the whole of this type of accommodation was in five-storey balcony-access flat blocks, with the living-rooms and most bedrooms arranged on the side with the better aspect while on the other side were kitchens and access balconies. Each flat extended the full depth of the block thereby giving through ventilation, and access was by communal staircases to the balconies.[14]

China Walk was one of these block developments by the LCC and was begun in 1928 to a density of 58.6 dwellings to the acre (145/ha). Wedgewood House was designed to provide a large quadrangle of 95 by 500 feet (29 by 152 m) as a garden, but this was railed-off and no children were allowed on the grass. The amenities of the scheme were ten barrow sheds, five workshops and an estate workshop.[15]

Disappointment with housing estates was on two fronts. Dormitory suburbs involved loneliness, expensive commuter journeys and lack of essential social life, while flatted estates without gardens in congested areas divorced their occupants from the advantages of countryside light and air. High flats were also unsuitable for both the young and the old. Opinion, however, came down in favour of the suburb. Sir Miles E. Mitchell, a former Lord Mayor of Manchester, in addressing the National Housing and Town Planning Council remarked 'there is no doubt that all persons interested in housing matters are strongly of the opinion that rehousing in cottages rather than in multi-storey flats is desirable in normal circumstances'.[16] Indeed, to check this claim it seemed, a deputation from Birmingham visited the Continent to see for themselves the best experiments in flat development and reported 'we are unanimously of the opinion that the most satisfactory system for housing the people, provided the requisite land and other facilities are available, is that which prevails in Birmingham at the present time, viz. the single or self-contained house with its own plot of garden ground attached thereto'.[17]

This prevailing attitude of the 1930s was accentuated by the war.[18] Post-war concentration was on numbers. It has been demonstrated[19] how the major effort of housing manifested itself in further proliferation of the pre-war suburb, with a slow-to-start new town programme in enactment of wartime plans for decentralisation. The principal wartime landmark, as far as urban areas were concerned, was the *County of London Plan* of 1943 by J. R. Forshaw and Patrick Abercrombie,[20] in which community grouping, social facilities, shops and schools were advocated as integral parts of schemes having a mixture of houses and flats to give residential densities, in zones around the city, of from 100 to 200 persons to the acre (247 to 494/ha). Disappointment with the results of immediate post-war efforts led in the 1950s to renewed concentration on the slum clearance redevelopment areas of London in particular.[21] But before this reorientation took place a few developments in the first years after the war picked up the pre-war modern movement's relatively minor contribution and continued it in a manner that was to provide the basis for subsequent urban redevelopment schemes.

One such connection between pre- and post-war thought was made by Tecton under Lubetkin's direction in its project at Spa Green, Finsbury. Two eight-storey flat blocks and one four-storey block in a curvilinear plan gave 129 flats at 235 persons per acre (580/ha). This project was also significant in that it was the first large-scale 'box frame' structure in Britain, having been brought here by Ove Arup from Denmark where it had been developed during the war. Spa Green's solution of large slabs, arranged to give a geometry of blocks with cubic spaces between them and humanised by planting in romantic forms, became a frequent London solution.[22]

During the war the themes of the modern movement had been applied in Sweden which was one of the few countries unaffected by a halt on construction. In 1942–45 clusters of point blocks were developed, among the earliest of which was Danviksklippen by Backström and Reinius. None of these schemes was on a vast scale, the largest, according to Pevsner, being Reimersholm with 888 flats, yet it was learned how to group high blocks.[23] Early LCC estates of flats, such as Ocean and Woodberry Down, remotely conveyed these Swedish examples in their flat roofs and wide eaves. Standards of planning improved; staircase instead of balcony access was introduced and block heights increased from five to eight and nine storeys by an introduction of lifts, often in too generous proportions due to low post-war costs of labour and materials – a situation that was soon to change.[24]

Fig. 4.3 Woodberry Down LCC Estate (*Department of Architecture Slide Library, University of Nottingham*)

In 1946 Westminster City Council, which was to prove an enlightened sponsor of post-war innovation, promoted an open competition for the planning of a 32 acre (12.95 ha) bomb-damaged site alongside the Thames opposite Battersea power station. It was won by two young architects, Philip Powell and Hidalgo Moya, who proposed tall slabs at right angles to the Thames with four-storey blocks between them so giving a series of courts in which were gardens, trees, lawns and children's play areas. It was a cubic layout that was clearly connected in inspiration to Gropius's Siemensstädt project, and it became a layout form later applied in many LCC schemes. In detail Powell and Moya provided, to Abercrombie's inner-area density of 200 persons to the acre (494/ha), 62 per cent of dwellings in nine- to eleven-storey flatted slabs, 37 per cent in four- to seven-storey maisonette blocks and 1 per cent in three-storey terrace houses.[25]

A variety of building types was offered and this was to prove a necessary solution. Decentralisation was thought to obviate the need for higher densities, despite Abercrombie's pyramidal zoning for urban areas in the *County of London Plan*. Fear of nineteenth-century squalor and the prevailing overcrowding of central London made high densities and the corollary of flat-living undesirable. Thus when the first inner London sites came to be developed with flats to Abercrombie's densities, it was a natural reaction to question motives. The same duality in housing as had existed pre-war was occurring again: low-density suburbs of houses with gardens and high-density inner schemes of flats. The desire in both areas, inner and outer, was for more space, air and light. In the inner areas, if more space was to be

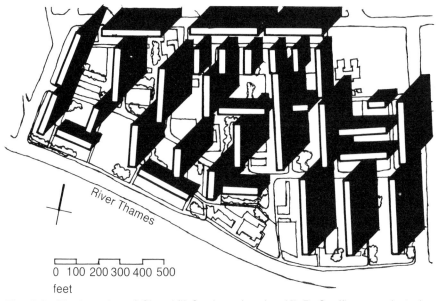

Fig. 4.4 Shadow plan of Churchill Gardens, London (*E. R. Scoffham – adapted from drawing by Powell and Moya*)

found between the hitherto closely packed five-storey flat blocks, an increase in height was seen to be the answer and the higher densities thereby gained could be used to advantage by a lowering of the heights of certain other blocks to achieve the required density. A greater sense of openness and more ground area for landscaping and playspace was the result – a result that society found acceptable immediately after the war.[26]

But the deficiency of this argument was that in order to create openness, dwellings had been placed on top of one another to an increased extent, thus accentuating the break in the traditional English connection of house and garden – a tradition that suburbia and the first new towns came to satisfy. A debate on the question of houses or flats inevitably followed. Flats were regarded as a necessary evil due to conflicts of interests which were social as well as economic in nature, and this tended to confound any rational policy for their existence. Marianne Walker did, however, put one forward,[27] but its premiss – that a policy for flats should be based on a detailed survey of population and family structure which would reveal for whom flats should be built, how many and where – was not heeded. It was not heeded until the 1950s when events had shown deficiencies in the results of decentralisation in the new towns and in the suburbs. Mrs Walker's rationalisation of the statistical basis for the disposition of flats was matched by Powell and Moya's solution which demonstrated, as a beginning, how a policy of mixing dwelling types might be achieved architecturally, while providing the much-sought-after light, air and space. Churchill Gardens became a forerunner, on its completion in 1949, of later LCC thinking.

Le Corbusier had by this time succeeded in building the ideas he had been publishing, so influentially, during the 1920s. But he was not building the new cities he had envisaged. In 1945 he had started work on a 'Unité d'Habitation' at Marseilles: an 18-storey block of 337 flats. Within the same building were a crèche, kindergarten, rooftop swimming pool, children's

Fig. 4.5 Churchill Gardens from across the Thames (*Department of Architecture Slide Library, University of Nottingham*)

playground, gymnasium, running track and solarium, while within the 8.5 acre (3.4 ha) site were a garage, swimming bath and sports ground. Le Corbusier described it, somewhat unfortunately, as a 'box of homes'.[28] It was not to be completed until 1952 but its building became well documented in the architectural press, and consequently it proved to have a deep influence throughout the LCC and the world. Le Corbusier's imagery of a 'new architecture' was finding built expression and architects eager to prove that they could create the setting for a 'new society' fell under his spell.

REFERENCES

1. J. L. Sert, *Can our Cities Survive?* 1942
2. H. Bruckmann and D. L. Lewis, *New Housing in Great Britain*, 1960, p. 19.
3. J. N. Tarn, *Working Class Housing in Nineteenth Century Britain*, 1971.
4. Le Corbusier, *Ville Contemporaire*, 1922.
5. Le Corbusier, *Plan Voisin*, 1925.
6. Le Corbusier, *Vers une Architecture*, 1923.
7. N. Pevsner, 'Roehampton, LCC Housing and the Picturesque Tradition', *Architectural Review*, July, 1959.
8. Ibid.
9. N. Pevsner, op. cit.
10. H. Bruckmann and D. L. Lewis, op. cit., p. 19.
11. *Architectural Review*, **77**, 1935, pp. 188 ff.
12. J. M. Richards, *An Introduction to Modern Architecture*, 1956 edn, p. 142.
13. Greater London Council, *85 Years of Housing by LCC and GLC Architects*, 1973.
14. G. and E. G. McAllister, *Town and Country Planning*, 1941, p. 118.
15. Ibid., p. 120.
16. Quoted by G. and E. G. McAllister, Ibid., pp. 117–18.
17. Quoted by G. and E. G. McAllister, Ibid., p. 125.
18. See Ch. 1.
19. See Ch. 2.
20. J. R. Forshaw and P. Abercrombie, *County of London Plan*, 1943.
21. See Ch. 2.
22. H. Bruckmann and D. L. Lewis, op. cit., p. 22.
23. N. Pevsner, op. cit.
24. Greater London Council, op. cit.
25. *Architects' Journal*, 30 May 1946, and 17 Apr. 1947.
26. H. Bruckmann and D. L. Lewis, op. cit. pp. 74–6.
27. M. Walker, 'Flats, their numbers, types and distribution', *Architects' Journal*, 6 Feb. 1947.
28. Le Corbusier, *Oeuvre Complete 1910–1965*, vol. 6, 1952–7 p. 154, 1962.

5 CITY OF TOWERS

The 1944 Dudley Report had said that 'there is a need for a mixed development of family houses mingled with blocks of flats for smaller households'. But neither Lord Dudley nor the 1944 *Housing Manual* took the idea any further.[1]

After the retirement of J. R. Forshaw in 1947, a reorganised LCC Architects Department under Robert Matthew made a significant break between the polarity of inner urban flats and outer suburban cottages. It fell to Whitfield Lewis, as Principal Housing Architect, and Michael Powell to bring in a pattern of housing that became standard for the LCC, and subsequently, by variation and by misapplication, for practically all city housing authorities for some 15 years.[2] Reorganisation started what became the largest and most prolific architectural department in the world during the 1950s. Arthur Ling, following his earlier work on the Greater London Plan, was Senior Planning Officer, and the Department was joined by such people as Percy Johnson-Marshall, Graeme Shankland, Walter Bor, Gordon Logie and Bruno Schlaffenberg.[3]

That pattern of housing was a continuation of the one Powell and Moya had begun at Churchill Gardens. It was developed by the addition of the point block which, properly, is a block of compact shape, substantially greater in height than in width or breadth, with small ground coverage and no horizontal circulation.[4] It did not come into its own at once for the long eleven-storey slab block, usually on 'pilotti', was a serious rival at the beginning. This slab block brought a break with the earlier five-storey flatted blocks. Its inspiration was Le Corbusier's Unité at Marseilles. It expressed the individual maisonette or flat units within it on the façade by emphasising balcony fronts, floor slabs and crosswalls. It was a simple, clear idiom. However, the large slab lost favour because its size was too dominating and overshadowing. It had limited orientation and was thus difficult to use on inner higher density sites. The point block had a wider range of orientation and a smaller shadow, and as such was more flexible in use. Later, due to economic pressures to put more flats to each floor, it became more bulky so losing many of its siting advantages.[5]

With these new block forms at their disposal the intention of LCC architects was to break down the polarity between inner and outer urban areas. Ground level freed by using these blocks could provide space for lower blocks: terrace houses and four-storey maisonette blocks, which would give large families garden space and ground-level access. The rigidity of choice between town flat and suburban house would be broken.[6]

Reinforcement for this new thinking came from the 1949 *Housing Manual* which suggested that 'unity and character are best achieved in low-density areas by the use of terraced and semi-detached houses in contrast with blocks of flats and public buildings, and in other areas by a mixture of three-storey terraces and multi-storey flats and maisonettes'.[7] The *Manual* went on to state that where sites were large enough in the 100–110 persons per acre (247–271/ha) zones, it was possible to provide 'approximately two-thirds of the total number of habitable rooms in three-storey blocks of terrace houses, or maisonettes and flats, and the balance in eight-storey blocks'.[8] The three-dimensional aspects of grouping blocks of different height were stressed, while it was stated that they should not be grouped around enclosed courts as these would be noisy, prevent circulation of air and exclude the sun – an obvious reaction against previous five-storey flatted blocks. Means of access was an aspect given considered attention. Balcony access was admitted to be the cheapest form, staircase access thought most convenient for low blocks, and lifts necessary in blocks where the entrance to the top dwelling was three or more storeys off the ground, with best lift use in blocks not less than five storeys high. The problems of balconies for sitting out, of ground-level storage, of means of escape in case of fire and of refuse disposal, all peculiar to living off the ground, were introduced.[9]

After Churchill Gardens one of the first examples of this new mixed development was the Somerford Estate for Hackney Borough Council designed by Frederick Gibberd and built between 1947 and 1949. This estate was in Churchill Gardens vein using slab blocks of different heights.[10] The new towns, however, were reluctant to build flats as they did not seem to measure up to garden city concepts,[11] and it comes as a contradiction to find that Britain's first point block was in Frederick Gibberd's The Lawn, at Harlow, built in 1950, a development of point block, three-storey flats and two storey houses.[12] But this contradiction is readily explained when it is realised that mixed development took the creation of openness, light and air as one of its objectives, just as the originators of the garden city movement had done earlier in the century.

At Lansbury the LCC developed an 8 acre (3.2 ha) 'comprehensive development area', a revolutionary planning achievement then and a necessary model, as an exhibition of architecture and planning for the Festival of Britain in 1951. In this Percy Johnson-Marshall had a large part. It provided 43 per cent of the dwellings at ground level while 60 per cent of its families had young children.[13]

The LCC's new ideas, and its first point block, were tried out at the Ackroyden estate on Wimbledon Parkside in 1952. The first eleven-storey point blocks had three flats per floor and were of traditional construction. They reduced ground cover and allowed lower blocks to be provided in the space gained, and despite some Council opposition the Housing Manager was able to charge higher rents for the upper floors because of their popularity. In the event three flats per floor proved uneconomic because of the high cost of lifts, and subsequent point blocks were designed with four flats to a floor.

The development of this point block plan, together with narrow frontage four-storey maisonette blocks, marked the beginning of a new range of type plans for mixed development schemes.[14]

Also in 1952 the Corporation of the City of London announced the results of an open competition it had promoted a year earlier for the redevelopment of a 7 acre (2.8 ha) site bombed during the war.[15] The Corporation was concerned about an imbalance of activities if some residential use was not included in central areas, and the site posed the problem that a solution should be introverted enough to protect inhabitants from outside disturbances, while providing an adequate replacement for open space which was not to be found in the vicinity. Geoffrey Powell won the competition with a solution that laid out the whole site as a series of pedestrian courts: some raised and reached by wide steps, some sunken and reached by ramps, with lawns and a pool. These became the theme of the design, linking cubic spaces around which were blocks of varying heights, the whole entered from Golden Lane through a colonnade. Golden Lane was to become a landmark in post-war housing in other ways,[16] but at the time it provided a much-needed example of mixed development on an inner urban site, so successfully executed, that as such it has rarely been surpassed. Its success was in the design of the space between buildings; in providing the whole site as a pedestrian precinct, in meeting current daylight standards so avoiding undue overshadowing, and in satisfying regulations about firefighting and means of escape, in planning blocks contrasting both in height and character and in dividing the site into interrelated courts.[17]

Golden Lane was indeed a much-needed example, for the increasing trend towards higher flat blocks was causing concern. The original arguments for mixed development were being obscured, particularly in inner high-density areas. Many of those responsible for providing such housing accommodation thought that high-density gave them no option but to build high flats.

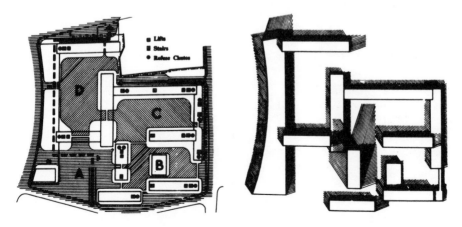

Figs. 5.1 and 5.2   Golden Lane, layout of courts and shadow diagram
(*RIBA Journal, 1969*)

Consequently a subcommittee of the Minister's Central Housing Advisory Committee was appointed under the chairmanship of Lord Brooke to report on the problems of living in flats.[18] It reported in 1952 with a restatement of the policy of mixed development that was currently being developed by the LCC, and had been earlier aired in the 1949 *Housing Manual*. Quoting figures from the LCC that between 1945 and 1951, on their flatted estates, they had built 81 houses and 13,012 flats, while the metropolitan borough councils had built 2,630 houses and 13,374 flats, the report went on to stress that it was still desirable to provide, in all areas, the maximum amount of accommodation for families with children in houses and maisonettes rather than in flats. Lansbury was quoted as an example where houses had been provided in a high-density area, and methods of grouping blocks of differing heights to give the required densities were cited. Privacy and noise were seen to be the two major objections to flat-living, the lack of an enclosed garden coming second. Thus, the report said, flats should be provided only for those to whom they offered advantages. Families with children and infirm older people were better located in alternative types of accommodation. As in the 1949 *Housing Manual*, Lord Brooke stressed the importance of careful design in such problems as access, private open space, children's play areas,

Fig. 5.3 Golden Lane tower block (*Merfyn Davies*)

balconies, communal facilities, laundries, car space, and refuse disposal. Indeed, almost as a forecast of events to come, evidence from the National Council of Social Service stated that some of the failure of flats 'arises because the block and not the individual home, is thought of as the important entity'.[19] That this situation arose because architects were attempting to build the image of a new architecture created by Le Corbusier was not questioned. Only later did disasters demonstrate an inability to cope with the fundamental problems Brooke had raised and awaken these image-making architects to the realities of living off the ground.

A spate of information appeared at this time in amplification of detailed aspects of flat-living and a policy of mixed development. In 1951 a British Standard Code of Practice had been issued on the problem of refuse chutes,[20] playgrounds were dealt with in 1952 by the National Playing Fields Associ-

Fig. 5.4 Interior of courtyard at Golden Lane (*Merfyn Davies*)

ation,[21] and the density problems of mixed development also received some guidance from the Ministry in 1952.[22]

The reasons for this preponderance of flats over other alternatives were attributed by Brooke to the subsidy machinery which favoured their development. Accordingly, the Conservative Government, as part of its policy of allowing increased participation in housing by private enterprise, made a number of policy changes during the first half of the 1950s. The 1946 Act[23] had provided subsidies for flats built on expensive sites according to a prescribed scale. It also made a subsidy available for houses in a mixed development of houses and flats, and it gave assistance towards the cost of lifts when these were in blocks of four storeys or more. The subsidies for flats and lifts caused the spate of flat-building, despite the 1949 Act which amended subsidies for expensive sites so as to disallow excessive grants at high densities.[24] In 1954 local authorities were required to prepare progammes of dwellings to be cleared over the next 5 years and this identified a tremendous backlog of unfit dwellings.[25] The following subsidy changes gave an inducement to authorities to clear them on a piecemeal basis. An Order in Council in 1955 reduced by one-sixth the subsidies provided by the 1944 Act[26] for slum clearance and overcrowding which had been extended to the post-war housing shortage. In 1956 the Housing Subsidies Act[27] further reduced subsidies on houses for the general need. These were abolished altogether in November 1956, while the subsidy was kept for slum clearance dwellings and it was increased for new towns and overspill areas. Thus a series of differential subsidies for urban decongestion and slum clearance were introduced. The subsidy on one-bedroomed dwellings, mainly to help old-age pensioners and movement from under-occupied houses, was kept after November 1956. It was by these changes that the policy of mixed development to rehouse people from slum clearance areas was considerably aided.

Golden Lane marked the establishment of mixed development as a permanent feature of the London housing scene. From this point on, aided by progressive subsidy changes, the LCC pursued the theme to its mature development at Roehampton in the late 1950s through a variety of schemes. Two streams of mixed development can be traced: one used the concrete-framed slabs inspired by Le Corbusier's Unité, and the other relied on more traditional materials, a concrete frame clad in brick with glazed panels or 'hole in the wall' windows.[28]

Of the latter, Alton East at Roehampton, followed Ackroyden from 1952. It was designed by Michael Powell, Cleeve Barr, Oliver Cox, Rosemary Stjernstedt, J. N. Wall and H. P. Harrison working under Whitfield Lewis as Principal Housing Architect, and Leslie Lane, in succession to Arthur Ling, as Senior Planning Officer. The new square point block, derived from earlier failings at Ackroyden, was used together with narrow-frontage maisonettes and a new range of cottage types.[29] Pale cream brick facings were used to the point blocks which had an irregular outline and the maisonettes and cottages had gently pitched roofs. The whole, according to

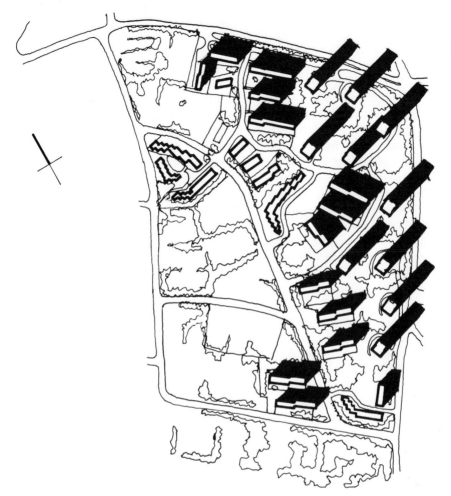

Fig. 5.5 Shadow plan of Alton East, Roehampton (*E. R. Scoffham – adapted from drawing by London County Council*)

Pevsner, 'combines perfectly with the picturesque plan, the winding streets and informally placed trees'.[30]

Meanwhile another team in the LCC Housing Division was following the Corbusian lead, and was applying his ideologies, including Le Modulor, to the design of the eleven-storey slab blocks at Bentham Road, Hackney. This estate became one of the forerunners of Alton West and of a spate of regrettable 'beton brut' structures in housing, as they were later to be called. Bentham Road contained a curious mixture in that its two-storey cottages were in the traditional or Ackroyden vein, apparently at odds with the adjacent tall blocks.[31]

Another forerunner of Alton West was the Loughborough estate. Some of the incongruities of Bentham Road were avoided; a greater degree of sophistication was achieved between the design of the seven-storey maisonettes, eleven-storey flats and the four- and six-storey maisonettes, yet the two-storey houses still remained as unresolved as before.[32] The eleven-storey maisonette block was developed further, and became a standard model for the LCC's housing programme. It used a new narrow-frontage, 12 feet (3.7 m) wide maisonette, developed in a full-size mock-up, which economised on external wall area and increased density. It involved the use of internal mechanically-ventilated bathrooms which became a standard feature, yet surprisingly these maisonettes were designed with solid fuel fires. Central heating was not yet a normal part of council housing and as a result almost impossible problems attracted a great deal of technical ingenuity. Coal had to be delivered via lifts, stored, and burned; smoke then passed through a multiple series of flues, one to each maisonette, and thence to cowls and wind deflectors on the roofs, leaving the residual ash to be disposed of by chute or lift. The narrow-frontage plan aggravated the problem of the location of a fuel store and the grouping of multiple flues so as not to lose too much floor area. Separate developments in smokeless fuels, and zones, only worsened the problem. Branched flues later solved some of the immediate planning problems of locating, at the higher levels of the building, the accumulation of flues from below.[33] Yet in spite of these difficulties the narrow-frontage three-room maisonette had advantages over flats – a greater privacy and more of the feeling of a 'house'.[34]

Loughborough Road was built from 1954–57 on a 38 acre (15.38 ha) site in South London to a density of 136 persons to the acre (336/ha). Its 1,031 dwellings were distributed as follows: 61 per cent in eleven-storey flatted slabs, 31 per cent in four-storey maisonette blocks and 8 per cent in two-storey terrace houses.[35]

Alton West was the mature development of the mixed development idea in a very English manner. It is on the site adjacent to Alton East yet design work did not start until the earlier scheme had been completed in 1952. In 1953 Leslie Martin took over from Robert Matthew as Chief Architect to the LCC, and the design team for Alton West was John Partridge, Bill Howell, John Killick, Stanley Amis, J. R. Galley and R. Stout, under the leadership of Kenneth Campbell, in succession to Michael Powell and Colin Lucas. Grouped point blocks and eleven-storey slab blocks on 'pilotti' exploited the advantages of a wooded landscape, while lines of four-storey family houses led up to the edge of Richmond Park. The contrast between the two Altons was marked; both followed separate themes in the mixed development idea. Alton East was directly descended from pre-war Swedish examples and the post-war traditional construction and detailing of Ackroyden and its ilk; whereas Alton West was a descendant of Le Corbusier's 1920 Utopias and their partly realised ambition in the Marseilles Unité. These two streams of development exist side-by-side, they were designed by different teams, under different chief architects, one continued a vernacular tradition while the other introduced an exacting, precise and intellectual architecture almost to the point of ruthlessness, but stopping short of brutalism.[36]

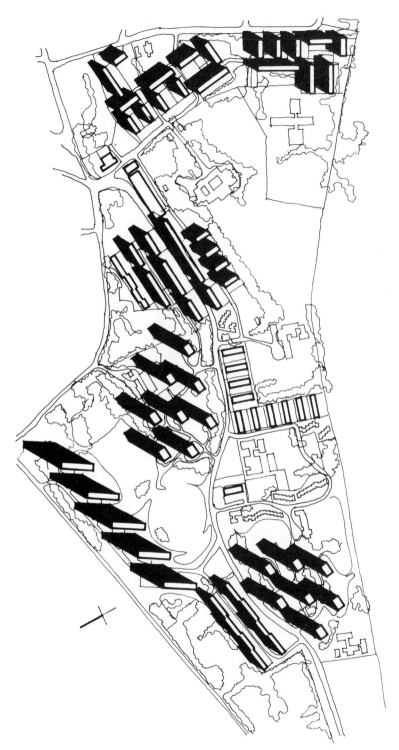

Fig. 5.6 Shadow plan of Alton West, Roehampton (E. R. Scoffham – *adapted from drawing by London County Council*)

The two streams demonstrated a dichotomy that was to frustrate later mass housing in the 1960s. That Alton West stopped short of brutality was undoubtedly due to the intelligence of its designers who were aided immeasurably by an attractive parkland site. Later developments on this theme did not show the same intelligence, they became brutal and inhuman, and on less fortunate sites gained for high-rise flat development much of its sad reputation.

But the uniqueness of Roehampton, both East and West, was in the site. Once this was a parkland of villas, many of which were removed while others were retained as social buildings to create a traditional English setting.[37] In both the severe Alton West and the more humane Alton East slabs and points rise among the trees in apparent informality, thus carrying on the tradition of park and garden at a communal level that is peculiar to English planning from the village green, the squares of London and Gropius and Fry's St Leonard's Hill scheme of 1935.

In total the Roehampton estates accommodated approximately 13,000 people at 100 persons per acre (247/ha). The 2,611 dwellings were located as follows: 41 per cent in eleven- to twelve-storey point blocks of one- and two-bedroomed flats, 12.5 per cent in eleven-storey point blocks of two-bedroomed maisonettes, 31 per cent in four-storey slabs of three-bedroomed maisonettes, 14 per cent in two- and three-storey terrace houses of three and four bedrooms, and 1.5 per cent in single-storey old persons' houses.[38] Thus full play of the mixed development idea was made in a manner which established it as a device for mass housing that was so much abused and misunderstood by others with less rational motives than the LCC teams of the 1950s. Unfortunately, as it happened, the car provision of the original design was a mere 5 per cent of all dwellings, and the spine road intended as a link to the whole estate now acts as a barrier.

But in 1959, when reviewing Roehampton, David Lewis provided a warning that while an immediately understandable scale of development was easy to achieve with tall buildings and open spaces, if maximum choice was to be given to the individual there must be large areas of low buildings related to gardens, and these must not be so ingenious in their planning to high densities 'that the amenities we are striving for are lost'.[39] Alton West was the built reality of an image of the city provided by Le Corbusier in the 1920s, as translated by a group of then young architects at the LCC. But as it turned out later, and was apparent even then, the building of images, whether those of Le Corbusier or Ebenezer Howard, did not create satisfactory housing. In this respect Roehampton was academic architecture – intellectually rational; but as housing it was misplaced. Yet it came to be repeated, and debased, just as Howard's Utopia had been debased by many after Unwin, until the next generation of architects tried out another version of Utopia.

At Eugenia Road, a first part of the Silwood estate, the Bentham Road slab was used at a time when its weaknesses were becoming apparent. Increasing cost restrictions meant that the sophisticated finishes and technology of Alton West disappeared. Plain concrete was adopted in a much more pol-

Figs. 5.7 and 5.8   Towers in an English park at Alton West, Roehampton (*Merfyn Davies*)

luted atmosphere than Roehampton, and the drabness which became un-acceptable was obvious in this high-density scheme.[40]

The traditional technology and materials of Alton East continued mainly in low- and medium-density developments, such as the Quadrant estate at Highbury and Tor Gardens in Kensington. It was a theme that was used predominantly in the relatively low-density estates of the old inner suburbs. Saint Martins at Tulse Hill began with two-storey cottages and three-storey flats, and in the mid-1960s it used a number of the five- and six-storey point blocks developed at Brooklands Park. Here in Blackheath on a good well treed site the low five-storey point block was used in combination with two-storey terraced cottages. Forest estate also used the same block and combination of types. In the late 1950s the existing Fayland estate was extended and developed in what became the last mixed cottage and six-storey block estate. The higher blocks had a 'pergola' at the sixth floor instead of the pitched roof of the former five-storey block. Later yardstick problems made the use of this low point block in a mixed development uneconomic.[41]

Fitzhugh estate continued the main openness theme of mixed development in a unique low-density scheme of entirely eleven-storey point blocks among fine trees on the edge of Wandsworth Common. The Warwick estate in Westminster combined two-storey housing, four-storey flats and twenty-one-storey flat and maisonette blocks. This latter block was a composite unit half way between a point and a slab, in which the two-storey high central corridors had maisonettes on either side and one- and two-bedroom flats at the south end. It became a frequently used block in the late 1950s and early 1960s since it was supposed that a maisonette was preferable to a flat as it involved a separate bedroom floor.[42]

Variations of the by now well established vocabulary of mixed development thus became the main preoccupation of its practitioners during the latter half of the 1950s and early 1960s. The point block moved away from the four-square plan of Roehampton, through T-shaped and Y-shaped plan forms to cruciform plans, but contained essentially similar flat units to the earlier blocks. New plan developments adopted internal bathrooms based on further advances in mechanical ventilation, and more flats per floor were included for economic reasons thus increasing the bulk of the block. For largely aesthetic considerations, the height was increased upwards to twenty storeys and sometimes more.[43]

Slab blocks developed similar more complicated forms to achieve high densities for reasons of economy. Central corridor access, as an alternative to staircase and balcony access, was developed, one of the early examples being at Camberwell when F. O. Hayes was Borough Architect in 1959.[44] Subsequently ever more complex arrangements of interlocking maisonettes, or maisonettes and flats, were developed by the LCC. Their 'scissors block' of cross-over maisonettes achieved the objective of higher densities, but had to be discontinued later owing to the complexity, and high cost, of its construction. The Banner estate, at 216 persons per acre (533/ha) the highest of the post-war period by the LCC, included such slab blocks. Despite the

Figs. 5.9 and 5.10 Traditional materials at the Quadrant Estate, Highbury (*Merfyn Davies*)

high density 14 per cent of its dwellings were at ground level with a small garden, providing an example of reasonable development at a density now considered to be intolerable.[45]

Because of the increasing complexity and inevitably higher costs of such developments the Ministry felt it necessary in 1958 to issue a guide on the design of layouts in the mixed development theme in order to achieve greater economy.[46] The overriding consideration, one which has often needed stressing to those involved in building high flats, was that the basic objective was to keep down the proportion of dwellings in high buildings. Consequently schemes on a number of different sites were given as comparisons of how to gain cost savings by reducing block heights, while still achieving the same densities.

Daylighting was proving to be one of the main bugbears in layout. The Ministry recognised this and established criteria for laying out different heights of blocks to the highest possible density. By using blocks spaced to their highest density it should then be possible to reduce the average height of building over the whole of a given site. Often authorities were spacing blocks too far apart, either in a misunderstanding of daylight considerations, or simply to be on the safe side. *Flats and Houses* went on to reiterate many of the criteria that had been stressed over and again since 1949 in numerous publications, but which were too often going unheeded. Balcony access was still regarded as the cheapest method of access, but when it was exposed at four storeys or more above ground it became inhospitable. For this reason the internal corridor had been devised, a solution that reached its ultimate development in the 'scissors block'. Narrow frontage, a theme followed since the Government's 1952 economy drive,[47] was again favoured to obtain higher densities both for two- and three-storey houses and for slab maisonette blocks of different heights.

Internal bathrooms, in both low and high blocks, were given emphasis by the winter of 1955–56 when 18 per cent of post-war local authority houses in England and Wales suffered frost damage to their water services. As a result the Ministry developed a 'frost proof' house which was exhibited at the Ideal Homes Exhibition in 1956. It contained all its plumbing, supply and waste services within the external walls, a development that favoured narrow-frontage, internal bathroom plans, once the effect of the 1953 Model By-Laws, to rectify an obsolete prohibition that sanitary plumbing could not be taken to ground inside dwellings, had been assimilated by building inspectors.[48]

Balconies were one of those aspects to fall foul of architectural imagery. They were invaluable in flats and maisonettes for a whole range of purposes: plants, prams, drying washing, airing, sitting out and so on, but unfortunately they were often allocated to dwellings with a view to the pattern they made on the elevation rather than on their usefulness to tenants.[49]

Mixed development was not limited to the London area. Elsewhere the City of Sheffield, under Lewis Womersley, was one of its leading exponents. The Gleadless estate, started in 1955, was 300 acres (121 ha) of steeply sloping land. It was developed with two-storey houses, three-storey flats and four- to six-storey maisonettes, with three thirteen-storey point blocks on the highest hilltop. It represented on a wooded site in suburbia, just as Roehampton did, another branch of the garden city idea to a high density – the openness and air, the reaction to the slum, a marriage of the two vastly different Utopias of Howard and Le Corbusier.[50]

Fig. 5.11 Mixed development at Scotswood, Newcastle-upon-Tyne (*John Ford*)

Fig. 5.12 More mixed development at Gateshead (*John Ford*)

Final expression of the mainstream of mixed development by the LCC came in 1963 with the building of the Canada estate. High building continued on other projects but Canada was one of the last to accept the basic tenets of mixed development: to provide a variety of accommodation for different family sizes and types, to give a variety of architectural form in contrasting building heights and shapes, to provide good outdoor amenities because of the space between buildings and to provide a pattern within which it was possible to obtain an economic balance of expensive high and relatively inexpensive low buildings.[51] On its completion Canada received architectural acclaim. The tall blocks had a heavy modulation reflecting the internal

Figs. 5.13 and 5.14 Traditional technology in a park at the Dacres Estate, Lewisham (*Merfyn Davies*)

arrangement of flats, they were in a 'brutalist' idiom with exposed concrete structure, dark grey brick and black pointing.[52] But the reaction of residents to this architectural setting was hostile. The use of 'tough' finishes provoked some 'tough' treatment, thus raising a whole host of other questions which had to be answered in different ways.[53]

Perhaps the most outstanding example of all that mixed development involved, closely interwoven with another theme to which it was linked, occurs in the Barbican. Now at last finally completed, the Barbican involved the idea of comprehensive redevelopment that had been earlier tried at Lansbury for the Festival of Britain. A mixture of uses, residential accommodation, commercial, shopping, cultural and educational, occurs simultaneously with the theme of mixed development. The residential area provides accommodation for 6,500 people in some 2,100 flats and houses, to a density, originally planned at 300 persons per acre (741/ha), of 230 persons per acre (568/ha).[54]

The Barbican was a direct descendant of Golden Lane. Chamberlin, Powell and Bon were the architects and they received the commission largely due to their success on the nearby Golden Lane. It has taken some 30 years to develop and is in the same idiom: a series of inter-related courts, with varied building heights and forms. Its achievement is tremendous. Such consistency of architectural quality over such a long period of time, and an undaunted attempt to integrate and humanise urban buildings are outstanding. But the Barbican is not for council tenants. Its rents are high, the city executive will largely be its resident, and he does not have the same requirements as a low-income family with children from a slum clearance area.[55]

Exhaustion of the mixed development theme, one which many architects today still believe valid if used in the manner for which it was originally developed, came in a series of schemes in the 1960s. Pepys estate, Deptford, used an eight-storey crossover maisonette block, two-, three- and four-storey flats and three elegant twenty-four-storey slab blocks. It was the final statement of the traditional design approach which began for the LCC at Ackroyden 10 years earlier.

At both Brandon and Swedenborg Square the tall block was carried to

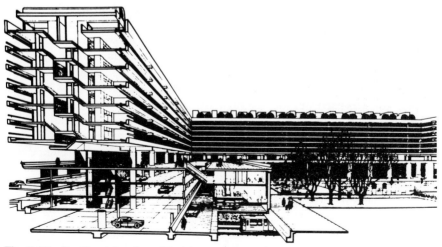

Fig. 5.15 Sectional drawing of Barbican courtyard (*Architectural Review, August 1973*)

Fig. 5.16   The finality of mixed development; Pepys Estate, Deptford (*Department of Architecture Slide Library, University of Nottingham*)

its limit. Swedenborg used a 'swastika' plan which was probably the most efficient devised, but was aptly named in view of the then prevailing demise of high living on sociological grounds. As Pepys represented the final expression of the traditional school, so the Ferrier estate at Kidbrook Green represented that of the Corbusian concrete school begun at Bentham Road and Loughborough Road. Its discipline, through two-storey houses, five-storey maisonettes and eleven-storey point blocks, was rigid and formal; the scheme worked as precisely as its appearance suggested.[56]

But the growing storm of criticism of tall blocks on sociological grounds derived from the unintended and unforeseen presence in them of families with children, for whom they were never intended.[57] This criticism was brought to a head by the disastrous collapse of the Ronan Point block in 1968.[58] Ronan Point was a belated disaster for high rise and for mixed development, for almost as soon as the idea had got off the ground in the early 1950s another group of architects, more closely attached to the basic premises of CIAM, had seen that what was happening was not a new architecture embodying the 'heart and content of society' as Sert has described. Together they moved in a different direction and it is from them that the progression of built form into the 1960s must be traced.

Fig. 5.17   Point blocks, Brandon Estate (*Merfyn Davies*)

REFERENCES

1. W. H. E. Dudley, *The Design of Dwellings* (Dudley Report), 1944.
2. K. Campbell, 'Home sweet home', *Building*, 31 Aug. 1973, pp. 47–54.
3. J. Craig, 'London planning in retrospect', *Official Architecture and Planning*, May 1965, pp. 677–81.
4. A. W. C. Barr, *Public Authority Housing*, 1958, p. 63.
5. K. Campbell, op. cit., pp. 50–3.
6. Ibid., p. 50.
7. *Housing Manual*, 1949.
8. Ibid., p. 33.
9. Ibid., pp. 82–4.
10. A. W. C. Barr, op. cit., p. 35.
11. F. Schaffer, *The New Town Story*, 1972, p. 112.
12. A. W. C. Barr, op. cit., p. 35.
13. J. Craig, op. cit., p. 679.

14. Greater London Council, *85 Years of LCC and GLC Housing*, 1973.
15. *Architects' Journal*, 6 Mar. 1952.
16. See Ch. 6.
17. H. Bruckmann and D. L. Lewis, *New Housing in Great Britain*, 1960, p. 58.
18. Lord H. Brooke, *Living in Flats* (Brooke Report), 1952.
19. Ibid., p. 14.
20. *Refuse Chutes in Multi-Storey Buildings*, BS 1703, HMSO 1951.
21. National Playing Fields Association, *Playgrounds for Blocks of Flats*, 1952.
22. *The Density of Residential Areas*, 1952.
23. Housing (Financial and Miscellaneous Provisions) Act, 1946.
24. Housing Act, 1949.
25. Housing (Repairs and Rents) Act, 1954.
26. Housing (Temporary Provisions) Act, 1944.
27. Housing Subsidies Act, 1956.
28. Greater London Council, op. cit.
29. H. Bruckmann and D. L. Lewis, op. cit.
30. N. Pevsner, 'Roehampton, LCC and the Picturesque Tradition', *Architectural Review*, July, 1959.
31. Greater London Council, op. cit.
32. Ibid.
33. A. W. C. Barr, op. cit., p. 74.
34. H. Bruckmann and D. L. Lewis, op. cit., p. 85.
35. Ibid., p. 68.
36. N. Pevsner, op. cit.
37. D. L. Lewis, *Architectural Design*, Jan. 1959, p. 21.
38. H. Bruckmann and D. L. Lewis, op. cit., p. 60.
39. D. L. Lewis, op. cit., p. 21.
40. Greater London Council, op. cit.
41. Ibid.
42. Ibid.
43. A. W. C. Barr, op. cit. p. 63.
44. H. Bruckmann and D. L. Lewis, op. cit., p. 63.
45. Greater London Council, op. cit.
46. *Flats and Houses*, 1958.
47. *Houses 1952* and *Houses 1953*.
48. A. W. C. Barr, op. cit., pp. 93–4.
49. M. Willis, *Private Balconies*, 1956.
50. *Architectural Design*, Sept. 1961.
51. A. W. C. Barr, op. cit., p. 36.
52. Greater London Council, op. cit.
53. See D. Turin, 'The Seamy Side', *Architects' Journal*, 23 Sept. 1964.
54. J. Tetlow and A. Goss, *Homes, Towns and Traffic*, 1965, pp. 164–5.
55. C. G. L. Shankland, 'Barbican and the Elephant' *Architectural Design*, Oct. 1959.
56. Greater London Council, op. cit.
57. K. Campbell, op. cit.
58. *Report of the Inquiry into the Collapse of Flats at Ronan Point, Canning Town*, 1968.

6 STREETS IN THE AIR

Mixed development, and its unfortunate corollary, high rise, had been the built realisation of an image provided principally by Le Corbusier, but also by Gropius and architects in Sweden during the 1920s and 1930s.[1] It was a curious hybrid of a variety of ideas, the most influential and historically earliest of which were those of Le Corbusier. Like Howard's Garden City, Le Corbusier's city for 3 million and his later *Ville Radieuse* were social arguments against the oppression and overcrowding of the nineteenth century. But Le Corbusier was an architect and he transmitted his thesis as a built form solution, not in organisational, social and literary terms as Howard had done. Howard had needed architects, Parker and Unwin, to bring his vision towards reality; Le Corbusier had not. Where Howard's thesis had suffered for its lack of a three-dimensional image, Le Corbusier's suffered from being socially less resolved, an imposed architectural solution. Yet both men strove for openness, light, air and trees as the setting for a balanced community. Howard, and particularly Unwin, saw the solution in low-density development, while Le Corbusier saw it in just the opposite: a higher-than-ever density of development. Unwin provided the socially more acceptable houses in ample gardens, and Le Corbusier gave us dwellings stacked upon one another to provide the open space that high buildings inevitably generate between them.

Le Corbusier's line was followed by those bringing in a policy of mixed development from 1947 to 1952 in order to marry the dual advantages of town and country within the congested city,[2] whereas Howard, Unwin and Reith had performed the same marriage to decongest the city outside its boundaries.[3] Howard's Garden City had trod an eventful path and had been much maligned and misunderstood, before it gained official blessing in the 1946 New Towns Act, and thereafter continued to produce much the same built form solutions that it had spawned in the inter-war suburbs. Le Corbusier's city had no such gestation period; it was adopted virtually from the drawing board and the exhibition screens of CIAM. Built evidence was almost non-existent.

Because of this what first got built was very much the literal interpretation of an image, despite the current building of Le Corbusier's Unité d'Habitation at Marseilles. Had the content and reality of the Unité and its origin in Le Corbusier's writing and drawings been examined at the time, rather than the external image it created, events might have been significantly different. The Unité was a part realisation of Le Corbusier's project for

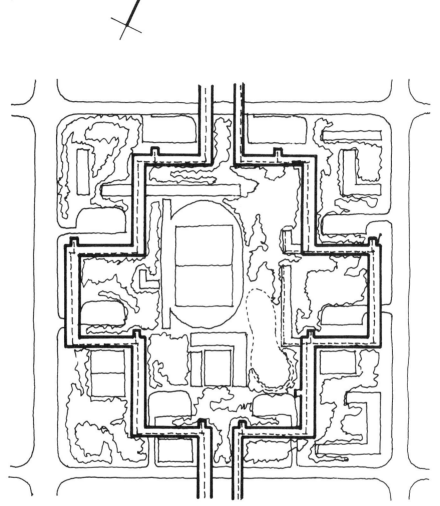

Fig. 6.1 Grid block from Ville Radieuse (*E. R. Scoffham – adapted from drawing by Le Corbusier*)

Algiers of 1930,[4] developed and explained in his *Ville Radieuse* of 1933.[5] *Ville Radieuse* in turn was a development, rationalisation and improvement upon his earlier *Plan Voisin*[6] and city for 3 million.[7] Le Corbusier at least progressed his ideas, even if those who followed and attempted to copy him did not.

The first expression of Le Corbusier by the LCC at Bentham Road and Loughborough Road[8] took the elevations and block form of the Unité as its model – an expression of the dwellings within, by emphasised balcony fronts, crosswalls and infill panels in concrete. Yet it was the plan and section that were Le Corbusier's prime contribution, and their origin must be traced from his *Ville Radieuse*.

This originated as a 'reply to Moscow' – a reply to a questionnaire sent to Le Corbusier by Russian authorities asking him to give his solutions for the future of the capital; and the answer 'became the logical sequel to my previous researches'.[9] Le Corbusier was concerned about the spread and lack of urbanity inherent in garden city arguments, and proposed an intensification of people in high-rise buildings, which because of their nature, would free the ground for cars, parks and gardens. He never disputed the premiss of the garden city enthusiasts that new towns should be self-contained communities providing every facility for home, work and play, or that they should be divided into sections, each a self-contained part of the whole. He answered the objectives of the garden city movement in a manner which made full use of developing technology. High buildings were served by lifts, and the growth of car ownership was foreseen. His solution was technical, and rigorously precise.

Buildings were separated from roads. Roads were independent traffic routes crossing open parkland in a gridiron pattern, and buildings stood in parkland away from these roads. Gone was the traditional street of pedestrians and vehicles. 'The house no longer needs to rise above the street; the street is no longer at the foot of the house.'[10] Having postulated a high density of development, up to 1,000 persons per acre (2,471/ha), Le Corbusier was then concerned to provide a method of access and a way of living in these high blocks. He dismissed walking up more than three flights of steps as a crime, used the lift to give access to higher levels and proposed a notion of 'interior streets' at various intervals in height throughout his building blocks.[11] These 'streets in the air', as he termed them, were horizontal, they were served by lifts every 100 metres (330 feet) and as a result his building became a continuous ribbon of dwellings which could be bent and modelled to provide enclosed courts, to obtain sunlight in all dwellings and to give a view of parkland from each dwelling. His 'street in the air' linked communal amenities and provided access to children's playgrounds, all within the building, and it protected inhabitants from inclement weather.

At Marseilles the Unité d'Habitation was a small slice of this ribbon of building. It contained the horizontal 'streets in the air', linked dwellings to lifts and to amenities, and it protected from the weather. Yet this seemed not to be realised by architects working at the LCC until much later when the course of mixed development was unalterable. Only one London authority took the content of the Unité and translated it in a British context, and this was the Borough of Camberwell under Frank Hayes.[12] But by the time this had happened in the late-1950s, other developments had interpreted Le Corbusier's *Ville Radieuse* on a much larger and more meaningful scale.

These developments owe much to the work of a small international group of architects who were part of CIAM, and who were to assume some of its intentions when it finally foundered in 1956 at Dubrovnik.[13] It had been realised during the 1953 Congress at Aix-en-Provence that CIAM had lost its purpose. There were too many members and its organisation was unwieldy. Consequently a group of individuals emerged who had formed a

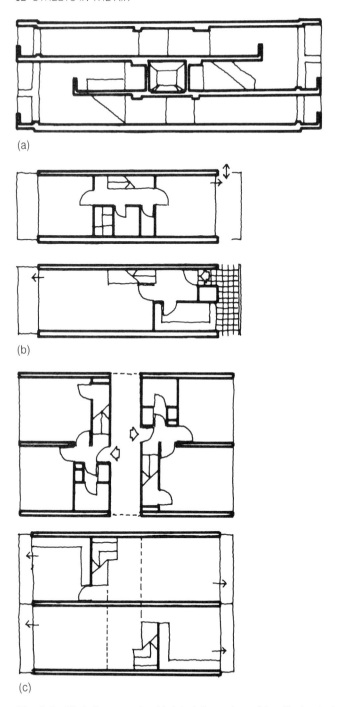

Fig. 6.2 Variations on the Unité: (a) section of Le Corbusier's Marseilles block. (b) LCC Alton West block, plan indicating access balcony, and (c) Camberwell central corridor block, plan (*E. R. Scoffham – adapted from drawings by Le Corbusier, London County Council and Camberwell Borough Council*)

close working relationship and had started work on projects that seemed to them important. That group was called Team 10. Among its members were two young British architects, Alison and Peter Smithson, and among their projects was an entry for the Golden Lane competition in 1952.

Their entry was unplaced; Geoffrey Powell had carried off the prize. Yet in 1953 Team 10 was left in possession of CIAM's organisation for the Dubrovnik Congress in 1956. They met at Doorn in 1954 and at Otterlo in 1959,[14] and through their various publications the Smithsons' unpremiated entry was seen by many. Their Golden Lane project was elaborated into a general theory and was first presented to the Aix-en-Provence Congress in 1953.[15]

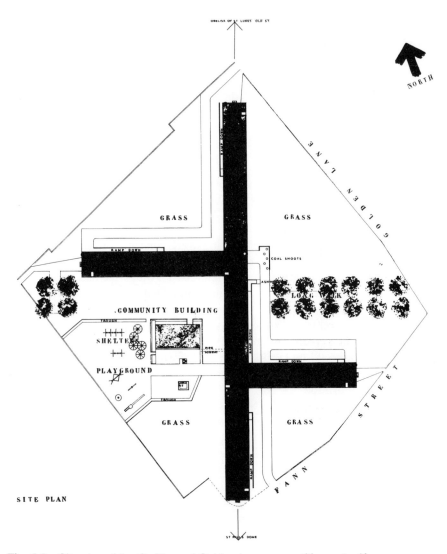

Fig. 6.3 Site plan of the Smithsons' Golden Lane competition entry (*from Ordinariness and Light by Alison and Peter Smithson, Faber & Faber*)

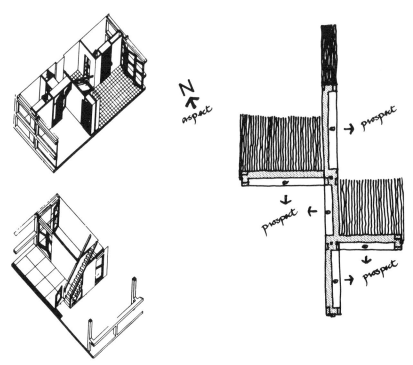

Fig. 6.4 Diagram of principles for the Smithsons' Golden Lane entry (*from Urban Structuring by Alison and Peter Smithson, Studio Vista*)

Essential ingredients in their thinking were concepts of 'association' and 'identity'. Identity was a quality they argued was missing from official sociological division of the city into different-sized groups. It had more to do with the physical grouping of dwellings and facilities, and parallels were drawn in the social coherence of the by-law street. A community they argued comprised a hierarchy of 'associations' – a complex pattern of movement between different persons' interests. Both concepts were to them irretrievably linked and should be facilitated by built forms. It was a theory 'in direct opposition to the arbitrary isolation of the so-called communities of the Unité and the 'neighbourhood' '.[16]

At the 1953 Congress the Smithsons proposed a multi-level city with 'streets in the air' linking a continuous residential complex, and connected as necessary to work places and those ground elements necessary at each level of 'association'. The house and the street were basic elements of this complex.[17] Their Golden Lane entry was a part of this concept of the city, much as Le Corbusier's Unité had been a part of his *Ville Radieuse*. Le Corbusier had started from a concept of the city and had later built the Unité as a portion of it. The Smithsons appeared to work from the opposite direction – their project was expanded to a notion of the city.

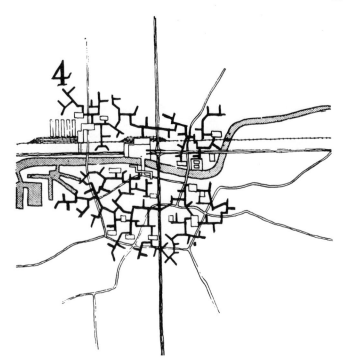

Fig. 6.5 The Smithsons' expansion of their Golden Lane entry into a city structuring diagram (*From Team 10 Primer by Alison and Peter Smithson, MIT Press*)

Yet the similarities in the two solutions were remarkable. Both adopted the 'street in the air' as an essential part of their arguments. 'Streets would be places and not corridors or balconies, thoroughfares where there are shops, postboxes, telephone kiosks.'[18] But here the similarities end, for whereas Le Corbusier's street was an internal one, the Smithsons' was open to the air although covered over, giving views outwards to parkland and open space.

Unlike Le Corbusier, the Smithsons were working in a period when high-flat living was becoming an increasing part of the urban scene. Their proposals were a reaction to the apparent inhumanity of the methods of access and conditions of living in these high balcony- and staircase-access blocks. Le Corbusier's solution was a direct reaction to the darkness and squalor of the nineteenth century. Both the Smithsons and Le Corbusier were part of the CIAM, at different times, that carried the message of the modern movement from 1928 to 1956.

Considerable difference in approach was thus demonstrated between those who took the images of Le Corbusier, and those who perhaps tried to understand what he said and what his drawings actually contained. Peter Smithson explained, 'our current aesthetic and ideological aims are not 'castles in the air' but rather a sort of new realism and new objectivity, a sort

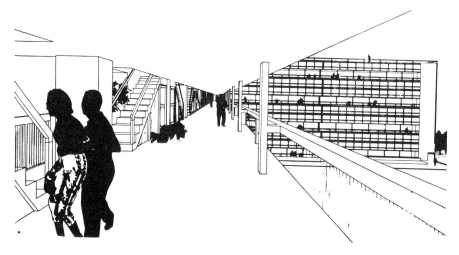

Fig. 6.6 'Streets in the air' at Golden Lane (*from Team 10 Primer by Alison and Peter Smithson, MIT Press*)

of radicalism about social and building matters; and a matter of acting in a given situation'.[19]

Another of the Smithsons' concepts of urban form was that of 'cluster'; a grouping of the traditional units of house, street and so on, and one which they introduced to the final CIAM Congress at Dubrovnik in 1956. The term 'cluster' was made public in America through an article by Kevin Lynch in 1954,[20] where he defined it as a 'unit of natural aggregation'. He also introduced the idea of 'grain' as an assessment of the distribution of functions according to their size and mixture. Both terms found expression in the work of Denis Lasdun, himself a member of CIAM. In 1955 he designed two so-called 'cluster-blocks' in the Usk Street Development at Bethnal Green.[21] He was concerned, as were the Smithsons, not to perpetuate the kind of diagrammatic building that was coming from many of the London authorities and new towns. He designed two eight-storey blocks of a split-butterfly plan that attempted to create ground-level spaces of the same urban 'grain' as the adjacent nineteenth-century streets. The blocks themselves were made up of maisonettes about the size of a semi-detached house and this unit was expressed on the exterior as a 'cluster' of homes around vertical services. His later Claredale Street block was intended to be seen as a kind of 'vertical street' of stairs, lifts, services and public spaces, flanked by two-storey, two-maisonette units of semi-detached house scale.

In approach it was almost the antithesis of Le Corbusier's and the Smithsons' horizontal 'streets in the air'. Yet Lasdun was concerned to group dwellings in some more meaningful way about 'vertical streets' in the air. Both solutions were aimed at the same end-product – a more realistic and less diagrammatic interpretation of methods of putting human beings into buildings at an urban scale. In influence Lasdun's work was marked. Later point

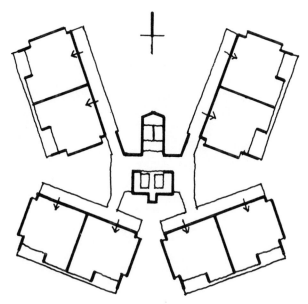

Fig. 6.7 Diagram of plan principle for Denis Lasdun's cluster blocks (*E. R. Scoffham – adapted from drawing by Denis Lasdun and Partners*)

and slab blocks in London did make some attempt to identify the individual dwelling in what was too often an anonymous straight-sided block, and the LCC's Canada estate demonstrated the end-product of developments along this theme. But Usk and Claredale were still high flat-blocks and did not answer the basic questions the Smithsons had posed.

In 1953 the Smithsons entered another competition for the design of buildings for Sheffield University. While not housing, the solution and the image it created had much in common with what was soon to happen in that same city. The Golden Lane theme was extended – patterns of pedestrian movement were seen to be the key to the architectural organisation of the buildings, and 'streets in the air' appeared again.[22]

Park Hill, behind Sheffield's Midland Station, became the first built realisation of Le Corbusier's theme of 'streets in the air' in Britain. It was designed from 1953 onwards, started on site in 1957, and completed in 1961. Despite dispute it is generally resolved that Ivor Smith, Jack Lynn and Ted Nicklin, working for the then city architect Lewis Womersley, were its job architects, assisted by G. I. Richmond and A. V. Smith. Their solution is not surprising when it is realised that Jack Lynn, working for Gordon Ryder and Peter Yates, had entered the Golden Lane competition with a solution that offered high-level street decks without actually using the term, and had been as unplaced as had the Smithsons, who incidentally had introduced him to Ivor Smith in connection with the latter's housing thesis at the Architectural Association. There can be no doubt that Le Corbusier provided each entry with the germ of the idea in his Unité, and that his *Ville Radieuse* was the original model for them all.

Fig. 6.8 Urban structure at Park Hill, Sheffield (*John Ford*)

Fig. 6.9 Repetitive monotony at Park Hill, Sheffield (*John Ford*)

Park Hill has been extensively published and reviewed since it was first revealed in 1955.[23,24] It contains 995 dwellings, 500 being maisonettes and 495 being flats. There are 31 shops, 4 pubs, a laundry, 74 lock-up garages and 100 parking spaces. A sloping site offered the opportunity to give access to the street decks at ground level from the top of the site, with lifts to the shopping centre at the lower, Sheaf Valley, end. The decks were located every three floors vertically, and the block heights varied from four storeys at the top end, to fourteen storeys at the lower end of the site. One continuous building, the horizontal street decks within it, stretched for half a mile (0.8 km) and was folded at angles of 112.5° and 135°, to enclose spaces for play, both hard and soft. Decks passed from one side of the block to the other at junctions, so achieving alternating views across the city, and into internal spaces; they were planned 10 feet (3 m) wide, so as to be adequate for milk floats, children's play, and so on, and to give access to the flats and maisonettes above and below the deck.

According to the architects, street decks at Park Hill followed from an analysis of working-class life in Sheffield, and they were intended to offer the same kind of community focus to working people's lives as did the by-law street – similar reasoning to that adopted by the Smithsons. It became clear that the deck was a social device as well as a means of access, and in this context it is interesting to record the comparison with balcony access. Balcony access had long been regarded as the cheapest means of access to high flats but was inhospitable above about four storeys. It was a method used on the early slab blocks of the LCC at Bentham and Loughborough Road, and on pre- and post-war flatted estates throughout the country. To use balcony access efficiently the maximum number of flats had to be served from any one lift point. At Park Hill the usual 4 foot (1.2 m) wide balcony on every floor was replaced by street decks, 10 feet (3 m) wide, on every third floor.[25] By virtue of continuous buildings the decks were also continuous and so achieved a far greater economy in use than did balcony access in slab blocks, but with the added social advantages of 'street life', protection from the weather and safety.

Thus Park Hill was a housing scheme that became one complete building rather than a series of separate dwellings or blocks assembled into a layout. It offered a fresh notion of urbanity in housing; it offered an alternative to traditional concepts of the house and its grouping that the Smithsons, Team 10 and CIAM had tried so hard to achieve after Le Corbusier. It was a 'new architecture' which satisfied those who saw one in terms of an image, and also those who wanted a deeper social meaning – a greater objectivity. It seemed the end of a line, a happy marriage of two very different approaches, both of which started from the same Unité at Marseilles.

Sheffield City went on to build the Hyde Park scheme higher up the hill behind Park Hill in the 1960s. It was larger and higher, and lost much of the precision and consistency of organisation that had been demonstrated at Park Hill.[26]

While Park Hill was building the London Borough of Camberwell had developed the central corridor maisonette block – another variation of the Unité translated into English local authority housing standards. The LCC had persisted in using outside balcony access in its versions of the Unité on such sites as Loughborough Road. The Camberwell version was nearer to Le Corbusier's original in that the access was central – an internal corridor street.

But this version was used in mixed development schemes so that the block incorporating the internal street was not continuous as Le Corbusier had intended it, but an independent slab.

Such blocks were used at Sceaux Gardens in 1957,[27] Mansion Street in 1959 and Pelican Yard in 1960, all by Camberwell under Frank Hayes.[28] These derivations were all regressions from the original model of Le Corbusier. Only Alton West achieved, in its sophisticated external styling, the visual image of the Unité, while Park Hill came nearest to the total city concept that Le Corbusier had in mind.

It was the City of Westminster who provided the next step. In 1960 it had sponsored a competition for the design of housing on an urban site at Lillington Street in Pimlico, not far from its earlier competition site at Churchill Gardens. The results demonstrated that the 'street in the air' concept had arrived, for the first two premiated schemes adopted this approach to the problem of accommodating families at a density in excess of 200 persons to the acre (494/ha). It was interesting to find that the assessor, Geoffrey Powell, had moved his position from mixed development; for it was he who had won the Golden Lane competition in 1952 with a, then acceptable, mixed development solution, while unpremiated entries had included the deck access alternative now built at Sheffield. First premium went to John Darbourne, and second premium to Alec Collerton, Winston Barnett and Newman Smith.[29]

John Darbourne's solution introduced to deck access the use of traditional materials and detailing that the LCC had followed in a chain of schemes from the Ackroyden estate.[30] In appearance it owed nothing to Le Corbusier; only

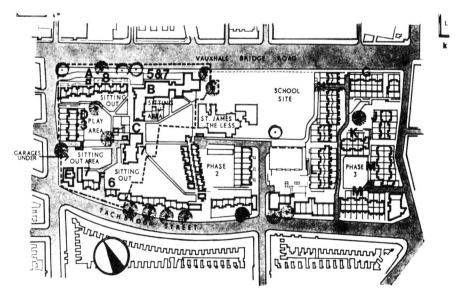

Fig. 6.10 Site plan of Lillington Street (Gardens) indicating three phases of development (*Architects' Journal, October 1969*)

in its organisation was there any similarity. Darbourne managed to achieve interest and variety, and an expression of individual dwelling units in the modelling of his blocks that Park Hill had concealed behind a rigid structural module and flat façades. The decks themselves were not the straight lines of Park Hill; they continually changed direction because the structural bays of the blocks were staggered and the sizes of the individual dwelling units were allowed to vary the width and shape of the block from bay to bay. The decks were humanised by planting on the outer edge, and they were partly covered and brick-paved thereby avoiding the seemingly unending repetition of Park Hill.[31]

'Streets in the air' now offered a means of allowing families with children to live at a distance from the ground, especially when the street deck met ground level naturally, or lifts led to a point of community interest. By this means prams, deliveries, small trolleys, bicycles and so on could be brought to the front door of each dwelling. The advantages this offered prompted the Ministry in 1961 to suggest that 'ways of meeting the need for outdoor space may come to be found in newer forms of access to the dwelling associated with covered space in the open air at the level of the home, and providing some of the virtues of the back yard and the pedestrian street'.[32]

Lillington Gardens, as it was named, took a long time to build largely because of its complexity. Stages 1 and 2 were built more-or-less as originally designed, but stage 3 develops the street deck theme further. Here the deck was not located on one side of the block giving access to dwellings on the other, better-aspect, side. Instead it was positioned in the centre of the block, was open to the sky and gave access to dwellings on each side. It became a familiar street with houses on both sides, while being open to the weather it attempted to avoid the impression of being within a building. It could, in fact, have been a street on the ground.[33]

Because of the length of time in construction Lillington Gardens was overtaken by other street deck schemes which were designed after the date of the competition. The first of these was at Washington in County Durham,

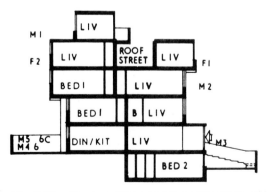

Fig. 6.11 Block section used in section three of Lillington Street (*Architects' Journal, October 1969*)

designed by the second-prizewinners of the Lillington Street competition, Alec Collerton and Winston Barnett working with J. H. Napper and Partners.[34] Here a 16 acre (6.5 ha) gently sloping site was developed with continuous three-, four- and five-storey deck access blocks to 136 persons per acre (336/ha), the deck running one floor down from the top storey in all the blocks so that at the highest point of the site nearest to the town centre it was possible to ramp off the deck naturally. It was in the same traditional materials as Lillington Gardens but without the complexity of block configuration. The street deck was part open, part covered, and surfaced as a pavement with paving slabs. Two communal laundries were provided along its length. Perhaps the main achievements of the scheme, however, were in accommodating 60 per cent car provision from the outset, and not least in building to such a density and in such a manner in a mining village in County Durham that only later became the core of a new town. Building started in 1964 and was completed in 1967.

After the Ministry had accepted the idea of street decks in the Parker-Morris Report of 1961, it followed this up in a scheme at St Mary's in Oldham designed by the Research and Development Group, then led by Oliver Cox, in collaboration with Max Lock and Partners and Tom Cartlidge, Oldham's borough architect.[35] However, the Ministry did not get free of ideas of mixed development as the scheme included family houses on the ground in addition to the street deck blocks of three, four and five storeys. In addition to this, because of Government encouragement of industrialised building from the early 1960s, the scheme was built by Laings in a modified version of its Jespersen system. The unresolved and often clumsy detailing of this early venture into large-scale industrialisation resulted in a reversion to the more brutal aspects of Park Hill including a straight street deck, completely covered but with columns on the open side to support the upper floor, and straight-sided blocks.

These initial schemes were followed by a multitude of others in various parts of the country, many misunderstanding some of the fundamental principles of the theme, and often taking them out of their original context to disastrous effect; demonstrating yet again how easy it was to take an image and use it out of the context for which it had been originally developed. From 1966 there were many schemes: St Anne's, Rotherham, by Gillinson, Barnett and Partners,[36] Pleasant Vale, Southampton, by Wilson and Womersley[37] and Packington Street, Islington by Co-operative Planning Ltd.[38] The Yorkshire Development Group (YDG), under Martin Richardson, started the first of its industrialised street-deck schemes at Leek Street in Leeds in 1966, to be followed by others in like manner at Hull, Sheffield and Nottingham.[39]

London County Council architects never accepted the mainstream development of 'streets in the air' in any of their work. They were far too committed to a mixed development policy so that when a change was made, because high building had fallen into disrepute in the mid-1960s, events had already moved architectural thinking away from living off the ground whatever the method of access to dwellings. The LCC missed the mainstream of

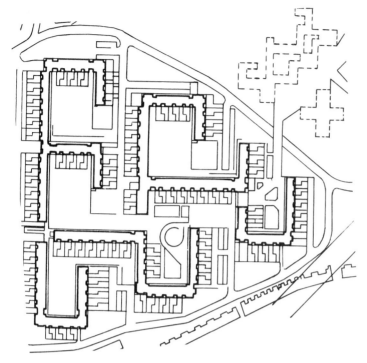

Fig. 6.12 Continuous blocks enclosing courtyards at Edith Avenue, Washington, plan (*from Architects' Journal, July 1963*)

Fig. 6.13 Street deck junction at Edith Avenue, Washington (*E. R. Scoffham*)

street decks, but later did adopt something of their influence in a minor way, still wrapped up in by now dated concepts of mixed development. In fact Thamesmead, as a prime example of this mixture of different approaches, appeared not to fall into any one category. Yet if one was put it would have to be that of mixed development.

Thamesmead was intended as a new township and was developed by the LCC on the Erith marshes, for which design work started in 1965. It was conceived as a visual image, to be seen to best effect from the river. It used block forms of various shapes and configurations to give an artificial topography to the town.[40] Among these block forms were point blocks, high and low slab blocks and orthodox ground-level houses in the traditional mixed development manner. But one block form was different and appeared to be derived from Park Hill and Lillington Gardens. This was a continuous deck access block which meandered through the town and acted as a 'spine' or 'link' between different parts. It was clearly in the tradition of *Ville Radieuse* and the multi-level city the Smithsons had derived from their Golden Lane entry.

Alison and Peter Smithson had rejected the arbitrary social divisions of mixed development and neighbourhood and had provided an alternative form of physical organisation. At Thamesmead that form was used in combination with the very blocks the Smithsons had been at pains to reject. It had been used to link districts, to provide a focus in a visual sense and in the arbitrary manner the Smithsons had attempted to prevent. The whole con-

Fig. 6.14 'Spine' block at Thamesmead (*Department of Architecture Slide Library, University of Nottingham*)

cept of Thamesmead seemed to be based on a visual image using the deck access block as an integral part of that image, and in a manner diametrically opposed to that for which it had originally been developed. Similarly it used the point block, low slab and terraced house out of their original mixed development context. From Lillington Street, Thamesmead appeared to take the expression of individual dwellings in the modelling of this 'spine' block. Dwellings were located on, over, projecting from and making recesses into, the street deck in a visual manner that attempted to express the progressive growth of the traditional city. Yet it was an imposed architectural solution, an image of that city.

To unify the wide range of built form solutions the whole town was built in the Balency industrialised system. It was the final phase of the LCC's long line of progression from Bentham Road, through Loughborough Road, Alton West and the Ferrier estate[41] in the concrete idiom motivated by Le Corbusier's Unité in 1947. Its density was that of Roehampton, 100 persons per acre (247/ha); its sophistication, ruthlessness without brutality, and intellectual honesty, equalled that of Alton West on a vast scale and through a greater variety of built forms. But as with Alton West this was not housing, only the image of it.

Similarly Dawsons Heights in Southwark represented the progression of Frank Hayes's department's thinking from its central corridor maisonettes of 1957 at Sceaux Gardens, now picking up Park Hill's 'streets in the air' and Lillington Gardens' expression of individual dwellings in its block formation. This, too, was an image; but whereas Thamesmead represented the concrete school, Dawsons Heights represented the traditional.[42]

High blocks were now seen to be unsatisfactory, and street decks merely an alternative, more humane means of providing access within them. Ronan Point was largely responsible for accelerating this decline, but the demise of high living was a cumulative one and more complex than sociological disadvantages would infer. Sociological problems there obviously were in high blocks;[43] but research by the Ministry[44] did not entirely support this view. The Ministry found that more conclusive rejection came if an estate was not attractive, was ill-maintained, or if there was a poor outlook from the windows of dwellings, and this was irrespective of height above ground. Park Hill was one of the estates surveyed and its grim appearance was highly criticised by its residents, as was the Canada estate. Such criticism obscured the organisational motives of the different approaches behind these two schemes. Their residents appeared not to be aware of any differences that affected their lives one way or the other. This somewhat negative conclusion underlined the growing failure of architecture to provide satisfactory housing whatever the intellectual basis behind it. As a result 'streets in the air' became another arbitrary planning and architectural device, just as mixed development had been, classified by the Smithsons along with that neighbourhood.

Ironically Alison and Peter Smithson built street-deck housing only once at Robin Hood Gardens in the London Borough of Tower Hamlets which was completed in 1970.[45]

Fig. 6.15 Expressions of high-rise living. City of Towers at World's End, Chelsea by Eric Lyons and H. Cadbury-Brown (*from A Broken Wave by Lionel Esher, Penguin Books, 1983*)

Fig. 6.16 Streets in the air at Lillington Gardens, Pimlico, by Darbourne and Darke (*from The State of British Architecture by Sutherland Lyall, The Architectural Press, 1980*)

REFERENCES

1. See Ch. 4.
2. See Ch. 5.
3. See Ch. 1.
4. Le Corbusier, *Ville Radieuse*, 1967 edn, pp. 57 ff.
5. Le Corbusier, *Ville Radieuse*, 1933.
6. Le Corbusier, *Plan Voisin de Paris*, 1925.
7. Le Corbusier, *Une Ville Contemporaire de 3 Millions d'Habitants*, 1922.
8. See Ch. 5.
9. Le Corbusier, *Ville Radieuse*, 1967 edn, op. cit., p. 91.
10. Ibid., p. 39.
11. Ibid., p. 39 and 113.
12. *Architects' Journal*, 7 Jan. 1960.
13. J. Voelcker, 'What happened to CIAM', *Architectural Design*, May 1960, pp. 177 ff.
14. A. and P. Smithson, *Urban Structuring*, 1967, Introduction p. 7.
15. A. and P. Smithson, op. cit., p. 14.
16. A. and P. Smithson, *Team 10 Primer*, 1960, p. 31.
17. A. and P. Smithson, 'Golden Lane project', *Architects' Year Book* 5.
18. Ibid.
19. P. Smithson in A. Smithson (ed.), *Team 10 Primer*, op. cit., p. 35.
20. K. Lynch, 'The Form of Cities', *Scientific American*, 1954.
21. *Architectural Review*, May 1960; *Architectural Design*, June 1960.
22. A. and P. Smithson, *Urban Structuring*, 1967 pp. 46–9; *Architectural Review*, Dec. 1955.
23. *Architectural Design*, Aug. 1955, (first published).
24. *Architectural Design*, Sept. 1961; *Architectural Review*, Dec. 1961; *Architect and Building News*, 25 July 1962; *RIBA Journal*, Dec. 1962; *RIBA Journal*, July 1963; *Architects' Journal*, 15 Jan. 1964 and 21 July 1965.
25. Quoted by H. Bruckmann and D. L. Lewis, *New Housing in Great Britain*, 1960.
26. *Architects' Journal*, 21 July 1965.
27. *Architects' Journal*, 7 Jan. 1960.
28. R. Padovan, 'Housing in Southwark', *Architects' Journal*, 25 Apr. 1973.
29. *Architects' Journal*, 2 Aug. 1961.
30. See Chapter 5.
31. *Architects' Journal*, 1 Oct. 1969, pp. 807 ff.
32. Sir G. Parker-Morris, *Homes for Today and Tomorrow* (Parker-Morris Report), 1961.
33. *Architects' Journal*, 1 Oct. 1969, pp. 813 ff, and 12 Jan. 1972.
34. *Architects' Journal*, 17 July 1963, and 9 July 1969; *Architectural Review*, Jan. 1964.
35. *Architects' Journal*, 26 July 1967.
36. *Architects' Journal*, 9 July 1969.
37. *Architects' Journal*, 11 Jun. 1969.
38. *Architects' Journal*, 3 Sept. 1969.
39. *Architects' Journal*, 6 Aug. 1969 and 9 Sept. 1970.
40. *Architects' Journal*, 11 Oct. 1972.
41. See Chapter 7.
42. *Architects' Journal*, 25 Apr. 1973.

43. K. Wharton, 'Sad storeys for children', *Architect and Building News*, 1 Oct. 1970.
44. I. Reynolds and C. Nicholson, 'Living off the ground', *Architects' Journal*, 20 Aug. 1969.
45. A. and P. Smithson, *Ordinariness and Light*, 1970.

7 THE ALIEN CASBAH

The progression of built form into what became generically termed low rise–high density was a historical regression. Traditionally towns had conformed to a dense low-rise pattern prior to the development of transport and the growth of the garden city movement from the end of the nineteenth century. Historically, then, it has been a relatively recent phenomenon that urban development should move away from a well-established and previously essential built form. However, this form emerged anew during the 1960s through a progression of events that caused it to be seen almost as an original idea, and it is this progression that must be looked at closely.

Low rise–high density should be taken as a relative expression. Low rise being a lower rise than hitherto in post-war urban redevelopment schemes, and high density being a higher density than had been usual in post-war low-rise suburban and new town schemes. It was a merging of the higher densities achieved in high-rise schemes of all forms of access and block configuration, and the advantages of low-rise living in closeness to the ground. Inevitably it meant a densely packed grouping of buildings and because of this low rise–high density was unable to develop earlier in post-war developments as a viable alternative.

It has been shown[1] that immediate post-war concentration was on the provision of more openness, light and air, both in the new towns and later in urban renewal mixed developments. The overriding desire was to get rid of the last vestiges of the nineteenth century and to prevent conurbations from spreading by a policy of planned decentralisation and decongestion. Any continuation of built form solutions that did not aid this policy, either in image or reality, could not find a place. It thus took time for the inherent advantages of low rise–high density to be assimilated and acted upon, and these were only realised due to the increasing failure of solutions that had been devised in conformity with that policy of decentralisation and decongestion.

Initial new town and suburban development was criticised during the 1950s[2] for its lack of urbanity, for a deficiency of social amenities, a destruction of sociability and the high cost of travelling to work in the conurbation. Mixed development declined through abuse and misunderstanding. It declined due to an inability to cope with the needs of growing families which resulted in their living in the high-rise blocks for whom these were not intended. It declined due to the high cost of high buildings, and finally it declined because of the dismal appearance and outlook of too many developments. 'Streets in the air', a social device to counter the mechanical and diagrammatic planning of mixed development, suffered the same fate as mixed development, for many of the schemes it spawned were equally as high-rise and as dismal in appearance and outlook. Yet the approach of those involved in early 'streets in the air' schemes, to find a more meaningful way of assembling dwelling units into a social order, led more logically into low rise–high density.

Warnings were sounded during the 1950s about the dangers inherent in the density proposals of both the New Towns Act,[3] where Raymond Unwin's arguments for 12 houses per acre (30/ha) were supported,[4] and Patrick Abercrombie's density zoning for the Greater London area.[5] Elizabeth Denby demonstrated the statistical fallacies upon which these policies had been based;[6] for the towns where overcrowding was being tackled were not in fact overcrowded in terms of density. They were being tackled with 'pre-war town-hating attitudes of mind' resulting in further sprawl. Indeed, Elizabeth Denby went further to show, by using a Georgian, an early Victorian and an early twentieth-century revival example, how densities of between 120–150 persons per acre (296–370/ha) had been achieved in two- and three-storey terraced development around squares with private gardens and ample public open space.[7]

Ruth Glass, a sociologist in London University's Department of Town Planning, had earlier pursued this theme[8] to demonstrate that density statistics and their calculation was a 'game' the clever could play to support whatever they wanted to do; and she showed that while densities might mean something on paper they meant relatively little in practice. Her argument was similar to that of many at the time, including architects, for a return to the kind of town where 'the relativity of space and distance is recognised and, indeed, exploited to advantage'.[9] In fact, for density to be seen as the result of a built form solution that provided civilised living conditions, rather than it being the simple objective of built form.

Other sociologists, notably Willmot and Young,[10] had found merit in the close knit family relationships of the crowded older areas of the metropolis. Agriculturalists naturally supported any move that would limit encroachment on farmland, and rising car ownership introduced an increasing design problem into urban communities. 'Privacy, safety and urbanity became the watch-words of the time.'[11]

After their development and exposition of a 'streets in the air' alternative to high-density urban housing, Alison and Peter Smithson continued their search for an organisational technique for the town. They concluded in 1959 that 'family living, except in exceptional circumstances, is best served by relatively low-density development, wherever its location'.[12] While this appeared to support garden city low densities, the key was the 'relative' nature of low density. The Smithsons qualified this by stating that none of the needs of family life 'can be met simply and pleasurably at densities much above 70 persons per acre'.[13] This was a density that at the time was almost double the 36 persons per acre (89/ha) being achieved in the new towns, and it was at the lower end of Abercrombie's density pyramid.[14]

Economy measures in the early 1950s had led to an increased use of the terrace house in layouts both in the inner and outer town. A closer proximity of houses was the result but without any general raising of densities, for these were imposed standards to be obeyed. In inner areas the terrace became an integral part of the mixed development idea without its advantages being used in isolation. Only in a few schemes in the early 1950s was the closer proximity of houses in terraces used to advantage, and hence the greater intensity of land use they achieved realised. Among them was a group of six four-storey terrace houses in Hampstead by Stanley Amis and Bill Howell in 1956, on the site of four bombed Victorian houses.[15] Although these houses were built for individuals, including the two architects, they provided a then extreme case of low-rise housing. In isolation certain parts of large housing developments provided similar examples. Horndean Close, a two-storey area of Alton East, Roehampton, was built in 1955 and the residential density is 70 people per acre (173/ha) although it is part of the Roehampton estates whose overall density is 100 people per acre (247/ha), this including the large amounts of open space that mixed development held so dear.[16]

The reluctance to take up the advantages of these developments was a by-product of fear of the kind of development which took place under nine-teenth-century by-law control. While many architects were aware of the shortcomings of both high rise and sprawl, they were prevented from achieving a more compact, urban alternative by regulations governing road widths, traffic movement, daylighting and services which were devised and enforced by authorities who saw their infringement as the thin end of a wedge that would permit inferior speculative development.[17] Eric Lyon's develop-ments for Span were a minority among speculative schemes, and were to relatively low densities as they were located on the outskirts of the conur-bation; but they provided a much-needed example of what could be done.[18]

A breakthrough in the use of more compact building on a large scale came at Cumbernauld new town from 1957 onwards. Two initial estates, Carbrain and Kildrum, designed under Hugh Wilson's direction as Chief Architect, achieved densities of 85–90 persons per acre (210–222/ha) using two-, three- and four-storey blocks. A similar integrity to that which had caused Cumbernauld to be progressive in ideas of vehicular and pedestrian segregation was permeating the layout of housing areas, and the planning of dwellings within them. Terraces of dwellings in different block types were used to create a closer grouping of buildings than hitherto in either the post-war new towns or in the conurbations. Buildings enclosed garden squares and contracted to provide narrow alleys, while a sloping site was used to advantage to tuck garages under blocks.[19] Later developments demonstrated that it was possible to provide adequate living conditions and 100 per cent car provision using solely two-storey houses to densities around 60 persons per acre (148/ha). Many of Cumbernauld's inventive ideas were concerned

Fig. 7.1 Span development at Parkleys. Ham Common (*Department of Architecture Slide Library, University of Nottingham*)

with traffic and pedestrian segregation and, as has been shown,[20] a revalidation of house–garden–car positions was fundamental. Wider-frontage houses, and the separation of car from house were derivations in layout that aided the achievement of higher densities in low-rise developments. By separating car from house the dwelling blocks need not be spaced apart by dimensions based on traffic requirements. They were in a portion of the site that was wholly pedestrian and as a result could be spaced to the requirements of people rather than to those of cars and service vehicles. In fact their spacing was controlled by privacy distances between facing windows and by daylight and sunlight considerations. A single-aspect dwelling obviated privacy distances, around 70 feet (21 m) and a closer spacing depending entirely on environmental criteria was achieved.

Cumbernauld was thus in complete contrast to the attitude of mind that strove for maximum open space about dwellings. It recognised the virtues of the dwelling on, or close to, the ground as providing better conditions for British family living, and it was a turn-about in the garden city philosophy that gave birth to Cumbernauld in favour of dropping low densities and large gardens. In a Scottish context Cumbernauld's achievement can perhaps be interpreted: for Scotland has an urban tradition of apartment living almost akin to Europe, and Cumbernauld as a result required a relatively high proportion of flats. The private garden was not an established tradition; smaller gardens than in the earlier English new towns could be provided, and a larger proportion of blocks containing apartments closer to the ground than in current urban developments could be achieved.

It was from the Continent that the inroads made at Cumbernauld were reinforced. Europe had not been moved to the same extent as had Britain by garden city objectives, and the creation of new towns. A dense building fabric was an established norm that was continuing, and within which variations of block configuration and dwelling type, predominantly flats, were devised. Claims for the small house as a serious competitor in high-density housing were not regarded seriously in most European countries in the inter-war years. Holland was an exception where high-density layouts had successfully coped with Dutch preference for the small house. In 1927 J. J. P. Oud had designed the Kiefhoek scheme in Rotterdam and demonstrated the claims of the small house as offering a valid alternative to the flat. Amsterdam city promoted a competition in 1933 which included among its unpremiated entries a scheme by Leppla consisting entirely of small two-storey terrace houses to a high density, while more orthodox entries provided four- to six-storey flatted blocks in single- or double-row layouts. Other entries to this competition included the point block and tall slab, themes that were subsequently adopted in post-war English mixed development.[21]

It was against this background that a form of house developed that proved instrumental in Britain in moving built form away from mixed development and high rise towards more compact layouts. This development was the single-storey courtyard house when used in mass housing schemes rather than as an individual one-off dwelling. Hugo Haring, a Berliner, had devised a house in 1924 which had windows only to those rooms which needed a view. These he specified as the living-rooms, the remaining rooms in a one-storey house could be rooflit. The defects of this single-aspect house he later corrected in his 1928 L-house. Simply, this was a single-aspect house placed at right angles to the road, the L-shape being formed by a high screen and porch from which the house was entered. Haring managed to get five of these houses built in 1932 for the Werkbundsiedlung Lainz in Austria.[22] Adjoining these five houses are two L-shaped courtyard houses designed by Austrian Anton Brenner. Brenner had taught at the Bauhaus while Hannes Mayer was Director and Ludwig Hilberseimer was Instructor in Housing and Town Planning. Between them Mayer and Hilberseimer developed the L-shaped courtyard house. Mayer won a competition in 1928 for the German Trades Union School in Bernau with a series of two-storey houses in parallel, but linked along one side by single-storey wings, on the roofs of which were terraces. From this developed the layout of the Dessau Torten housing project of 1928–29. It is not clear which of the two actually designed it for it is attributed to Mayer, but in 1929 Hilberseimer produced similar plans giving the credit for developing courtyard housing to Hugo Haring.[23]

Hilberseimer went on to develop the L-shaped house as we know it in Britain today. In 1930 he developed his 'Growing' house with living-rooms and bedrooms in separate wings, and showed how it could be built in stages, and 1931 saw his E-type house which corrected the outward aspect of the

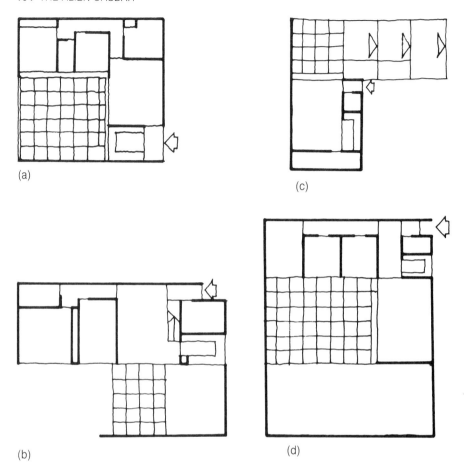

Fig. 7.2 Development of the courtyard house: (a) Anton Brenner at 1932 Vienna exhibition, (b) Mayer, Dessau Torten housing, (c) Hilberseimer, 1930 'Growing' house, and (d) Hilberseimer, E-type house (*E. R. Scoffham – adapted from drawings by Macintosh*)

earlier house to look inwards to a court, and grouped kitchen and bathroom to economise on plumbing.[24]

In 1931 a competition in Vienna, and in 1932 another in Berlin, were both won by entries comprising single-storey houses that expanded into L-shaped courtyard houses.[25] It was an expandable house that the National Building Agency was to advocate in 1971 for young married couples.[26] Yet in 1930 at the Brussels CIAM Sigfried Giedion had objected that the authorities were advocating low-rise housing due to the English garden city movement. Gropius took up this theme and criticised low-rise housing while making out advantages for high-rise living that would change the life-style of inhabitants and promote public spirit. More objectively, however, Gropius criticised low-rise housing on grounds of density and construction. These Hilberseimer answered in social terms, and provided examples to show how courtyard housing might achieve densities, using his E-type house, of 131 persons per acre (323/ha), then of course excluding cars and public open spaces. He showed, by using the same shadow angle as Gropius had in his slab blocks, that he achieved the same density as Gropius while using courtyard housing covering 50 per cent of the ground by buildings.[27]

As we have seen,[28] history records that Gropius won – mixed development and high rise were the results in Britain during the 1950s. Yet during the 1930s many continental architects took up the courtyard theme including Mies van der Rohe; but this was not mass housing, for most of his clients were individuals. The most decisive influence on post-war developments was that of Haring, Mayer and Hilberseimer.[29] The transition to Britain was almost entirely due to the publications of Walter Segal who had, before coming to Britain, designed a courtyard house in Berlin in 1931 and another in Majorca in 1934.[30] In 1943 he published an article which dealt in very full terms with two-storey single-aspect courtyard houses.[31] This article was later included in his book *Home and Environment*,[32] along with other developments including a single-storey L-shaped house and groupings of houses alongside a common green to densities of 101 persons per acre (250/ha) for two-storey, and 56 persons per acre (138/ha) for single-storey houses. As density was the major concern of Segal's book it was widely read and later it had considerable influence that materialised into buildings once events had cleared the path. In 1948 policies of mixed development and of decentralisation were the major preoccupations; society was not then ready to recognise Segal's alternatives, not until these policies had been tried and found lacking.

In 1952 Chamberlin, Powell and Bon had devised a split-level courtyard house with footpath access, to a high density, but with the courtyard over-shadowed by the higher bedroom wing.[33] The first courtyard houses to be built in Britain included these split-level types. They were designed by Frank Perry for the 1956 Fort Leith competition in Edinburgh.[34] Courtyard houses were grouped into clusters that were repeated to give a variety of appearance that was often lacking in later courtyard schemes. Again Scotland's tradition of apartment-living may explain why the small courtyard house was first used there rather than in the supposedly more progressive South East of England. Chamberlin, Powell and Bon were also to provide a repeating cluster of one- and two-storey courtyard houses in their 1958 Living Suburb Project, to a density of 89 persons per acre (221/ha).[35]

Meanwhile in Scandinavia the 1950s had seen parallel developments in single-storey houses that provided a variation of the courtyard. Alvar Aalto had designed for himself a summer house at Muuratsalo in 1952–53, which was an open-ended courtyard house, the house wrapping round three sides of the court. In 1953 Mogelvang and Utzon won a competition with a house that was to be expanded around the edge of its site, eventually enclosing what the Romans in particular had called an atrium. This scheme was the precursor of Utzon's noted courtyard schemes at Helsingfors and Fredensborg in 1956, both having pitched tiled roofs sloping inwards towards the courtyards.[36] A development of this atrium idea occurred in Alison and Peter Smithson's

House of the Future at the 1956 Ideal Home Exhibition.[37] This was a home for a childless couple, one which they later developed into a 'carpet' layout, excluding cars, to 60 persons per acre (148/ha).[38]

Houses similar to those advocated by Walter Segal were designed at the War Office in 1960 under the direction of Roger Walters, later to become GLC Chief Architect and who for a time had worked as an assistant to Segal.[39] These provided accommodation for army personnel at Talavera Lines, Aldershot. The two-storey wing of the house was parallel to the access way rather than at right angles to it and the 170 houses achieved 45 persons per acre (104/ha), including 128 maisonettes and open space.

In 1960 the LCC designed a small scheme of experimental low-rise housing at Angrave Street, Shoreditch, completely against the run of its mixed development theme. This achieved a density of 120 persons per acre (296/ha) with garaging for 50 per cent of the dwellings. The houses were back-to-back on each side of pedestrian lanes while in the centre of the scheme was an open courtyard for public use.[40]

It was Michael Neylan's prizewinning entry for the Bishopsfield competition at Harlow in 1961 that was to act as the initiator of the bulk of innovative work on low rise–high density housing during the 1960s. It re-established a compact mode of arranging dwellings as a permanent part of British housing, and it is notable that the second prize to Geoffrey Darke and Robert Blom van Assendelft was for a similar arrangement of dwellings.[41] Both schemes adopted the courtyard house. Michael Neylan used two: the

Fig. 7.3 Sketch of pedestrian lane at Angrave Street, Shoreditch (*Architectural Design*)

L-shaped plan which he arranged back-to-back around access ways radiating from a central core of dwellings above car parking, and an introvert U-shaped plan which was used on the top floor of these central dwellings.[42] A more complex and integrated built form of different house types was thus devised, and the central core of dwellings above car parking was a theme that came to be adopted and developed to many later low rise–high density schemes in order to achieve adequate car provision coupled to adequate density.

Compact housing patterns were explored in a more thoroughgoing manner than at Cumbernauld by the LCC's Hook new town team.[43] Standard new town corporation-maintained front greens and draughty open corners, due to an apparent inability to design terraces to turn a right angle, provided an excessive amount of expensive open space to little social or visual advantage. At Hook these spaces were concentrated into more useful park areas; the houses were closer together, and each was given reasonable private open space by a small courtyard or garden, even dwellings off the ground. Vehicles were separated from pedestrians vertically as well as horizontally; it was a town designed in terms of the motor car which at the same time still managed to create an acceptable environment for the pedestrian. Cumbernauld's housing schemes and Angrave Street were quoted as examples of the kind

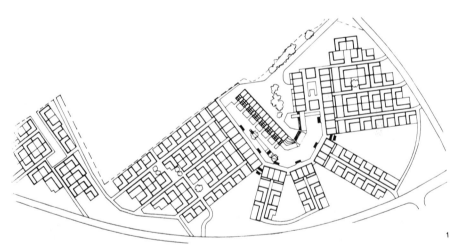

Fig. 7.4 Site plan of Bishopsfield, Harlow (*Architectural Design*)

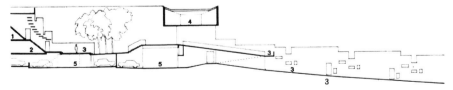

Fig. 7.5 Site section, Bishopsfield (*Architectural Design*)

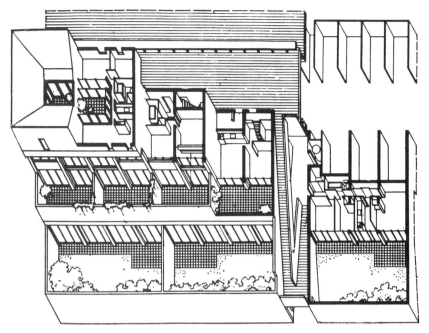

Fig. 7.6 Axonometric of central block, Bishopsfield (*Architectural Design*)

Fig. 7.7 Courtyard house form, Bishopsfield (*John Ford*)

of approach to house design that was necessary to achieve Hook's objectives.

Courtyard houses were adopted in a scheme carried out by the Edinburgh University Architectural Research Unit in 1961 at Prestonpans.[44] Forty-five L-shaped single-storey houses were designed after the team had toured low-rise developments on the Continent. Houses were linked by a series of covered ways reminiscent of Eske Christensen's 'twig' housing in Copenhagen. The scheme achieved a density of 10 houses per acre (26/ha) and was built for local authority tenants. Similar courtyard housing adopting covered pedestrian routes was built as part of the Ardler development at Dundee by Baxter, Clark and Paul in 1963,[45] and both these schemes were surveyed by the Edinburgh University Architectural Research Unit between 1962 and 1965.[46]

The complexity and ingenuity of low rise–high density schemes from this point was notable. Two major competitions occurred in 1961: Lillington Gardens and Bishopsfield. Both established their respective built forms as permanent parts of housing in the 1960s, and both developed in parallel until 'streets in the air' became enmeshed in the later demise of high-rise living. Nevertheless the idea it contained, a more pleasant and less impersonal means of access to dwellings off the ground, continued and became absorbed into the development of evermore ingenious low-rise solutions. It should be noted that Geoffrey Darke went into partnership with John Darbourne, so it was not too remarkable perhaps that phase 3 of Lillington Gardens contained a number of modifications to the original design or that the firm's later work merged the two approaches. Both were very similar in concept, to provide a more urban and sociable method of accommodating ordinary people.

Courtyard housing of various types became acceptable mainly because the desire for greater compactness meant greater intrusion on individual privacy. Privacy became a major preoccupation and was relevant at different levels: visual, acoustic and psychological. Previous 70 feet (21.3 m) privacy distances between facing windows, introduced by Tudor-Walters in 1918, were no longer necessary as by inward facing courtyard dwellings, by interlocking, and by the avoidance of facing windows, a closer proximity of blocks could be achieved. A closer proximity of dwellings also meant a closer proximity of cars, and this, too, became a major preoccupation. Rising car ownership during the 1960s, particularly after Buchanan's predictions in 1962, generated larger car-parking areas which were recognised from the early Radburn examples as being unsightly. A frequent solution was to locate as many cars as possible underneath dwelling blocks. This was very much a policy of 'out of sight, out of mind'. The apparent visual problem of the car outdoors had been dealt with; but that the car might be less convenient so accommodated, or that the parking place itself might be more unsightly than cars grouped on the surface or that it might provide opportunities for antisocial activity, were only realised later, when economic and social pressures forced changes.

It was the rising graph of car ownership that raised fundamental questions about parking for tall blocks. It can be understood that the higher dwellings were stacked the more acute became the parking problem at ground level. It became so acute that the spread of cars on the surface was unacceptable, and was to be seen at Roehampton from the mid-1960s where adequate car provision had evidently been lacking from the original design. Underground garages were similarly vast, and in terms of cost often prohibitive except in

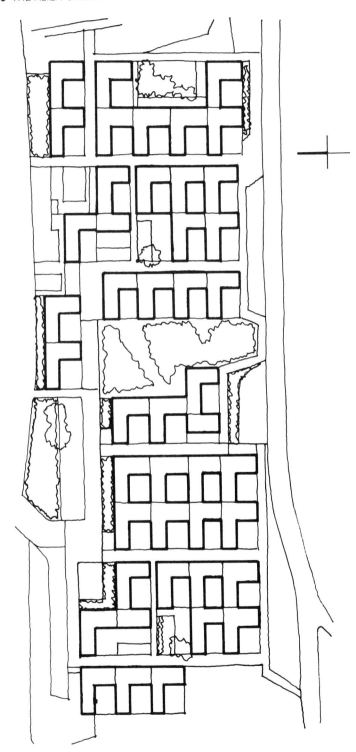

Fig. 7.8 Layout of courtyard housing at Prestonpans (E. R. Scoffham – adapted from drawing by Architectural Research Unit, Edinburgh University)

very high-density urban schemes. Consequently a lowering of height was necessary in order satisfactorily to deal with car provision at a more humane and economical level.

Progressive schemes were not necessarily all for local authorities or new towns. In 1961 Clifford Culpin had won a competition in Harlow, sponsored by the Royal Institute of British Architects and *Ideal Home* magazine, for private-enterprise housing to a density of 60 persons per acre (148/ha) and with a then high provision of car accommodation located in groups away from dwellings.[47] From the private sector, too, an example in Switzerland proved to be of considerable influence. Seidlung Halen near Bern, by Atelier 5, represented one of the most logical attempts at putting the idea of low rise–high density housing into practice. It accommodates seventy-nine dwellings on a south-facing slope in an economical manner – economical in that a dense pattern of building is achieved while providing privacy to individual dwellings, a view from, and direct sunlight into, each dwelling, a group of shops, sports and playground facilities, a swimming pool and an underground garage. As it is isolated from any adjoining development, it represents a self-contained 'village', complete with a central square of shops. It is entered by way of a communal garage, and the houses are grouped in terraces forming alleyways and small courtyards between them. It is a total building in the same manner as the Unité and Park Hill, but in compact low-rise form. The scheme was designed from 1958 and completed in 1961.[48] On the success of this scheme Wates Ltd commissioned Atelier 5, in 1967, to design its St Bernard's estate at Croydon,[49] which was unfortunately never completed as originally intended.

The development of low rise–high density was hampered by the often too conscientiously applied daylighting code.[50] This was devised after the war to prevent a too-close positioning of buildings for reasons of daylight provision, in fear of a return to nineteenth-century conditions. As a result it had been largely responsible for the openness so characteristic of mixed development, early new town and post-war suburban housing. Rigidly applied to more closely-knit schemes it meant protracted negotiations to decide which windows were critical for daylighting purposes, and which were not. An attitude of mind had to be overcome in order to allow a more concentrated form of building to develop, and this was a slow process. Comparisons made by Kenneth Browne showed that application of the codes would mean destruction of many characteristic London streets of three- and four-storey Georgian houses more effectively than by the Luftwaffe.[51] But the LCC had earlier shown that Angrave Street could have been built in compliance with the daylighting codes while still maintaining urbanity by a careful design of buildings and the location of windows.[52] Design problems thus became more complicated resulting in slow progression on all but a small number of schemes. For many it was easier to continue to build in a lower-density less-compact manner out of town, and to a mixed development theme, or simply high rise, in the conurbations.

From America came ideas of a courtyard house of a different type to that which had developed in Europe. Linear patio house types had been developed by Chester Nagel in 1953, and he built one at Five Fields, Massachusetts, in which the rooms were contained within two parallel walls and alternated with enclosed patios. In 1956 Morse Payne, a member of the Architects' Collaborative with Chester Nagel, took the pattern a stage further by introducing more patios and arranging similar houses in terraced fashion on narrow crosswall dimensions. The circulation within this house was acute as narrow passages connected the different parts. Still later the idea was taken up by Serge Chermayeff, teaching at Harvard from 1953 to 1961, and by some of his students. Of particular concern to them was privacy within the house and for this reason it was divided into areas having different privacy requirements, both visual and acoustic, each separated from the other by patios.[53] Five of these plans were published in 1957, and four more in 1963 when Serge Chermayeff and Christopher Alexander published *Community and Privacy*.[54] Houses are divided into 'domains', each having different requirements, particularly in terms of privacy. This resulted in extensive circulation and compartmentalisation within the dwelling. Chermayeff's own house at New Haven, built in 1962, was more simplified, as the built projects using the linear patio house have been in California, where the type first proved acceptable.[55]

Coincidental with the American publication of *Community and Privacy* in 1963 was the building of a co-operative scheme of linear patio houses at Hatfield by Peter Phippen.[56] Michael Baily, the originator of the Cockaigne Housing Group in 1962, stated his objectives were 'to create a new initiative in housing design' and to 'set a new pattern in development and urban renewal'. Broad issues for a small group, but significant in the context of low rise–high density. Compartmentalisation within these houses was less rigid than in Chermayeff's types. Crosswalls were at 23 feet (7 m) centres with two structural bays, and the variety and permutation of the twenty-eight houses within this framework was the scheme's major design achievement. Yet it was rejected by the local planning authority at first, because it was thought to be substandard and have light wells.[57] So successful has this scheme been that it was recommended by the committee led by Lady Dartmouth to report on the Human Habitat for the 1972 United Nations Stockholm conference on the human environment.[58] It was the method of the project's management, a then relatively unprecedented co-operative venture in which each house-owner took part, and the design of a range of plans within a consistent framework that make this scheme the more significant as time passes. It proved to be a pattern for future housing, which was reinforced by the Housing and Planning Act in 1974[59] to encourage co-ownership and housing association schemes, and by the National Building Agency's re-orientation of many of its activities under Lord Goodman.

Courtyard housing achieved high densities in the mid-1960s when it was used extensively by Lambeth Borough Council under Ted Hollamby on small urban sites such as Alexandra Drive in 1967, where it was found to be popular with tenants, and by Colin John Collins who managed to approach

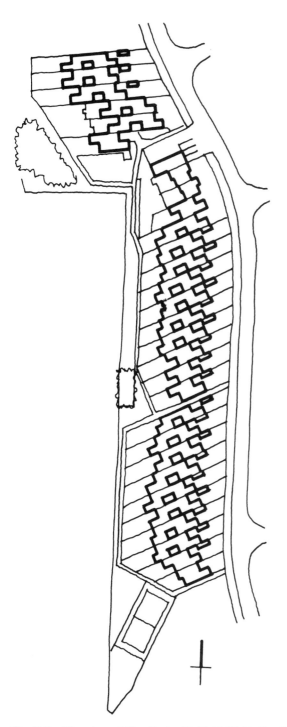

Fig. 7.9 Site plan of The Ryde, Hatfield (*E. R. Scoffham – adapted from drawing by Peter Phippen of Phippen, Randall and Parkes*)

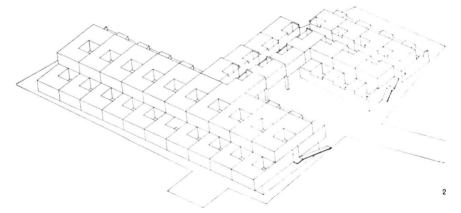

2

Fig. 7.10 Axonometric of Brentwood courtyard housing on two levels
(*Architectural Design*)

Hilberseimer's density in a scheme at Brentwood, to 124 persons per acre
(311/ha), using courtyard housing on two levels with garages below.[60]

For the LCC the Cedars Road scheme close to Clapham Common
marked the beginning of a transition away from mixed development.[61] The
project was opened in 1964 and consists of, for the most part, four-storey
maisonettes, giving half the families in them a garden, and was to a density
of 95 persons per acre (235/ha), which was achieved by folding the standard
four-storey maisonette block on plan to form small recessed courts. As a built
form it was so economical in site use that it proved possible to provide a large
landscaped area for play and leisure activities. It was a popular scheme with
tenants, but might have been more successful had it not been executed in
shiny white bricks, which, while they reflected light into the recessed courts,
did attract comments about public conveniences.

On their out-of-town estates the GLC made similar transitions. At
Haverhill in west Suffolk the Clements Lane scheme broke away from the
cottage tradition and provided 17.5 houses to the acre (43.23/ha) grouped in
tight protective courts, with garages provided for all households.[62] Both here,
and at schemes for their Andover town expansion, emphasis was placed on
the orientation of houses, ideally west or south, the organisation of open
space, and on provision for cars.

Back in town, Michael Neylan, now joined in partnership by William
Ungless, followed up his Bishopsfield success bv being commissioned to
design a scheme at Linden Grove, near Peckham Rye. Neylan was concerned
to reduce the distinction between housing and flats by giving both similar
amenities; he was concerned about individual privacy and the intensification
of individual and dwelling, and a desire to generate a sense of place and
community within a larger urban fabric.[63] Sixty dwellings were provided,
forty for families and twenty in the form of 'sheltered' accommodation for
old people. Dwellings were located back-to-back along a pedestrian 'spine'
which widened out adjacent to the sheltered accommodation. This was an

Z ←

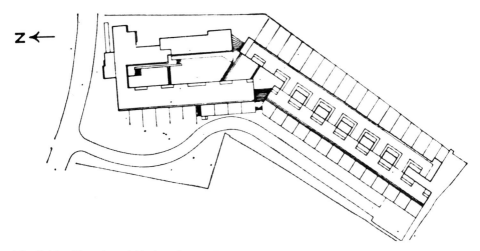

Fig. 7.11 Site plan of Linden Grove, Peckham Rye (*Architectural Design*)

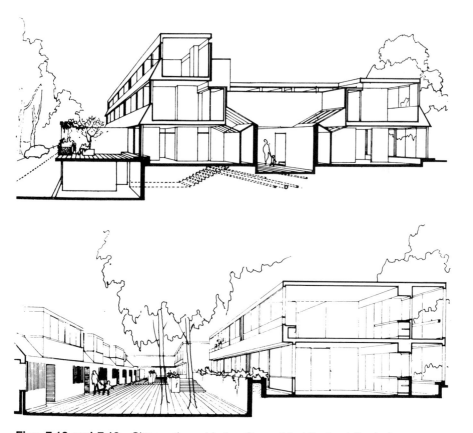

Figs. 7.12 and 7.13 Site sections, Linden Grove (*Architectural Design*)

arrangement similar to the radiating spurs of Bishopsfield but used two-storey single-aspect houses to the narrow part of the 'spine', while cars were tucked under the gardens of houses on the north side. In terms of construction it was, like Bishopsfield and Neylan's later schemes,[64] built of traditional materials and used traditional devices such as pitched roofs in original manner. It was a rejection of the ideals of those architects who sought a new architecture through new materials and construction techniques.

Higgins, Ney and Partners designed their Reporton Road scheme in Hammersmith,[65] using similar construction and aesthetic techniques. Here a density of 136 persons per acre (336/ha) with 100 per cent garaging was achieved by parallel runs of four-storey flat and maisonette blocks back-to-back along a 'spine' of car parking which was roofed-over to provide a pedestrian walkway, or vestigial 'street in the air', to the upper maisonettes which were stepped on both sides to avoid facing windows and had their front doors opening directly off the paved deck which was open to the sky. Unfortunately none of the dwellings had a private garden, though balconies were provided on the outer façades of the block. It is notable that this scheme was the prototype for a progressive redevelopment of areas of typical Victorian housing in Fulham, a policy which was reconsidered in the light of later

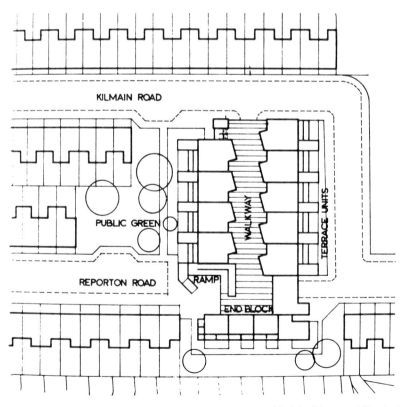

Fig. 7.14 Site plan of Reporton Road, Hammersmith (*Architectural Design*)

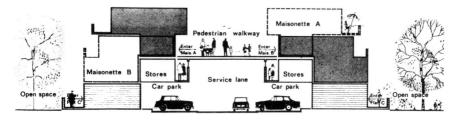

Fig. 7.15 Section through Reporton Road Block (*Architectural Design*)

concern for the improvement of older houses rather than for their replacement.[66] Yet a further project on similar lines was built at Moore Park Road in Hammersmith.

After publication of the Parker-Morris Report in 1961[67] the Ministry's Research and Development Group, notably Oliver Cox and Michael Wellbank, built a demonstration project at West Ham in 1964 to test the report's proposals. The scheme comprised thirty-nine dwellings in a low-rise idiom with dwellings ranging from one to three storeys in height, all with private gardens, car parking and open space in accordance with the Parker-Morris Committee's recommendations.[68]

In 1965 Oliver Cox was one of the assessors of a competition for the design of a village extension at Broadclyst, sponsored by the National Trust.[69] An intense pattern of land use was proposed by the winners H. Werner Rosenthal in association with Eldred Evans, Denis Gailey and David Shalev. The assessors reported that a break away from then fashionable village extension patterns had been made; it was a concept developed out of ideas for management of the motor car while creating an acceptable environment for people. Indeed, as at Reporton Road, the car was located off a 'spine' road which ran through the development, and pedestrians gained access to houses from a pedestrian deck at first-floor level. Houses were designed in narrow-frontage terraced blocks, which were arranged to follow the contours of the ground in similar manner to those of the Seidlung Halen at Bern.

Another competition in 1965 exposed a dilemma within the architectural profession. The winning scheme for Portsdown Hill at Portsmouth was an impeccably worked out mixed development by Theakston and Duell,[70] while subsequently published unplaced entries explored the virtues of low rise–high density forms to satisfy the same brief.[71] These unplaced entries contained among them a scheme by Birkin Haward, Martyn Haxworth and Peter Rich, and another by Michael Brawne, Michael Gold, Edward Jones and Paul Simpson, all of whom were soon to find expression of their ideas elsewhere. Both these schemes grouped dwellings closely together, following the slope of the site, over and around part basement car parking. Haward, Haxworth and Rich used a narrow-frontage terrace house in short blocks, grouped in close association with individual garage courts and a centrally placed four-storey block, an integral part of which was a communal garage; while the

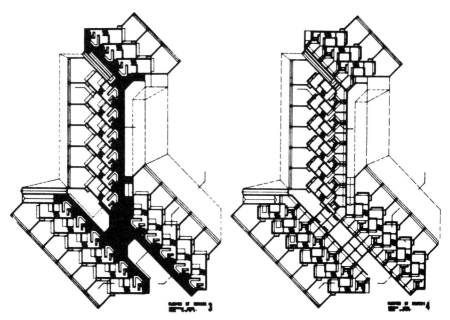

Fig. 7.16 Plans at pedestrian deck level and above, Broadclyst Village housing
(*Architectural Design*)

other team used a single-aspect wide-frontage house stepping down the slope
of the site, but with a long seven-storey slab block at the highest point.

What was happening in these schemes was a low and domestic scale of
building in terms of height, but a grouping of houses that was more crowded
than anything since late-Victorian times. In layout terms the disposition of
dwellings was becoming much more regular than earlier low rise–high
density solutions. It was as gridiron in pattern, and as dense in terms of buildings, as the by-law street. This apparent regression was explained by Peter
Rich:[72]

Present day layout technique has not yet thrown off its romantic and picturesque
origins. Those designers who still wish for irregularity and quote examples of past
'beauty' fail to realise that the irregularity of the past was never planned – it grew.
Whenever, the planners of the ancient world or medieval world had the chance,
they planned and built in regular forms.

Thus principles of design were evolved which demanded an 'absolute
clarity of organisation' if low rise–high density development was 'not to de-
generate into a maze.[73]

Reinforcing the earlier arguments of Chermayeff and Alexander in
Community and Privacy[74] Rich went on to state that his design principles were
based on an organisational 'hierarchy' of such aspects as pedestrian and car
routes, green space, play provision, supply services, drain runs, density and
visual considerations; all of which were laid upon one another, connecting
and crossing at well-defined points, until the final layout was composed of

an 'intricate system of well defined and interconnected hierarchies'.[75] In reality what happened was that the dimensioning of layouts came to be determined by physical factors such as fire brigade hose-reel lengths, or the maximum distance refuse collectors would tolerate from truck to furthest house, and from these the grouping of dwellings followed. As a result layouts at this time became notably more regular and grid-like in plan appearance.

In general the most common layout resulted in a low penetration of roads and open spaces, and with very few windows facing pedestrian paths a low-key public environment appeared, quite different from the orthodox street. This impression has been described as an 'alien casbah effect',[76] despite low rise–high density housing in Britain owing nothing to Moorish precedents; while Rich asserted that inspiration for his approach came from Greek island vernacular lanes and courtyard houses typified by Lindos in Rhodes, as well as Seidlung Halen, Prestonpans, and the recently finished Albertslund scheme in Denmark by Bredsdorff.[77]

Fig. 7.17 *'The alien casbah'* at Clarkhill, Harlow (*E. R. Scoffham*)

Perhaps the best scheme to demonstrate this approach is that at Clark-hill, Harlow, by Associated Architects and Consultants who employed Haward, Haxworth and Rich after their Architectural Association thesis about housing schemes on which they developed the theme. The site was immediately adjacent to Michael Neylan's Bishopsfield, with which the project made the same marked contrast tha ran through post-war housing of various built forms. The contrast was between the use of traditional materials in a progressive technical manner, and the development of a different aesthetic based on developing materials technology. Here Bishopsfield represented the former and Clarkhill the latter, just as Alton East had contrasted with Alton West and Park Hill had contrasted with Lillington Gardens.

Clarkhill used the same L-shaped courtyard house as Bishopsfield, organised to a density of 70 persons per acre (173/ha) into a close grid of dwellings surrounding an open green in the centre of the site, and flanked on each side by four-storey blocks of three floors of flats above basement car-parking.[78] It was intended that car parking should be restricted to the perimeter of the site, the car only penetrating the service culs-de-sac to give access for deliveries and in emergency. In practice this idealism breaks down for the cul-de-sac provided the opportunity for parking the car more conveniently accessible to the dwelling in an area where it could be watched over by passers-by. The basement car park as a result became underused and abused. While it hid the car visually and was paid for by a higher intensity of land use, the ground space thereby gained was often not beneficially utilised and the basement garage became an increasing social problem. This major defect was to some extent anticipated by the designers as they stressed in their *Residents' Handbook* that the culs-de-sac were only for service purposes and that cars 'must' go back to the garage or hardstanding outside the housing area.[79]

Unfortunately for the outcome of this scheme the decision was taken to build it using concrete panel industrialised techniques. From a visual point of view the result was as dreary as parallel developments in other built forms. It seemed clear that the decision to use industrialised techniques caused the unsatisfactory appearance of Clarkhill, rather then anything inherent in its built form. Yet nineteenth-century by-law streets had been criticised for their dreariness and Clarkhill provided a warning that the use of low rise–high density solutions on large schemes could give comparable results. A satisfactory solution to the use of low–high density techniques *en masse* so 'achieving clarity without monotony and complexity without confusion'[80] had yet to be found.

Subsequent large schemes ably demonstrated this failing, particularly when linked with industrialised or non-traditional construction and aesthetics. London County Council and GLC schemes designed in the mid-1960s, such as Beaver's Farm, did not show any evidence of attempts to achieve popularity by the use of traditional materials or a vernacular aesthetic. They did, however, achieve a more domestic atmosphere through lower buildings, but with little compromise in other architectural logic. Beaver's Farm was entirely of two-, three- and four-storey blocks geometrically arranged in rectangular patterns. It was built in a heavy panel concrete system of construction and achieved high standards of acoustic insulation beneath the flight path to Heathrow Airport, and as such its 600 dwellings were popular with tenants.[81] Napper and Partners 70 acre (28.3 ha) Bessemer Park at Spennymoor in County Durham, designed at the same time as Clarkhill to 90 persons per acre (222/ha), was equally as dreary in total appearance, despite the integrity with which the layout had been clearly and methodically organised. A continuous five-storey deck access block meandered through the centre of the scheme so providing large open spaces by enclosing courtyards, and a visual difference in what would otherwise be a vast densely packed two-storey layout; again showing that the two approaches of deck access and low rise–high density developed in parallel throughout the 1960s.[82]

A similar layout approach in the use of two distinct built forms occurred in 1966 at Corby new town under Chief Architect John Stedman. The Kingswood estate contained a similar 'spine' building to Bessemer Park, but not of deck access. Pedestrian routes were in the main on the ground, around which various dwelling types and assemblies of dwellings were stacked in apparently unending permutation, in similar manner to Thamesmead's 'spine' deck access blocks. The surrounding housing was lower in intensity, yet high by comparison with earlier new town housing, and it was organised on conventional Radburn principles using garage courts.[83]

Both these schemes demonstrated the hangover of an image of ordering a town by dwelling blocks that had been one of the motivations of mixed development and which had been reinforced by Park Hill on its completion in 1961. That these blocks were being used in a diagrammatic fashion as a device to prevent plan monotony was not yet apparently realised. That they might be equally disastrous to live in, from a social point of view, as high point blocks went unmentioned. Architects were particularly prone to devising shapes and diagrams which satisfied their aesthetic judgements while making merely token concessions to the social and visual problems that society expected them to solve. Indeed Basildon's large Laindon 5 area[84] designed under Chief Architect D. Galloway compacted the dwellings in courtyards above garages in such manner that provoked local residents to castigate it as 'the ugliest post-war housing development in Britain';[85] and this criticism for a scheme that made, in its architectural critic's eye, a 'considerable achievement in advanced neighbourhood design' and 'imaginative housing'[86] to a density around 75 persons per acre (185/ha). Traditional materials were used at Basildon as they were in Gillinson, Barnett and Partners' The Lanes at Rotherham,[87] a layout of 230 single-storey, two-storey and courtyard houses to 68 persons per acre (168/ha), in the centre of an earlier very large scheme of semi-detached houses. The same question that Clarkhill raised of size of development for such a consistent built form approach was evident, but arguably better answered by a variety of house types and shapes and by the use of traditional materials.

In 1963 the Ministry of Housing had introduced housing cost yardsticks[88] which operated on local authority schemes according to a sliding scale

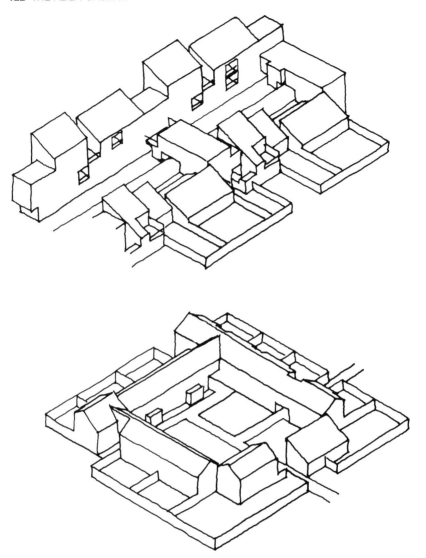

Fig. 7.18 Kingswood, Corby; diagram of (a) 'spine' building, and (b) enclosed courtyard (*E. R. Scoffham – adapted from drawing by Corby Borough Council*)

relating density to average house size. Higher densities attracted more money and so did a lower bedspace size – the maximum amount of money being allowed for schemes which complied entirely with the recommendations of the Parker-Morris Committee,[89] and correspondingly less, pro rata, for those that did not. Certain recommendations of the Parker-Morris Committee only became mandatory on the 1 January 1969 and in general these were concerned with space standards and heating.[90] The effect of these yardsticks was to encourage the social move towards low rise–high density housing, but they

Fig. 7.19   Laindon 5, Basildon (*Basildon Development Corporation*)

also had the effect of increasing the height of high-rise blocks, simplifying block arrangements, and making larger schemes more advantageous in terms of yardstick allowance. Obviously it was cheaper to build to lower storey heights, but it was also cheaper to increase the height of tall blocks to make optimum use of such expensive items as lifts, services and structure. Socially, low rise was preferred, but higher-rise blocks and a skimping of detail on all built forms were corollaries.

Housing subsidies were once again given attention in the Subsidies Act of 1967.[91] A range of subsidies was permitted for certain admissible items – basically superstructure, substructure and external works; but other items were inadmissible for subsidy purposes. Among these items was provision for cars. This resulted in a reappraisal of car accommodation as it was no longer possible to provide accommodation to an ideal 1 : 1 ratio unless there were sufficient families on the estate to pay for it. Any shortfall in car ownership meant that car provision in excess of that required would have to be subsidised by all rent payers, whether they owned a car or not. The net result was a gradual disappearance of car provision as an integral part of complex built forms.

Solutions such as Clarkhill, Reporton Road and Burghley Road, Camden,[92] were excessively expensive in terms of car costs to be passed on to tenants as rents, and as a result the spreading of cars alongside dwellings, on the surface, in courts or in other patterns, increased. Densities inevitably decreased to a certain extent because of the increased ground coverage required, and a more compact and rectangular layout, as exemplified at St Anne's Rotherham and the GLC's Cricketer's Way scheme at Andover[93] became more general.

It was naturally more economic to build on large sites where management could be concentrated, land might be cheaper bought in bulk and design could be simplified, all with consequent savings in time. But the disadvantages of low rise–high density solutions spread over large areas were beginning to be obvious, and it was the Brookvale competition at Runcorn new town in 1969 that provided some of the ideas for a way forward. The site was that of a complete neighbourhood of the town, broken down into four clusters and linked to the rest of the town by a rapid transit route passing through the neighbourhood centre of shops, welfare and community facilities and two churches, with the planning to include three schools and some local industry. The area was 165.2 acres (66.8 ha) to be developed at 65.1 persons per acre (161/ha) giving 8,042 persons in 2,300 dwellings – by far the largest housing competition site in post-war times. The purpose of the competition was for 'original' layout conceptions and an exploitation of industrialised or rationalised building methods within cost yardsticks and to the now mandatory Parker-Morris requirements. Entries demonstrated a variety of approaches to the problem of the size of the site.[94] The winning scheme by

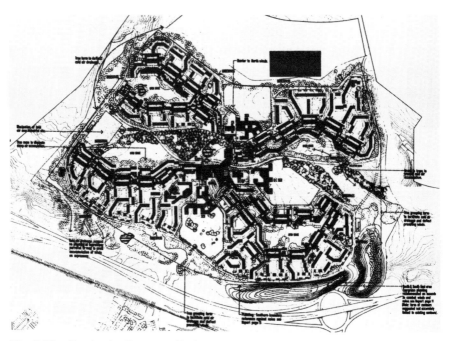

Fig. 7.20 Brookvale, Runcorn; Darbourne and Darke prizewinning entry, site layout (*RIBA Journal, June 1969*)

Darbourne and Darke, taking time off from the tedium of building Lillington Gardens, was an almost informal, unrepetitive, villagey layout with pitched roof houses and a pervading rural quality, yet with underground garages. Birkin Haward, in association with Johns, Slater and Haward, won second prize with a rectangular hierarchic layout, an enlargement of many of the principles earlier established at Portsdown and Clarkhill; while a commended entry by Christopher Cross and Jeremy Dixon proposed a strictly formal linear arrangement of terraced blocks across the site, the car having access directly to each house from a sunken roadway.

Fig. 7.21   Site sections of Darbourne and Darke entry, Brookvale (*RIBA Journal, June 1969*)

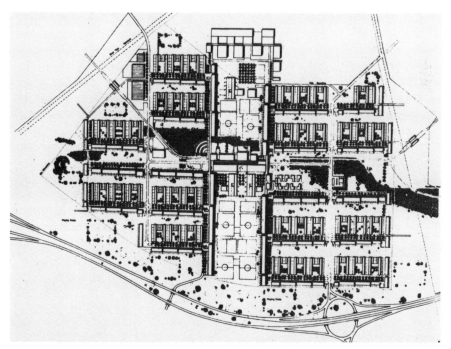

Fig. 7.22   Site layout of Birkin Haward entry, Brookvale (*RIBA Journal, June 1969*)

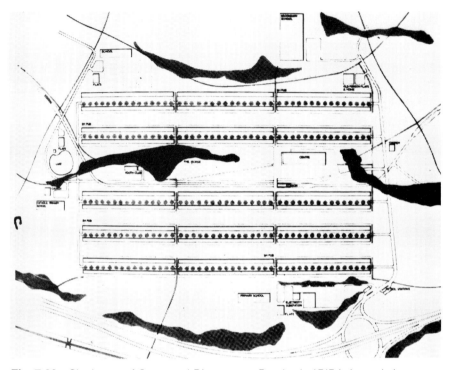

Fig. 7.23 Site layout of Cross and Dixon entry, Brookvale (*RIBA Journal, June 1969*)

Each of these approaches, from the relaxed informality of Darbourne and Darke, through the mainstream rectangularity of Birkin Haward, to the ruthless formalism of Cross and Dixon, was to gain expression elsewhere. The contrast between Darbourne and Darke's scheme and that of Cross and Dixon typified the two approaches to design that thread their way through the shape of post-war housing. From Ackroydon versus Bentham Road, Park Hill versus Lillington Gardens, Bishopsfield versus Clarkhill, the use of traditional materials and building shapes in apparent informality has vied with the desire to create new shapes and a new aesthetic out of developing technology. It has repeated the contrast between Garden City and Ville Radieuse, between Unwin and Le Corbusier, between social acceptability and architectural Utopia. The dilemma it posed was that which condemned architecture in relation to housing from the Unité d'Habitation to Ronan Point, and created the desire for individual expression, a greater degree of participation, and less interference by the architect, the planner and the bureaucrat.

REFERENCES

1. See Ch. 2 and 5.
2. See Ch. 2.
3. New Towns Act, 1946.

4. R. Unwin, *Nothing Gained by Overcrowding*, 1912.
5. J. H. Forshaw and P. Abercrombie, *Greater London Plan*, 1943.
6. Elizabeth Denby, 'Oversprawl', *Architectural Review*, Dec. 1956, pp. 427 ff.
7. *Architectural Review*, Dec. 1956, pp. 424 ff. (Examples quoted were: Paultons Square, Chelsea, dated 1840, at 16.3 houses per acre (40.3/ha); Cleaver Square, Lambeth, dated 1800–20, at 17.3 houses per acre (42.7/ha); and Courteney Square, Lambeth, dated 1914, at 24.8 houses per acre (61.3/ha).)
8. Ruth Glass, 'Higher or Lower', *Architectural Review*, Dec. 1953.
9. Lionel Brett, *Architectural Review*, July 1951, pp. 16–26; W. Manthorpe, *Architectural Review*, Dec. 1956; Gordon Cullen, *Architectural Review*, July 1953; I. Nairn, *Architectural Review*, Dec. 1956; N. Tweddell, *Architectural Review*, Sept. 1960, pp. 195–205.
10. P. Willmott and M. Young, *Family and Class in a London Suburb*, 1957.
11. F. Schaffer. *The New Town Story*, 1972, p. 106.
12. A. and P. Smithson, 'Scatter', *Architectural Design*, Apr. 1959.
13. Ibid.
14. J. H. Forshaw and P. Abercrombie, op. cit.
15. H. Hoffman, *One Family Housing in Groups*, 1967.
16. *Architectural Review*, Dec. 1956, p. 423.
17. W. Manthorpe, 'The machinery of sprawl', *Architectural Review*, Dec. 1956, pp. 409–22.
18. R. F. Jordan, 'Span', *Architectural Review*, Feb. 1959.
19. *Architectural Design*, Sept. 1960, p. 352.
20. See Chapter 3.
21. W. Segal, 'Changing Trends in Site Layout', *Arena*, Mar. 1966, pp. 231 ff.
22. D. Macintosh, *The Modern Courtyard House*, 1971, p. 27.
23. Ibid., pp. 28–30.
24. Ibid., pp. 31–32.
25. Ibid., p. 32.
26. *Architects' Journal*, 21 July 1971.
27. D. Macintosh, op. cit., pp. 34 – 5.
28. See Chapter 5.
29. D. Macintosh, op. cit., p. 35.
30. Ibid., p. 37.
31. *Architect and Building News*, 19 Feb. 1943.
32. W. Segal, *Home and Environment*, 1948.
33. *Architectural Design*, Oct, 1956.
34. *Architect and Building News*, 5 Feb. 1958, pp. 180–9.
35. *Ekistics*, 10, 1960, p. 355.
36. D. Macintosh, op. cit., pp. 25–6.
37. *Architectural Design*, Mar. 1956.
38. *Architectural Design*, Apr. 1959.
39. *Architects' Journal*, 18 Feb. 1960.
40. *Architectural Review*, Oct. 1962.
41. *Architects' Journal*, 25 May 1961.
42. *Architectural Design*, Sept. 1967, pp. 401.
43. London County Council, *The Planning of a New Town* (Hook Report), 1961.
44. *Architects' Journal*, 4 Mar. 1964 and 24 May 1967.
45. *Architects' Journal*, 14 Jan. 1970.
46. *Architects' Journal*, 24 May 1967 and 14 Jan. 1970.
47. J. Tetlow and A. Goss, *Homes, Towns and Traffic*, 1965, pp. 109.

48. *Architectural Review*, June 1966.
49. *Architects' Journal*, 17 June 1970.
50. Post War Building Studies No. 16, *The Lighting of Buildings and the Redevelopment of Central Areas*, 1947.
51. K. Browne, 'Straitjacket',*Architectural Review*, May 1962.
52. *Architectural Review*, Oct. 1962. (See also A Trystan Edwards, *Official Architectural and Planning*, Mar. and Apr. 1965.)
53. D. Macintosh, op. cit., pp. 17.
54. S. Chermayeff and C. Alexander, *Community and Privacy*, 1963.
55. *Progressive Architecture*, Jan. 1970. pp. 120 – 3.
56. *Architects' Journal*, 12 Oct. 1966 and 16 Aug. 1962.
57. P. Phippen, 27 Nov. 1968 at RIBA.
58. United Nations, A Report on the Human Habitat; *How Do you Want to Live?* 1972.
59. Housing and Planning Act, 1974.
60. D. Macintosh, op. cit., p. 41.
61. Greater London Council, *85 Years of LCC and GLC Housing*, 1973.
62. Ibid.
63. *Architects' Journal*, 3 Nov. 1971 and *Architectural Review*, Nov. 1971.
64. For example Emmanuel Road, *Architectural Review*, Nov. 1971.
65. *Architects' Journal*, 24 July 1968.
66. *Old Houses into New Homes*, Cmnd 3602, 1968.
67. Sir G. Parker-Morris, *Homes for Today and Tomorrow* (Parker-Morris Report), 1961.
68. H. Hoffman, op. cit., p. 40 – 3.
69. *Architects' Journal*, 14 July 1965.
70. *Architects' Journal*, 6 Oct. 1965.
71. *Arena*, Mar. 1966.
72. P. M. Rich, 'Notes on low rise–high density housing', *Arena*, Mar. 1966, pp. 242 ff.
73. Ibid., p. 243.
74. S. Chermayeff and C. Alexander, op. cit.
75. P. M. Rich, op. cit., p. 243.
76. D. Jones, 'The role of the courthouse in urban renewal', *Keystone*, Summer 1961.
77. P. M. Rich, op. cit.
78. *Official Architecture and Planning*, Mar. 1967, pp. 344 ff.
79. P. M. Rich, op. cit., p. 243.
80. D. Macintosh, op. cit., p. 42.
81. Greater London Council, op. cit.
82. *Official Architecture and Planning*, Mar. 1966.
83. *Architects' Journal*, 6 and 13 Nov. 1968.
84. *Interbuild*, Dec. 1965.
85. *Architects' Journal*, 9 Dec. 1970.
86. *Architects' Journal*, 16 Feb. 1972.
87. *Architects' Journal*, 21 Aprl 1971.
88. Ministry of Housing, Design Bulletin No. 7, *Housing Cost Yardsticks*, 1963.
89. Sir G. Parker-Morris, op. cit.
90. Circular No. 36/67, 1967.
91. Housing Subsidies Act, 1967.
92. *Architects' Journal*, 11 Sept. 1968, p. 553.
93. *Official Architecture and Planning*, Mar. 1969.
94. *Architects' Journal*, 30 Apr. 1969 and *RIBA Journal* June 1969.

8 TROJAN HORSE

Industrialisation of itself did not generate any new shapes in housing. It did, however, to a degree accentuate variations that were already in existence, and it hindered the development of others. Production techniques, whether in factory or on site, tended to be applicable to a particular built form, or a limited range of built forms, and as a result these became more-or-less accentuated by the success of a particular production technique. Post-war developments in industrialisation have been predominantly a story of the means justifying the end – the end being unacceptable to society for it was not devised with society in mind. But a by-product of industrialisation in the 1960s, an acceptance of the potential of industrialisation to meet the varied requirements of mass housing, did produce a built form variation that occupied the centre of later thinking.

Reference has already been made[1] to the temporary house-building programme at the end of the Second World War, a programme which was initiated by the Government as a means of countering the shortage of traditional building materials and labour in order to produce houses quickly.[2] These emergency factory-made dwellings, popularly known as 'pre-fabs', were all single-storey houses of identical plan. In total they numbered 159,000, most of them being built during 1946–47.[3] Their estimated life was 10 years, yet many are still occupied today and others have been dismantled for re-erection elsewhere. Each was 650 square feet (60.4 m²) in area, including an outside shed, and contained a living-room, two bedrooms, hall, kitchen, bathroom and separate w.c. They were all factory-made and were assembled on standard *in-situ* concrete site slabs. In services and equipment they were ahead of most permanent, traditional dwellings.[4]

Prefabrication using aluminium started in five former aircraft factories at the end of the war. This effort produced the Aluminium Bungalow, the most fully prefabricated and most expensive of all the experimental houses. At the height of production one bungalow was produced every 12 minutes.[5] Other manufacturers at the time produced the Arcon, the Uni-Seco and the Tarran, which with the Aluminium Bungalow comprised the four main types. The Arcon bungalow, devised by architects Edric Neel, Rodney Thomas, Raglan Squire and A. M. Gear, contained a number of pioneer inventive ideas, perhaps the best-known being the complete kitchen–bathroom unit which was subsequently replaced by a similar Ministry of Works unit.[6]

Yet this justifiable interest in prefabrication proved to be short-lived, for the opportunities offered in a return to aircraft production were an irresistible attraction.[7] The Government did, however, having launched the temporary

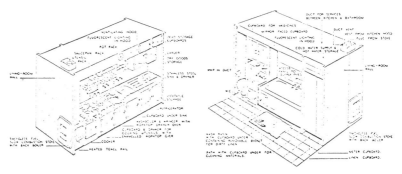

Fig. 8.1 Prefabricated kitchen-bathroom unit of the Arcon bungalow (*from Public Authority Housing by A. W. C. Barr, Batsford*)

dwellings programme, proceed to give backing to the development of 'permanent non-traditional' two-storey houses. Grants to firms for this purpose continued until 1947, after which local authorities were compelled to take these houses for a certain proportion of their housing programmes. New towns were obliged to provide 15 per cent of their programmes by non-traditional houses. As the availability of labour and materials improved from 1954 efforts in this direction were relaxed so that only those firms which could survive commercially remained.[8]

One of these aircraft factories developed a complete organisation for the design, production and building of permanent houses and this came as near as anything could, in immediate post-war years, to an economic break-through. But the company was under pressure to reduce costs and it found the factory and contracting organisations difficult to integrate, so that it, too, found the attractions of a return to aircraft production irresistible.[9]

The products of this permanent non-traditional programme were unre-markable, and were deemed to be architecturally disastrous, for they were the result of policies by most firms to camouflage factory-made products to look as much as possible like traditional houses; after all, they had to sell them. It was basically a search for alternative materials for an established traditional product[10] – a kind of Trojan Horse with which to resolve the problem. Other progressively-minded people such as the Committee for the Industrial and Scientific Provision of Housing, had thought in terms of producing houses like consumer goods so that they could benefit from the price reductions commonly associated with mass production. Yet this argu-ment, reinforced by such architects as Maxwell Fry,[11] was foiled, as it came to be later in the 1960s, because local preferences and prejudices for traditions were dominant. It was a situation summed up by Burnham Kelly in 1951, 'the largest marketing problem is found in the fact that houses are not mere consumer goods, to be used and thrown away when they fall apart. They are the focus of the basic social unit in our society.'[12]

In the immediate post-war programmes of both temporary and non-traditional houses concentration was on individually complete houses and not on the evolution of a series of component parts which could be assembled in a variety of ways to provide solutions to particular problems. Many of the advantages that the immediate post-war years gave us in terms of technical inventiveness went unrealised, because of an understandable situation that the Ministry embodied into the 1949 *Housing Manual*: 'the light construction of the present day, scientifically tested to the maximum load, stress or strain to which it would reasonably be subjected, and pared down to the minimum, cannot be expected to look as substantial as traditional building in brick or stone, but it can be designed in such a way that it neither imitates nor deliberately flaunts established tradition'.[13]

Without the benefit of long-term production there could be little chance of prefabrication being competitive with well-organised conventional building. Nevertheless the post-war years saw the development of a large number of so-called 'systems' of house construction, only a few of which achieved the security of continuous production. In fact many of these 'systems' contained little in the way of prefabrication, and this ironically accounted for their longevity. Nevertheless many of these, too, faltered or failed when, in the 1950s, materials and labour became plentiful again.[14]

During the later years of the 1950s some firms turned their attention to the currently developing multi-storey slab and point blocks. But the adaptation of existing systems led to aggravated problems of stability, noise insulation and fire resistance. It was the increasing numbers of high-rise flats, however, that gave expression to the development of prefabricated techniques vastly different from those of the immediate post-war years.[15] Manufacturers such as Wimpey who had developed techniques of 'no-fines' concrete using prefabricated shuttering, or others who had developed pre-cast concrete frames and claddings, or large wall units in concrete, found new opportunities being opened up for their systems; and in combination a more logical development of prefabricated components followed. This 'heavy' prefabrication of large wall-sized reinforced concrete structural wall, floor and staircase units, was particularly applicable to high-rise blocks where speed of completion, repetition and economy could be optimised.[16]

Alton West had been completed in 1959 and had demonstrated the sophisticated aesthetic that could result from the logical development and use of prefabricated concrete components on a large project. It provided an inspiration and progression from Le Corbusier's concrete idiom of the Unité. From Roehampton the step to large-scale prefabrication and to what subsequently developed as industrialisation was a short one. In parallel with the publication of the Parker-Morris Report in 1961[17] renewed emphasis was placed on the potential of prefabrication for house-building. The housing shortage was as acute as ever, production rates not having increased since Macmillan's economy drive of the early 1950s which achieved a resumption of pre-war annual house-building rates. The Government was expecting an expansion of the economy and feared a shortage of building labour, and in consequence it pressed authorities to use systems of industrialised building. In 1962 R. B. White provided the warnings that had been sounded for prefabrication since immediate post-war days.[18] Standardisation was still seen as the 'bogey of individualism', and he stressed the need to develop a components approach, rather than 'closed' systems based on the whims, economics and novelties of individual manufacturers; and for the architectural profession to work to 'avoid any dehumanising influences in the visual context'. Appropriate warnings these were in retrospect; for the development of industrialised building techniques following the Labour Government's pledge in 1965 for 500,000 houses a year by 1970,[19] was to lead to failures, just as had prefabrication, through misapplication and through a misunderstanding of the real nature of housing.

It was upon a guarantee of production with Government aid and backing that the proper development of industrialised and prefabricated techniques depended, and the Labour Government appeared to give this guarantee. A more prolific growth of 'systems' followed, both 'closed' and 'open' in nature to satisfy all manner of requirements. Production did rise, but not to the extent that Labour had promised, the highest annual rate being in 1968 when 413,000 houses were completed.[20] By then other events had overtaken the ability to produce and these had been precipitated by some of the failings White had anticipated. By 1964 21 per cent of all dwellings built by local authorities and new town corporations were in industrialised techniques and by 1967 the figure had risen to 42 per cent. Yet by 1970 it had fallen dramatically to 15 per cent.[21]

'Closed' systems were sold by enterprising sponsors to unsuspecting local authorities eager to achieve the targets Whitehall had set, often as a complete design-and-build 'package' requiring little effort on the part of the authority other than selection of site and approval of scheme. For many it seemed a means of freeing their time so that they might concentrate on other problems. That they might be creating for themselves a greater future problem went by in a rush to achieve statistics. Architects, too, fell under the spell that by adopting a 'system' developed and manufactured by others they could spend more time on layout problems and on the next more pressing job. The only result of this abdication of aesthetic and humane responsibilities was user dissatisfaction and a series of monuments to a mistaken easy-way-out that are proving to be an expensive legacy. The model of sophisticated prefabrication that Alton West had provided was rarely surpassed and only infrequently equalled.

Yet there were a number of developments by those who were not willing to abdicate from their architectural responsibilities in visual and social terms, and it is to this relative minority that attention must turn for the potential of industrialisation to be realised. The LCC had from 1960, almost immediately following the completion of Alton West, embarked on the use of industrialised techniques as the Government had advocated. Danish production methods were studied by a team which designed a range of three- and ten-storey flats using the Larsen–Neilsen system. Morris Walk was the first major scheme to be carried out on this basis. Flats were spacious and well-equipped but the layout suffered from a rigidity of alignment that was imposed by the adoption of this particular system.[22]

By 1966 about a dozen systems had been used by the LCC and GLC in various projects but few achieved the success of Morris Walk in its exploitation of this kind of closed system. In 1967 the promised shortage of manpower and materials had not come about, and as a result the use of industrialised techniques diminished so that by 1970 the GLC was using only three systems. Nevertheless, one group had developed reinforced plastic mouldings in three-storey-high panels which were used on four point blocks before cost yardstick limitations effectively put an end to tall blocks in the London area.[23]

Industrialisation as part of a policy for increasing housing output had occurred at the same time as the transition from mixed development and high rise towards low rise–high density alternatives. Thus a productivity deal was being sought at the same time as predominantly social pressures were bringing about a wider diversification of built form alternatives. As a consequence of this manufacturers tended to opt for one or other built form, generally dividing their options into heavy panel concrete systems for high-rise blocks, and lightweight systems using a variety of materials for low-rise blocks. Unfortunately for them the schemes currently being designed did not fall into one or other category of built form. Mixed development by its nature ranged from two-storey houses to eleven-storey slab blocks or even higher point blocks, and no single system would suit all block types – a situation that the LCC and GLC might have foreseen, for prior to Alton West mixed-development schemes had shown a difference in construction and aesthetic between high and low blocks. Only at Alton West were they unified – in appearance at least.

Thus it was difficult to find one system that would suit every block shape of a particular scheme. To an extent schemes tended to change to take advantage of the economics of a particular system, so that what might have been a mixed development scheme, or a scheme of different block formations for other social reasoning, became simplified to satisfy the limitations of one system. In this situation the hard sell by a manufacturer could influence design decisions in an adverse manner, and it resulted in the perpetuation of forms such as high point blocks when other developing alternatives were more suitable. In some situations it was possible to save money on one block type where a particular system was economic, so that the same system could be used on another block type where it was uneconomic, thereby achieving a balance in costs to meet yardstick limitations. But as yardsticks became more difficult to achieve, particularly in the London area, this kind of balancing act became increasingly problematical.

For the GLC the transition from mixed development to low rise–high density was done at the height of the industrialisation boom of the 1960s and the majority of schemes which made this transition used systems of construction. Thamesmead was designed in the Balency system using heavy concrete panels with a Scandinavian white marble aggregate. The GLC owned and operated the factory producing the units, and its capacity was far greater than could be absorbed by construction manpower in the area.[24]

Hyacinth Road was an extension to the Alton West estate at Roehampton and was built in Concrete Ltd's large panel concrete system at a time when industrialisation was already declining in popularity; and Beaver's Farm, beneath the flight path to Heathrow Airport also adopted a heavy precast panel system for its two-, three- and four-storey blocks.[25]

The difficulties of selecting a system to meet the increasing complexities of low rise–high density solutions were many. An increasing variety of block shapes meant that the apparent guarantee of numbers pledged by the Government was dissipated. Many manufacturers went out of business or adapted their factories to produce something other than housing, just as the aircraft factories had done in 1947–48. It became not so much a problem of production but a debate about what to produce. At Clarkhill the designers had found the same problem in the selection of a system with which to build both the courtyard and the four-storey peripheral blocks. In the event two systems were used, one for each block form, and a concrete panel with similar aggregate used as the device to unify the appearance of the two.[26]

Of all the developments of the drive towards the industrialisation of house-building in the mid-1960s, the first to exploit its potential in the manner that R. B. White had earlier outlined, was the Yorkshire Development Group (YDG). The YDG was established in 1962 to serve the housing needs of the cities of Leeds, Sheffield, Hull and Nottingham; and Martin Richardson, who had earlier worked on the LCC's Morris Walk scheme, was appointed its development architect. The manner in which Richardson and his team exploited the potential of industrialisation was by the development of a series of dwelling-type plans and constructional components, to suit a variety of sites in the four cities. At the time development work started Park Hill had just been completed in Sheffield and the Lillington Street competition had proved the acceptability of 'streets in the air'. It is not surprising, therefore, that by 1965 YDG had produced a range of deck-access type plans and a specification for a medium rise–high density concrete housing system to suit.[27] By the end of 1966 work had started on the Leek Street site in Leeds. The dwellings were treated as components which could be assembled in various ways, and standardised factory-made units made up the range of dwelling types which, it was claimed, met the housing requirements of the consortium of cities. Subsequent developments at Nottingham, Sheffield and Hull demonstrated the merits of the design for a variety of different site situations and provided some variation in appearance between the sites. Costs were reasonable; at Leeds tenders were received 6.4 per cent below the yardstick allowance, thus demonstrating the benefits to be gained from the consortia method and the design approach of Richardson and his team.[28]

Alas the union of the four cities had, by 1970, fragmented due to political changes, diverse local needs, and the general disillusionment with industrialised building on a national front. But more than this, a programme such

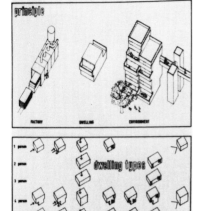

Fig. 8.2 Principles of design of YDG Mark I housing (*Architectural Design*)

as had been devised demanded management expertise, leadership and professional skills that were lacking in, not only YDG, but most of the housing consortia that had developed with similar aims in mind. Martin Richardson himself resigned in 1969.[29]

Nevertheless the approach that YDG had pursued, based on components and their interchangeability in a variety of situations, was followed by the GLC in their 'spine' deck access blocks at Thamesmead. Here there was more irregularity in the disposition of dwellings around the deck than in the YDG schemes – an attempt to convey the impression of randomness despite the dwellings having been deliberately so placed. But the 'spine' buildings at Thamesmead were part of a new township comprising various other more orthodox blocks in a conventional mixed development.[30]

At Runcorn, Darbourne and Darke's winning scheme for the Brookvale competition adopted a similar approach, used in an informal, relaxed, almost rural manner. The dwelling units were predominantly two- and three-storey houses, and the system of components was one of structural and wall elements that could be permutated to provide the apparently random and irregular disposition of dwellings.[31] Unfortunately the tenders for Darbourne and Darke's scheme came in so far above the yardstick that there appeared to be no chance of achieving adequate reductions in cost without severely changing the original concept, and the architects' commission was terminated.[32]

Despite this denial of the aim of industrialisation its potential in using a component rather than a 'closed' system approach was demonstrated by YDG, by Thamesmead, and here at Brookvale. The outcome of Brookvale demonstrated the perennial argument against the yardstick system of vetting costs and made a cogent case for its updating, or waiving, to deal with

Figs. 8.3 and 8.4 YDG at Balloon Wood, Nottingham (*E. R. Scoffham*)

Runcorn's case. Independently the question of components was being explored by the Ministry's Research and Development Group, and by the National Building Agency (NBA) which had been established to deal with the very management and co-ordination problems that industrialisation posed. After their initial ventures into industrialisation at St Mary's, Oldham, using Laing's Jesperson system, and the development of their own 5M system at Gloucester Road, Sheffield, the Research and Development Group settled

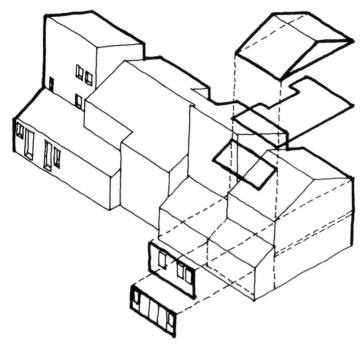

Fig. 8.5 Diagram of component assembly from Darbourne and Darke Brookvale entry (*E. R. Scoffham – adapted from drawing by Darbourne and Darke*)

down to develop a component approach based on the spatial recommendations of the Parker-Morris Committee of 1961. Inherent in the publication of Design Bulletins, dealing with internal house planning[33] and dimensional coordination,[34] was the derivation of a dimensional basis for house planning that had been based on user requirements, and which recognised certain elements such as staircases and bathroom fittings as being standard throughout all house types irrespective of size.[35] The NBA picked up this theme and evolved a series of generic house plans for one-, two- and three-storey houses[36] based on the group's earlier work. Subsequently the NBA standardised a range of house shells[37] within which certain layout objectives could be achieved and house-planning requirements met. The intention was to prevent abortive design time on fresh house types when analysis had shown that there was only a limited range of options within certain basic dimensions.

Industrialisation as a means of achieving national house-building programmes fell into disrepute through a variety of circumstances. The crudeness of detailing and finishes on many schemes led to early deterioration and inevitable complaint; the often appalling outlook from dwellings in system-built schemes provoked tenant unrest, and social and economic circumstances led housing away from the high-rise solutions where industrialisation was most beneficial. The final nail in the coffin of industrialisation

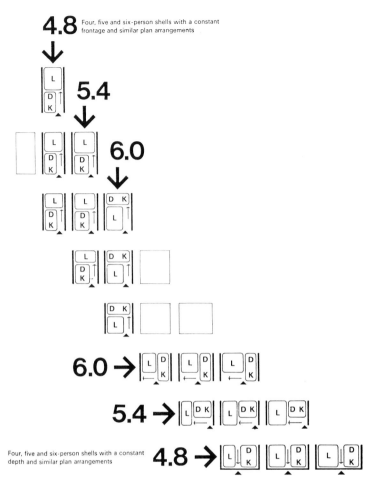

Fig. 8.6   House shells based on standard frontage dimensions by National
Building Agency (*N.B.A.*)

was undoubtedly placed by the disastrous collapse of the Ronan Point
block of flats in Canning Town in 1968, which was built by Taylor
Woodrow–Anglian Ltd using their Larsen–Nielsen system.[38] Although industrialisation was not held responsible in the report of the inquiry into the
collapse,[39] it was enough that progressive collapse was possible using such
a system for industrialisation and high rise to be the culprits in society's eyes.

Furthermore, the economics of industrialisation were only to be gained
on large schemes which provided sufficient repetition and quantity to make
factory production worth while. Schemes inevitably became larger, and
consortia to develop a number of small sites with similar solutions became
administratively difficult to organise. Dissatisfaction could only increase if a
design was inferior in any respect. Of these large schemes the Aylesbury
development in Southwark represented perhaps the ultimate in a pursuit of

Fig. 8.7 Industrialisation of mixed tower and deck access housing in Nottingham (*E. R. Scoffham*)

the statistical logic of industrialisation.[40] It became the largest single housing project ever undertaken by a London borough; it provided over 2,400 homes for some 8,000 people in deck access blocks varying in height from 4 to 14 storeys at a density of 175 bedspaces per acre (432.3/ha), and it was built in Laing's 12M Jespersen system. The enormity of this and similar schemes in visual and social terms, and in the large-scale repetition of blocks, some one-third of a mile long, others arranged in regimental geometry, raised serious questions over the problem of size. If large schemes were impracticable then a component approach to industrialisation, offering variety within a consistent dimensional framework, seemed the only way forward in satisfaction of dwelling numbers.

But housing, as the demise of industrialisation ably demonstrates, is not simply a question of numbers, it is a socio-economic problem. In this context mass production and standardisation are irrelevant; yet the inspiration given by the process of industrialisation during the 1960s made the connection between housing as a socio-economic problem and the potential of some form of standardisation on components. Flexibility, adaptability, choice and change became the watchwords of a socio-economic approach to housing – the ability to have what one wanted at a price one could afford. Components offered the potential of satisfying that ideal, once changes in the administration of mass housing had been made both in the public and private sectors, and Thamesmead provided the image of that potential. But the image that Thamesmead offered for greater flexibility and personalisation was more complex than mere components could explain. The social arguments and the images they in turn produced must be traced elsewhere.

REFERENCES

1. See Ch. 3.
2. Housing (Temporary Provisions) Act, 1944.
3. A. W. C. Barr, *Public Authority Housing*, 1958, p. 118.
4. Ibid., p. 118.
5. R. B. White, 'Prefabrication, Past, Present and Potential', *RIBA Journal*, Sept. 1962.
6. A. W. C. Barr, op. cit, p. 118.
7. R. B. White, op. cit.
8. A. W. C. Barr, op. cit., pp. 118–9.
9. R. B. White, op. cit.
10. Ibid.
11. R. M. Fry, *Fine Building*, 1944.
12. B. Kelly, *Prefabrication of Houses*, 1951.
13. *Housing Manual*, 1949.
14. R. B. White, op. cit.
15. Ibid.
16. Ibid.
17. Sir G. Parker-Morris, *Homes for Today and Tomorrow* (Parker-Morris Report), 1961.
18. R. B. White, op. cit.
19. Circular 73/65, 1965.
20. *Housing Statistics*, No. 24, Feb. 1972 (Extracted).
21. F. Schaffer, *The New Town Story*, 1972, p. 109.
22. Greater London Council, *85 Years of LCC and GLC Housing*, 1973.
23. Ibid.
24. Ibid.
25. Ibid.
26. *Official Architecture and Planning*, Mar. 1967, p. 344 ff.
27. *Architects' Journal*, 6 Aug. 1969.
28. *Architects' Journal*, 9 Sept. 1970.
29. Ibid.
30. Greater London Council, op. cit.
31. *Architects' Journal*, 30 Apr. 1968.
32. *Architects' Journal*, 31 Mar. 1971.

TROJAN HORSE 141

33. Ministry of Housing, Design Bulletin No. 6, *Space in the Home*, 1963 and 1968.
34. Ministry of Housing, Design Bulletin No. 16, *Metric Dimensional Framework*, 1968.
35. Patricia Tindale, 'Component development in the public sector', *Architectural Association Quarterly*, Jan. 1970.
36. National Building Agency, *Generic House Plans, Two and Three Storey Houses*, 1965.
37. National Building Agency, *Metric House Shells, Two Storey Houses*, 1968.
38. *Architects' Journal*, 22 May, 21 Aug. and 13 Nov. 1968.
39. *Report of the Inquiry into the Collapse of Flats at Ronan Point, Canning Town*, 1968.
40. Douglas Frank, 'The greatest happiness', *Architects' Journal*, 27 May 1970.

9 INTERVENTION

Mixed development had, by its very nature, been a consideration of housing in terms of blocks – terraces, slabs and points. Each was devised to satisfy the housing needs of a particular section of the community according to a set of social rules. Large families were to live in low-rise terrace houses, smaller families in four-storey maisonette blocks, childless families and single people in high slabs and point blocks. It was a neat division that allowed architecture to get on with the job of arranging the resultant mix of block types in a diagrammatic and rational manner that was termed 'civic design'. The weaknesses of this approach were all too evident once the smaller families in the four-storey maisonette blocks had grown larger, and the childless families in high blocks were no longer childless. The envisaged mobility between various block types did not occur to any significant extent and as a result social problems accrued in estates with a predominance of high-rise blocks.[1]

In suburbia on the other hand, and in the out-of-town estates and the new towns to a lesser extent, predominantly one type of family house was being built, whether terraced or semi-detached. This was the three-bedroom five-person norm, which, while it was repetitively simple to build and satisfied an average family requirement, was allocated to a wide variety of family sizes. For some families it was a tight fit to live in a civilised manner, while others had too much space.[2] Nevertheless the manner in which these families were housed, whether on public authority or private enterprise estates, had untold advantages over urban mixed developments.[3] There was a greater opportunity to exercise some form of individuality; there was a more recognisable and hence familiar dwelling, and as a corollary a greater sense of personal satisfaction. The anonymity of the flatted block failed to offer this, despite the introduction of architectural devices to emphasise the individual dwelling as at Denis Lasdun's Bethnal Green blocks[4] and the LCC's Canada estate.[5]

But neither of these two polarised approaches had produced a framework by means of which the residential area, and the town, could be organised in order to permit the advantages of the suburb within the order of architecture. The social relevance of Howard and the ordained discipline of Le Corbusier had not met. Yet in his Unité Le Corbusier had provided the germ of the idea for a town framework within which the individual dwelling was a part. It was a germ that none of those concerned with the origins of mixed development ever caught. It was the Smithsons who grasped the essential ingredient of Le Corbusier's thinking from his early writings, his *Ville Radieuse*, and its part realisation at Marseilles. Both Frank Hayes at Camberwell and the LCC teams who produced the crossover maisonettes used the block formation of the central corridor or internal 'street in the air' of the Unité, but never as an organisational device as Le Corbusier had originally intended.[6] Their blocks were always in traditional mixed developments, and the objective of the block was simply that of density. The Smithsons dismissed the diagrammatic nature of mixed development in their search for an urban order and supported Le Corbusier's main theme in their Golden Lane, and later city structuring projects.[7]

'Streets in the air', a fashionable trend in the late 1950s and early 1960s became the device for providing order and discipline, and in this respect Park Hill must be seen as a landmark in that it provided an image of the ordered city. While Ivor Smith and Jack Lynn, like the Smithsons, had seen the 'street in the air' as the organisational device, the building form that resulted was the image taken – in the same way that the content of the Unité had been submerged under the image of its concrete slab and façade detailing. But the Smithsons, and others, were pursuing the content of the theme; low-rise alternatives were devised using horizontal pedestrian routes, both on and off the ground, to provide a discipline for the arrangement of individual dwellings. The Smithsons' 'close houses' and 'strip appliance' house, and early Archigram work, notably by Ron Herron, were examples – the work of Ron

Fig. 9.1 Expression of individual dwellings in tower blocks at the LCC's Canada Estate (*from A Broken Wave by Lionel Esher, Penguin Books 1983*)

Herron developed the route as a tube and extended the attachment of dwellings to the tube in a manner that was at the same time both technological in approach and science fiction in image.[8]

Enough exploratory work on idealised projects was around for the idea of an urban structure to be established, and for the dwelling to be seen as part of a total organism that was vastly different from the civic designs of mixed development. It is to this approach, in its origins part sociological, but mainly a reactionary force that was easily supported by sociological evidence, that can be attributed architectural preoccupations with flexibility, adaptability, change and choice in housing. There can be little doubt that the somewhat diverse theorising of the Smithsons, and the built reality of Park Hill, had by 1961 influenced not a few minds to fresh thoughts about the nature of housing. Sociological evidence about all manner of living problems could be used to condemn the civic design approach and mixed development in particular.

In 1961 John Darbourne had won the Lillington Street competition with an urban structuring, or 'streets in the air' solution.[9] But more than this his scheme expressed the individuality of dwellings. The variety of different dwelling sizes was used to alter the block configuration in such a manner that they were seen almost as separate elements within the blocks. Here was a more mature development of an urban structure within which were a variety of dwellings, of families and of social differences. Park Hill was, by comparison, too authoritarian in the manner in which dwellings, and hence people, had been packaged into a ribbon of building, albeit with the 'street in the air' as its social focus. Lillington Street was more subtle, more sophisticated, more traditional and also more expensive. More traditional because, naively, of familiar brickwork and also because it gave an expression to individual dwellings that was found in emotive traditional towns and villages. More expensive by virtue of this complex block configuration – an aspect that was to hinder over-complexity of blocks in later schemes – and hence a mature development of the ideas John Darbourne had put forward.

But Lillington Gardens (as it was renamed) was a long time in building. It was overtaken by a number of significant schemes, particularly those in low rise-high density vein, and consequently many of its basic premises were submerged under the gradual unveiling of its sophisticated brickwork, landscaping and complex façades. Again the image of the solution had obscured the projects's inherent advances. Meanwhile Thamesmead had been started and its significant 'spine' blocks carried further the expression of individual dwellings that Lillington Gardens had shown, on a scheme that more than many is one of urban structuring. But unlike the Smithsons' arguments, unlike Park Hill and Lillington Gardens, Thamesmead was conceived as an image, in traditional mixed development, civic design manner.[10] The 'spine' blocks were but one ingredient in the recipe of block types that made Thamesmead; they were not seen as the products of a sociological argument but rather as a form-giving device. In this way it seemed almost incidental that they made, in isolation, the contribution they did to the idea of individual expression within an urban order. Here the link between the sociological arguments for variety of dwelling size, and the potential of prefabricated components to satisfy that desire was made in image – in image only, not in reality, for like Lillington Gardens the apparently random ordering of the individual dwellings was quite deliberate. No administrative machinery had yet been devised for the freedom and flexibility that Thamesmead's 'spine' blocks inferred – an interchangeability of dwelling types aided by the use of standardised components – to be implemented at this mass scale in public authority housing.

Darbourne and Darke's later abortive Brookvale competition entry in 1969 for Runcorn New Town inferred a similar flexibility of dwelling disposition. It inferred it in a more credible way through a layout and aesthetic that evoked the traditional village in its apparent informality. This process of accretion according to a time honoured vernacular style appeared to be the scheme's inspiration – a machinery of growth that was the antithesis of the vast scale of a single project that provided Brookvale's brief.[11]

In 1963 Peter Phippen had started work on a co-ownership housing scheme at Hatfield. Here, in a single-storey development the potential inferred at Thamesmead had been earlier tried out. This was a co-ownership venture at a time when these were rare in post-war years, and it was mainly due to the machinery of its administration that The Ryde proved to be such

Fig. 9.2 Lillington Gardens, Pimlico (*from A Broken Wave by Lionel Esher, Penguin Books, 1983*)

Fig. 9.3 'Spine' block, Thamesmead (*Department of Architecture Slide Library, University of Nottingham*)

a success. Individual owners had some say in the size, fittings and equipment of their dwellings and Peter Phippen satisfied their varied needs within a basic dimensional framework.[12] Indeed, since completion, one or two owners have extended their houses in a manner facilitated by the linear patio plan arrangement, while remaining within the dimensional and aesthetic disciplines of the original design.[13] From the success of this and other later housing associations, co-operative ventures and co-ownership schemes, came evidence that the manner of their administration was the key as it enabled greater individual participation. It was a factor that came to be recognised in the 1974 Housing and Planning Bill which established, among other things, the Housing Corporation to explore alternative forms of housing policy and to provide central control for housing associations.[14]

Participation, inferred at Lillington Gardens and Thamesmead, but never practised, and to a limited extent possible at The Ryde, became a fundamental issue at all levels of planning. The Utopian schemes of the Corbusian school of architects had been rejected by society at social and visual levels. The almost aggressive determination by architects involved in housing to impose their solutions on society because they believed them to be right resulted in an apparent rejection by society of architecture and planning in mass housing. The perennial dilemma of planning, to control individual choice, had been heightened.

In this context a Dutchman, Professor N. J. Habraken, provided an architectural argument that received much publicity in Britain. It is necessary to put Habraken into an historical context in order that his ideas may best be understood and appreciated, for they came to Britain by reputation and translation some 6–10 years after their origination in Holland. In 1961 Habraken published his ideas as *De Dragers en de Mensen*,[15] translated as *The Supports and the People*, but translation into the English language did not take place until 1972 when the Architectural Press published *Supports: an alternative to mass housing*.[16] It was not until 1965 that Habraken himself had any positive results from his ideas. Then he became Director of Research of the Stichting Architecten Research (SAR), a body established by ten leading Dutch architectural practices to finance independent research into housing; and after some success at consultancy work, he was, in 1966, invited to take the chairmanship of the Faculty of Architecture at Eindhoven Technical University, to which he removed the whole SAR establishment.[17] It is from 1967 onwards that Habraken's theories became available to the English-speaking world, when, through his position at Eindhoven, he was invited to write and speak outside Holland, in parallel with developing his studies through projects in Holland itself.[18]

In general what Habraken proposed was a social approach to housing – one which recognised the varying needs, aspirations and finance of different family groups. He was against the finite housing estate where every dwelling was designed to an absolute set of criteria established by people other than those who would live there. But he recognised the need for some form of controlling discipline, and for these reasons proposed the separation of what he termed the 'support' elements: structure, services and land, from the variable elements of the dwelling itself: partitions, fittings and equipment. In a tentative description of what a solution might be, for his book was deliberately devoid of any illustrative material, he envisaged continuous 'support structures', multi-storey in nature – for he admitted high densities were needed – within which individuals had a dwelling of their own choice, access to which was gained along horizontal decks from periodic lift towers.[19] The similarity between this description and Park Hill, completed one year earlier than the book, was marked and has been noted by Jack Lynn,[20] though there was no evidence from Habraken that he was influenced by it, or by the Smithsons, or even by *Ville Radieuse* to which it was a parallel in ultimate solutions. The similarity in assuming that high density equates with high rise was a product of the time it was written, but here the similarities ended. What Habraken had in mind was a kind of framework within which a social order for housing could find its own changing level. In descriptions of a reality it was crude, and the actuality of the argument had many holes. It was the possibility of an alternative to the housing estate designed to a finite end for unknown occupants that was its potential.

Habraken dismissed the industrialised approach which equated house production with that of cars and other consumer durables, yet he saw the potential of industrialisation once a clear understanding of the process of housing, rather than the end-product, had been made. In approach this was similar to the component argument that the Ministry of Housing and National Building Agency (NBA) had arrived at after the traumatic experiences of industrialisation in Britain during the 1960s.[21] Habraken provided the social arguments and the possibilities for their realisation in mass housing at a time when, in Britain, changes away from high rise and from the difficulties of industrialisation were occurring and when public participation was finding its voice. Thus his ideas found ready acceptance among those eager to find an alternative to the established twin Utopias of Howard and Le Corbusier, but a cautious reception from those to whom Habraken seemed yet another Utopian.[22] Habraken's ideas were built at Maakssen Broek, 12 miles (20 km) from Amsterdam, as a result of a competition entry by one of his research team, Fokke de Jong, with the aid of two other SAR members in 1969. Time had by now seen certain changes, for while a high density was achieved the built form was low rise, yet the 'supports' premiss was maintained.[23] Independently of this Wates Ltd had produced what appeared to equate with Habraken's theory at a new estate at Forestdale, Aldington,[24] where a brick and concrete framework capable of supporting a varied mix of dwelling units was proposed and the correct type of dwelling and finishes for the particular market situation were inserted later. Here the dwellings were not the interchangeable items that Habraken had envisaged but the potential was evident. It was something that appeared far easier to develop in the private or co-ownership sector, as Peter Phippen's The Ryde had demonstrated, than it was in the public sector.

Ironically enough some extremely illustrative material demonstrating virtually exactly what Habraken had in mind came from the Archigram group in 1961, the same year Habraken's book was first published.[25] Whereas Habraken was cautious in the extreme about committing himself to drawings, the Archigram group provided almost unending images of cities of the future based on a full exploitation of technological potential. The group's plug-in city was Habraken in pictures, for a vast megastructure was envisaged into which dwelling pods would be plugged as and when required, and then moved with the same facility. It was futuristic and still is, though Archigram would without doubt never admit it, just as Le Corbusier had never seen his cities as being for any time other than the present, but futuristic in that its visual appearance was foreign to society. Archigram was as Utopian as was Le Corbusier in the 1920s.

The detachable nature of whole dwelling units was given form in Moshe Safdie's 'Habitat' for the Montreal Exposition in 1967, and the theme recurred in the GLC's experimental site at Carysfort Road. Here an inspiration given by the freight container was used to suggest a potential in the easy transportation of a rigid, well-insulated box for a small housing programme of limited construction time.[26] The GLC then turned its attention in conjunction with the Timber Research and Development Association, to the complete prefabrication of timber boxes delivered to site fully fitted. But these were not interchangeable units within a basic framework as Archigram and Habraken had inferred, they were merely a device for speeding up site erection time and as such were a product of the mass production industrialised argument, not the social one.

Fig. 9.4 Prefabricated timber box construction at Carysfort Road (*Department of Architecture Slide Library, University of Nottingham*)

To an extent Habraken's arguments were implemented in Britain through the development of PSSHAK (Primary System Support Housing and Assembly Kits).[27] The system was established in 1967 by Nabeel Hamdi and Nic Wilkinson together with economics graduate John Evans, and with the help of SAR. In the subsequent 4 years a number of experimental and theoretical studies based on Habraken's ideas were undertaken. In 1970 Hamdi and Wilkinson met with former Minister of Housing, Anthony Greenwood, and Principal Housing Architect to the GLC, Kenneth Campbell. This resulted in the use of GLC facilities for a study of the relationship between PSSHAK methods, Ministry standards and GLC constraints. A site at Stamford Hill was used for the study, and after presentation of the scheme in May 1971 a pilot project was designated where building started in 1972.[28] In essence PSSHAK enabled the future tenant to decide on the relative sizes of rooms for himself, and when one family moved, or the children grew up, the size of the rooms or the size of the flat could be changed. Inevitably this meant that the tenant must be known in advance and different administrative procedures were thus demanded to deal satisfactorily with the demonstrated potential.

Structure was identified as independent of partitions, fittings and services, and a lightweight party wall was adopted to give a greater range of flat sizes. These ideas were not new having been used in Sweden, in the Department of the Environment's own flexible house for the Ideal Home Exhibition, and in development work on the 5M system, but the significance was that a large

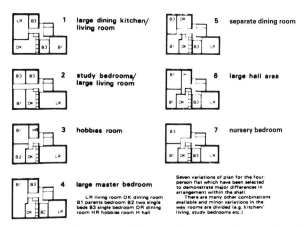

1 large dining kitchen/ living room

2 study bedrooms/ large living room

3 hobbies room

4 large master bedroom

LR living room DK dining room B1 parents bedroom B2 two single beds B3 single bedroom DR dining room HR hobbies room H hall

5 separate dining room

6 large hall area

7 nursery bedroom

Seven variations of plan for the four-person flat which have been selected to demonstrate major differences in arrangement within the shell.
There are many other combinations available and minor variations in the way rooms are divided (e.g. kitchen/living, study bedrooms etc.)

Fig. 9.5 PSSHAK variations within a standard shell at Stamford Road (*Architectural Design*)

housing authority had seen fit to commission the project. Being admittedly experimental the project was aimed to discover the potential of this kind of flexibility and changeability on grounds of cost, the degree of flexibility demanded and found necessary, whether the location and setting of the dwelling were more important than flexibility and whether occupancy rates were likely to change.[29] As it turned out, Stamford Hill fell victim to bureaucracy and its outcome was visually monotonous despite its ingenuity. Hamdi classed it as a necessary learning experience; yet while it was under construction Kenneth Campbell had seen fit to attempt a second project at Adelaide Road. The result here was much improved on the prototype. The range of the scheme was between 32- and 64-dwelling units; each block containing a maximum of 8 units as 6 single-person units and 2 two-person units. In reality the range of choice in layout was limited to fairly ordinary dwelling arrangements. The problem was that of local authority housing standards which forced the flexible shell to be tightly planned to space and fittings constraints, and this in turn limited the potential in use of the demountable rearrangeable partitions.[30]

Almost coincidental with the publicity given to Habraken's ideas John Turner had written a book based on his experience on self-help housing in South America.[31] In application to Britain's housing it exposed the dilemma of the imposition of standardised solutions by any, albeit well-meaning, authority. What Turner sought was a framework within which there was flexibility of choice about the use of individual resources, as long as in doing so neighbours had the same flexibility. It was an argument that put an end to packaged housing, as the evidence indicated this used up more energy and had a shorter life-span than a 'loose parts' approach assembled by local builders in response to local demands.

This 'custom built' approach was in a sense recognised in a Government White Paper, *Widening the Choice: the next steps in housing*, in 1973,[32] and

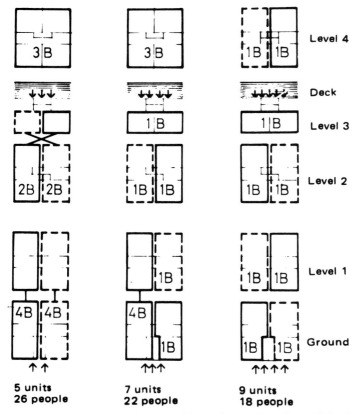

Level 4

Deck

Level 3

Level 2

Level 1

Ground

3 B
3 B
1B 1B

1 B
1 B
1 B

2B 2B
1B 1B
1B 1B

4B 4B
4B
1B
1B 1B

1B
1B 1B

**5 units
26 people**

**7 units
22 people**

**9 units
18 people**

Fig. 9.6 Plan permutations at Millman Street; Farrell and Grimshaw (*Architectural Design*)

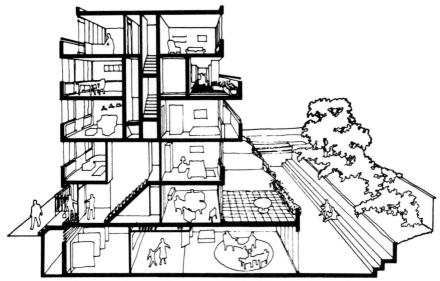

Fig. 9.7 Block section, Millman Street (*Architectural Design*)

implemented by the formation of the Housing Corporation to explore alternative forms of housing policy through the 1974 Housing and Planning Act.[33]

Meanwhile the issues of choice, change and participation had been considerably emphasised by an increasing trend towards the rehabilitation and improvement of older houses. It became increasingly evident that the attention given to policies of improvement was altering thinking about the nature of new housing. Local authority grants for individual house improvement and conversion had been available long before they were given publicity in the late 1960s, but they had only been made use of sporadically and not as part of a general policy. Indeed, the LCC had undertaken the rehabilitation and preservation of existing early nineteenth-century terraces from the Brandon estate of the mid-1950s onwards.[34] Here, in streets adjacent to the Brandon mixed development scheme, the repair and conversion of terraces into flats, both horizontally and vertically, to bring them up to contemporary standards of housing had proceeded in parallel with the new estate.

Rehabilitation continued at a variety of scales in LCC work: from the restoration of areas such as Porchester Square to the rescue of individual buildings. The Pepys estate, formerly the Royal Victoria Dock, contained the conversion and modernisation of eighteenth-century terraces, the alteration of two large warehouses into flats, and the modification of the colonnaded entrance offices into old people's dwellings.[35]

The bulk of more typical improvement came after 1966 when the plight of the nation's vast stock of older houses was focused upon by a committee under the chairmanship of Evelyn Denington. This report, *Our Older Homes: a call for action* established the basis for later legislation,[36] for it was becoming clear that industrialisation could not cope with the national house-building programme even if older areas could be acquired and cleared quickly enough. The 1950s had seen attention to slum problems being centred around demolition and replacement, and once the scale of this task had been realised it became obvious that it would be impossible even with the aid of large-scale industrialisation techniques. The improvement of those houses capable of rehabilitation, and the conversion of larger houses into a number of smaller dwelling units became an economic and statistical necessity.

In amplification of Mrs Denington's report the Ministry had demonstrated the potential of improvement in a study of the Deeplish area of Rochdale,[37] and in 1968 the Government published its White Paper, *Old Houses into New Homes*;[38] the general contents of which became law in the 1969 Housing Act.[39] Two aspects were important: the improvement and conversion of individual houses by means of a wider availability of the already existing grants, and the upgrading of the environment in which these houses were located by the designation of General Improvement Areas coupled with grants to local authorities for carrying out the necessary improvement work.

Also by 1969 the increasing pressures for public participation in the whole planning process, attributable to the general dissatisfaction by society with the products of planning and architecture, of which the condemnation of high rise and industrialised brutality in housing was only part of an argument which included new road proposals and planning blight, were given attention by a committee under the chairmanship of Sir Arthur Skeffington.[40] The committee's findings advocated wider participation in the planning process by means of public meetings and exhibitions, and through an extended communication by those concerned in planning with those for whom they were planning.

The general result of the 1969 Housing Act, and the shift in emphasis to greater participation by both public and planners, was an increasing awareness of environmental issues, and a desire to see these better resolved than before. Housing improvement was in essence a form of public participation: the individual could more easily control the outcome of his own household arrangements. There were, however, a vast number of unresolved issues, particularly where houses were in local authority ownership or in the hands of absentee landlords.

For architects, improvement and conversion was much less grand than the Utopian days of the 1950s, yet it brought greater satisfaction to householders, more so than their relocation into a contemporary estate might have achieved. Socially they were better off having stayed in their original house, an argument made years earlier by Young and Wilmott,[41] and in terms of standards and amenities they had seen improvements which were to some extent under their own control. There was little doubt that the progressive improvement and conversion of older houses would continue. The attitude of mind this brought about had repercussions within the architectural profession. The need and the desire to create the vast new communities of the 1950s and 1960s disappeared. So, too, did the need to adopt technological devices of unfamiliar aesthetics, and the use of mass-production techniques. A more gentle, and apparently more civilised attitude to housing developed.

As a corollary of this, new housing underwent changes. The potential for reshuffling the insides of eighteenth- and nineteenth-century houses to provide a rearrangement of living space for one or more families was paralleled in new housing. The PSSHAK had been an example, though admitted by its authors to have been based on a higher social objective. The shell approach to housing design, long advocated by the NBA and Ministry of Housing, offered options within dimensional limits. Older terrace houses were seen to provide admirable shells of ample dimensions, and they offered as a result a greater degree of flexibility in conversion and adaptation possibilities than did many metric house shells based on Parker-Morris area standards. Yet the idea was paralleled and this was important. The potential of an adequately-sized house shell within which a range of options was possible over a considerable length of time, rather than the mechanistically quick-to-change intentions of PSSHAK, became increasingly relevant and was demonstrated by an accelerating number of improvement examples,[42] despite the fact that the Act did not reach the people for whom it was intended. Better-off families had syphoned-off grants for improvements in a process of 'gentrification' and it was not until the 1974 Act that an attempt was made to correct this imbalance by the creation of Housing Action Areas.[43]

Perhaps the best-known, and in retrospect successful, improvement area was Black Road at Macclesfield. In this innovative project the architect, Rod Hackney, lived in the area, handled the accounting, managed the task on the basis of three contracts rather than by piecemeal improvements to individual houses and, significantly, involved self-help work with builders' co-operation.[44]

This latter innovation had been hinted at in the 1973 White Paper[45] in relation to the Housing Corporation in terms of 'informality' 'flexibility' and 'capacity for experiment', and in 1975 the Rents and Subsidies Act had encouraged the co-operative housing association where joint tenant management replaced the charitable trust or management committee.[46] All this suggested a change in the tenor of mass housing to, in John Maule McKean's phrase, 'housing by the masses, rather than for them',[47] and when this was related to new housing provision it suggested the professional team providing the background framework or skeleton which was filled in by the inhabitants themselves.

This self-determination approach was little more than a further development of Habraken; but quite different from his built expression through PSSHAK at Adelaide Road where the technical gadgetry of change now appeared to be almost irrelevant to the social objective. John Turner put it, 'as long as local makers and suppliers agree to standardised components, there can be very large numbers of small power tool makers'.[48] Such standardisation the Housing Development Directorate of the Ministry of Housing had been attempting to achieve in implementation of its dimensionally co-ordinated house plans throughout the 1960s.

The industrialisation argument thus came full-circle. A systems approach based on standardised components was attainable by those who saw it as a means of achieving social satisfaction, rather than by those who saw it as a means of architectural expression. It was Walter Segal who indicated the directions where effort was minimised and waste almost non-existent, in a method based on uncut, easily available manufactured pieces; one where everything was calculated leaving nothing to chance. It was a system that anyone could build using the simplest of power tools – a do-it-yourself architecture.[49]

But what impact had this architectural theorising in practice and especially in terms of housing form? At one level some traditional improvement and conversion devices found their way back into a new housing vocabulary. In a desire to find ways of extending and adapting new houses to future requirements Hillingdon Borough Council devised, in a project at Harehills, extendible housing that provided for planned vertical extension into the roofspace.[50] A large pitched roof had oversized ceiling joists and trimmers for staircases, dormers and rooflights built-in. Planning regulations allowed extension within the house as 'permitted development' – the extensions so achieved had little outward effect on the appearance of the scheme. It was a device that those concerned with the provision of more space in older

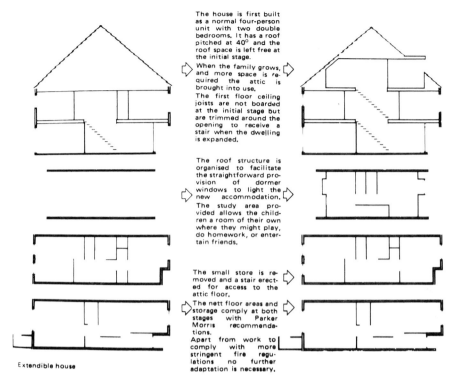

The house is first built as a normal four-person unit with two double bedrooms. It has a roof pitched at 40° and the roof space is left free at the initial stage.

When the family grows, and more space is required the attic is brought into use. The first floor ceiling joists are not boarded at the initial stage but are trimmed around the opening to receive a stair when the dwelling is expanded.

The roof structure is organised to facilitate the straightforward provision of dormer windows to light the new accommodation. The study area provided allows the children a room of their own where they might play, do homework, or entertain friends.

The small store is removed and a stair erected for access to the attic floor.

The nett floor areas and storage comply at both stages with Parker Morris recommendations. Apart from work to comply with more stringent fire regulations no further adaptation is necessary.

Extendible house

Fig. 9.8 Expansion and adaptation possibilities at Harehills, Hillingdon (*Architectural Design*)

Fig. 9.9 Elevational variations at Harehills (*Architectural Design*)

houses had used to advantage for a considerable number of years, and it was significant here to see it adopted in a local authority scheme where the public finance procedure implied that the additional costs of expansion potential must be absorbed into initial costs.

At another level the GLC and Department of the Environment developed Housing Action Kits – a sort of do-it-youself survey of attitudes and preferences. Project ASSIST was formed in Glasgow in 1972 to renovate tenement houses on a participatory basis, and in 1978, in a pilot scheme at Bromley, tenants were allocated individual architects to design their houses.

None of these interventionist ideas had yet found expression outside the bounds of the originally designed envelope; PSSHAK had swopped space, Harehills had extended within it. A number of projects attempted to do this but all of them, when in the public sector, ran up against the method of financial administration of public authority housing. As long as standards of space and equipment were related to initial cost yardsticks it was impossible fully to develop the participatory potential of Habraken and Turner. It was for the conversion of older houses, for the co-ownership sector, and for the private sector where extensions and modifications were a matter of course, to indicate directions along this line.

In the public sector the foremost interventionist project was Ralph Erskine's redevelopment of Byker in Newcastle upon Tyne. This participatory venture was started in 1970, before which Erskine had been involved in a private housing development at nearby Killingworth township where he had won a competition in 1967 with a solution that offered the concept of a traditional village on a lakeside. In 1968 he had been commissioned for a housing development at Studlands Park, Newmarket, where another village concept was proposed. The approach at Byker sought a middle route in participation. An office was established by the architect on the site which

Fig. 9.10 Lakeside village housing. Sketch by Ralph Erskine for Killingworth (*Architectural Design*)

future tenants were encouraged to visit and see what was going on. From the ensuing conversations a dialogue took place between users and designers that enabled the architects to achieve their stated objectives of maintaining the traditions of the area, its characteristics and its relationships with surroundings, and of rehousing those previously resident in the area without breaking family ties and valued traditions. The area office became an architect's shop and was located in a former funeral parlour, with the resident architect, Vernon Gracie, living in the flat upstairs. Janet Square was the first phase of the redevelopment built in 1971–72 where the aim, to create a friendly meeting place, was successful in the eyes of both architectural critic and inhabitant.

The second, and oft-quoted most interesting, phase of the redevelopment was The Wall. Here there was no tenant involvement as the task of The Wall was to shield the contained village from the noise of the proposed urban motorway and from cold winds. In concept The Wall was a 'street in the air' solution that curved in a manner similar to Le Corbusier's Algiers project of 1930, and the 1950s ideas of Team 10 of which Erskine was a member. While The Wall was the dominant element of the whole project, and a necessary one from the point of view of the protection it now offers from cold winds, it was perhaps the least satisfactory element in the eyes of Byker's inhabitants. No children live there, and it is becoming a Wall of old people. Ironically enough, the motorway which largely generated its form has not been built. Nevertheless, the phased redevelopment of the protected area The Wall encloses has been successful – phased in small sections of around 250 houses, with minimum disruption and maximum public involvement.

It is from the image it offers as well as from its participatory achievements that Byker has become a landmark. The atmosphere is one of friendliness and of familiarity, despite the varied building shapes. The detailing and use of materials suggest participation, arbitrariness and temporariness despite their having been deliberately designed, and within this looseness there is yet room for personalisation. Byker achieved a popularity in its approach and implied a popularity in its image. It was a continuing participatory exercise in design and continues to be so in reality. The point at which

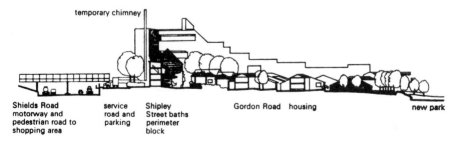

Fig. 9.11 Section through Byker redevelopment (*Architectural Review, December 1974*)

Fig. 9.12 Byker Wall (*John Ford*)

completion occurs has been blurred. Perhaps the most significant summing up of Byker's folksiness, its warmth and cheer, was that of an elderly couple arriving to spend their holidays with relatives – 'Just like a seaside village.' Peter Buchanan wondered whether there was any other modern housing development about which this might be said and which would be desirable for a holiday.[51]

The fun and fantasy notion that this observation conjures – a kind of urban holiday camp, was also a descriptive fragment of suburbia. 'We can devise a schizophrenic suburbia where on one flank there is a picture book tranquility, and on the other flank the gregariousness of seaside, zoo, playground, workshop, funfair, aesthetic free-for-all.'[52] The suburbia to which Byker alluded had, however, been on our doorstep since the efforts of Ebenezer Howard and his followers had provoked the misguided sprawl of the inter-war years. As J. M. Richards pointed out in 1946, suburbia

Fig. 9.13 Byker Wall (*John Ford*)

contained all the opportunities for 'individualism and anarchy', characteristics which could naturally be allowed expression; for, he went on, 'the suburb is the one hide-out of the amateur, on whose participation a living tradition must always depend'.[53] Obviously Richards' arguments became more relevant seen against Byker but they contained within them an appropriate warning. While greater freedom of choice, increased opportunities to adapt and change, and more individual expression might be sought, they also had to be controlled. 'Uncontrolled building of the suburban kind may, and does, add to the general architectural chaos of our time, but the suburb itself – at its best – has virtues peculiarly designed to bring comfort and fulfilment to many'.[54]

The eminent saleability and attractiveness of suburbia, in society's eyes, for all manner of personal motives, was its prime virtue. It represented the closest approach to a contemporary vernacular, a social alternative to the

Fig. 9.14 Byker's 'holiday homes' (*John Ford*)

dogmatic, Utopian, architectural view of the town. Architecture could, and should, show society how its aspirations might be achieved. It had within it the germ of a solution to the problems of choice and change. But the best means of bringing architecture to satisfy these aspirations might not necessarily be architectural ones. As has been shown, management processes, financial procedures and a change in legislation made the task that much easier. Yet the need for a vernacular style was increasingly evident while the gap between architecture and society appeared to be getting perceptively narrower. The manner in which this happened must now be studied.

REFERENCES

1. Walter Segal, 'Changing Trends in Site Layout', *Arena*, Mar. 1966. pp. 231–5.
2. Ruth Glass, 'Social determinants of housing design', *Official Architecture and Planning*, May 1965.
3. I. Reynolds and C. Nicholson, 'Living off the ground', *Architects' Journal*, 20 Aug. 1969, pp. 459–70
4. *Architectural Review*, May 1960, and *Architectural Design*, June 1960.
5. See Ch. 7.
6. See Ch. 7.
7. A. and P. Smithson, *Urban Structuring*, 1967.
8. See P. Cook, *Archigram 1–5*, 1961–64.
9. *Architects' Journal*, 1 Oct. 1969, pp. 807 ff. and pp. 813 ff.
10. *Architects' Journal*, 11 Oct. 1972.

11. *Archictects' Journal*, 30 Apr. 1969; *RIBA Journal*, June 1969.
12. *Architects' Journal*, 12 Oct. 1966.
13. *Architects' Journal*, 16 Aug. 1972.
14. Housing and Planning Act, 1974.
15. N. J. Habraken, *De Dragers en de Mensen*, 1961, Amsterdam.
16. N. J. Habraken, *Supports: an alternative to mass housing*, 1972.
17. M. Pawley, 'Mass housing', *Architectural Design*, Jan. 1970.
18. N. J. Habraken, 'Supports responsibilities and possibilities', *Architectural Association Quarterly*, Winter 1968–9, pp. 25–31; 'The perfect barracks and the support revolution', *Interbuild/Arena*, Oct. 1967, pp. 12–19.
19. N. J. Habraken, *Supports*, op. cit.
20. *Architects' Journal*, 12 July 1972.
21. See Design Bulletin No. 16, *Metric Dimensional Framework*, 1968; National Building Agency, *Metric House Shells, Two-Storey Houses*, 1968.
22. See comments on Habraken: *Supports* op. cit. in *Architects' Journal*, 12 July, 1972.
23. M. Pawley, op. cit.
24. Ibid.
25. P. Cook, op. cit.
26. *Architects' Journal*, 3 Oct. 1973, pp. 780–2.
27. Nabeel Hamdi and Nic Wilkinson, 'Public and private possibilities in housing', *Architectural Association Quarterly*, July 1970, pp. 44–9.
28. D. Frank, 'Habraken in Hackney', *Architects' Journal*, 15 Sept. 1971.
29. Ibid.
30. Andrew Rabeneck, 'The new PSSHAK', *Architectural Design*, Oct. 1975, pp. 629–33.
31. J. F. C. Turner and R. Fichter, *Freedom to Build*, 1973.
32. *Widening the Choice: the next steps in housing*, 1973.
33. Housing and Planning Act, 1974.
34. Greater London Council, *85 Years of LCC and GLC Housing*, 1973.
35. Ibid.
36. E. Denington, *Our Older Homes: a call for action* (Denington Report), 1966.
37. *The Deeplish Study*, 1966.
38. *Old Houses into New Homes*, Cmnd 3602, 1966.
39. Housing Act, 1969.
40. Sir A. Skeffington, *People and Planning* (Skeffington Report), 1969.
41. P. Willmott and M. Young, *Family and Class in a London Suburb*, 1957.
42. *Architects' Journal*, 10 June 1970, pp. 1447 ff, and 1 July 1970, pp. 15 ff.
43. Housing and Planning Act, 1974.
44. Tom Woolley, 'Housing improvement', *Architectural Design*, Aug. 1976, pp. 458–63.
45. *Widening the Choice*, op. cit.
46. Rents and Subsidies Act, 1975.
47. J. M. McKean, 'Self-Build housing', *Architectural Design*, Aug. 1976.
48. J. F. C. Turner, 'Housing the people, 7: the practice of housing' *Architectural Design*, Mar. 1976, pp. 170–3.
49. J. M. McKean, 'Walter Segal', *Architectural Design*, May 1976, pp. 288–95.
50. *Architects' Journal*, 9 May 1973, pp. 1132–3; *Architectural Design*, May 1974, p. 299.

51. Peter Buchanan, 'Byker, the spaces between', *Architectural Review*, Dec. 1980, pp. 331–43; see also *Architectural Review*, Dec. 1974, p. 346–62; *Architectural Design*, June 1975, pp. 333–8; *Architectural Design*, Nov.–Dec. 1977, pp. 823–41.
52. P. Cook, 'The suburban ethic', *Architectural Design*, Sept. 1974, pp. 563–4.
53. J. M. Richards, *The Castles on the Ground*, 1946, p. 58.
54. Ibid.; p. 70.

10 COMPROMISE

During the full flood of Corbusian fervour, whether through mixed development or 'streets in the air', there had always been architects who resisted the development of a new aesthetic based on developing technology. They preferred to use traditional materials and conventional details on buildings that were products of the ideas Le Corbusier and others had devised. To some extent these architects followed a Scandinavian theme, where natural materials were used in natural settings on the then developing high-rise flatted blocks. But their resistance can be seen as more than a simple preference for a Swedish aesthetic as opposed to a Corbusian one. It can be attributed to a wariness about the 'new architecture'; a reluctance to progress in advance of society's social and visual capabilities, and a traditional conservatism and respect for what was already built.

The parallels of this conflict: Alton East versus Alton West, Park Hill versus Lillington Gardens, have been described.[1] Indeed, initial high-rise buildings in Britain, such as Frederick Gibberd's The Lawn, at Harlow, and the LCC's Ackroyden estate, had been traditional in their use of materials. Only at Alton West was the break with tradition in terms of materials and aesthetic, but not in terms of its English parkland setting, made complete. From this sophisticated example the spate of far less worthy Unités accelerated. Yet the influence of the group that had resisted the new aesthetic, notably the one that had designed Alton East, continued at the LCC and GLC. For in its out-of-town estates, in its town expansion schemes and on a progression of central sites such as the Pepys estate, a kind of 'peoples detailing' can be traced.[2]

An early example of how to achieve this popularity within the order of architecture had been provided by James Stirling in 1955 in a Team 10 Village Project where parallel structural walls of varying configurations acted as supports for consistently pitched roofs in an apparently random manner.[3] Stirling and Gowan's housing project at Preston appeared to continue this idea through an idiosyncratic use of traditional materials and components.

With the arrival on the scene of low rise–high density alternatives the same conflict was apparent. Michael Neylan who was never to move away from a pursuit of traditional forms, established Bishopsfield at Harlow as the forerunner of a lower and denser built form, yet on the adjacent site the Clarkhill estate demonstrated the cruder result of a desire to use industrialised building techniques.[4] The movement towards lower built forms meant that technological solutions, so necessary in high-rise developments, were no

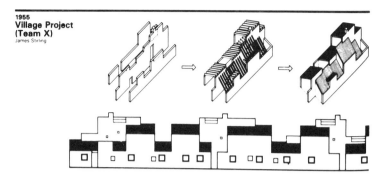

1955
**Village Project
(Team X)**
James Stirling

Fig. 10.1   1955 Team 10 Village project by James Stirling (*Architectural Design*)

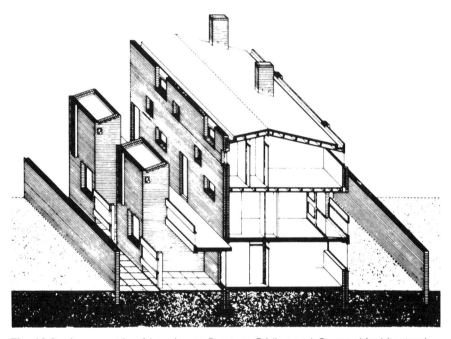

Fig. 10.2   Axonometric of housing at Preston; Stirling and Gowan (*Architectural Design*)

longer of prime importance. Little advantage could be taken of industrialised techniques when a spread-out development did not lend itself to quick construction methods. Yet the GLC made the transition from mixed development to low rise–high density on a few schemes using industrialisation at the height of its popularity; notably Cedars Road, Thamesmead, Hyacinth Road and Beaver's Farm.[5] But this was short-lived, and the subsequent establishment of low rise–high density, together with the demise of industrialisation, saw an increasing reliance on traditional and well-tried materials, forms and details.

However, the gradual resurgence of tradition was more than skin deep. Low rise–high density in itself was an historical regression – a reversion to a built form that was automatically essential before the growth of transportation and technological processes. Surprisingly the growth of car ownership appears to have aided this regression rather than having resulted in the derivation of fresh built forms.

It has been shown that Britain was ill-prepared to deal with an increase in car ownership that was inadequately forecast and reluctantly conceded.[6] Initial Radburn layouts confused the segregation of cars and people with broader environmental issues and hoped-for cost savings, thus hindering full development of its advantages until Cumbernauld provided the example. In general, low–density developments achieved segregation horizontally while high-density developments achieved it vertically. The major growth of car ownership, and provision for it, followed publication of the Parker-Morris Report,[7] and the Buchanan Report.[8] The implementation of these reports' recommendations came at a time when social pressures were already forcing a move away from high-rise solutions towards more compact, nearer-the-ground, alternatives. Subsequent schemes thus demonstrated a dilemma as to how to deal with the land taken by cars and roads in crowded layouts. Some adopted vertical separation with homes above underground car parks, while others attempted to make use of every available piece of land by grouping cars in courts separated horizontally from their respective housing areas. Again high density meant a general adoption of the former and low densities the latter.

Yet the suburban house, particularly when from speculative builders' hands, naturally had to accommodate the car within its plot on grounds of saleability; for the speculator was dealing with a, so-called, better-off and more middle-class person than were the local authorities. In 1946 Lord Reith advocated the building of a 'middle class' house by public authorities in order to break down the strict class divisions of inter-war housing estates,[9] and in the 1949 *Housing Manual* a Labour administration had seen fit to state that subsidised housing should not be for people who could afford to buy and run motor cars.[10] This dichotomy was taken up in 1966 by William Cowburn,[11] who, on sensing the profound social advantages of suburbia just as J. M. Richards had done in 1946,[12] advocated an adoption of some of its inherent principles. One such principle, that of attaching car to house was soon to develop in schemes designed by architects for local authority clients. More people were now falling within the terminology 'middle class' that Lord Reith had in mind, and the problem of what to do about increasing car ownership in high-density local authority schemes became an architectural difficulty.

By the mid-1960s, on LCC and GLC town expansion estates where the car was more essential to family life than it was in the conurbation, it had been located adjacent to front doors for the majority of houses. During the early 1960s garages had been in special courts away from the houses, until at Abbey Farm in Thetford 100 per cent garage provision was made, in many cases next to front doors, and 20 per cent parking provision was made for visitors.[13] At King Arthur's Way, Andover, garages were cut into the hillside and patio houses were placed on top of them, resulting in a land saving allowing the creation of large meadows for recreation as an integral part of the estate.[14]

This theme was continued by Haringey Borough on a central London site at Milton Road, where design work was started in 1965 under borough architect C. E. Jacob. This small site of 3.7 acres (1.5 ha) saw one of the last schemes to be built in the 5M system. Its virtue was that it grouped houses around three different kinds of open space, two of which were grassed and planted recreation and play areas separated from the surrounding roads by houses which were entered from the road side. It was a return to the tradition of semi-private open space at the backs of houses, which themselves were entered off public roads, that was to be found in eighteenth- and early nineteenth-century parts of London, particularly around Ladbroke Grove.[15] In essence it anticipated, by a year or so, the work of Leslie Martin and Lionel March at Cambridge, but without their mathematical basis.[16]

From Milton Road it was not such a long step to the development of a 'mews' theme for dealing with a closer proximity of car to house in a controlled manner. At Mildenhall, St John's Close was one of many such schemes developed by the GLC as part of its town expansion programme to minimise the space taken by garages and to make cars more accessible to residents.[17] Projects in 1971 by Phippen, Randall and Parkes at Crawley and Basildon were similar. In a scheme for the Urban District Council at Crawley the architect's intention was to avoid the car having a second-class environment; accordingly it was placed immediately in front of each house, as it was in their housing association scheme at Basildon.[18] The return to a traditional road–entrance–house–garden situation appeared, too, at Napper Errington Collerton Barnett's Ellenborough scheme at Maryport in Cumberland, where the access road to houses was deliberately played down as a limited service and entrance 'mews', complete with flats over garages.[19]

Two contrasting approaches, demonstrating on adjoining sites the progression from Radburn segregation to a more traditional integration of cars and people, exist at Halton Brook and Halton Brow, Runcorn. These schemes were designed for and by the Development Corporation, by R. L. E. Harrison as chief architect in succession to F. Lloyd Roche, who moved to Milton Keynes. Halton Brow represented a deliberate reversal of the Radburn segregation principles attempted at Halton Brook. In the Brow both people and cars use the access roads which were ingeniously designed so that drivers would respect the priority of pedestrians. The houses were informally, almost randomly, arranged, there were to be no garages, only parking areas, and the planting has been allowed to grow wild.[20] Here a break was made away from the diagrammatic and doctrinaire nature of Radburn; encouragement was given to a mutual respect between drivers and pedestrians, for at this density, 51 persons per acre (126/ha), and arguably at higher densities, both could mix satisfactorily once the car had been controlled. It was

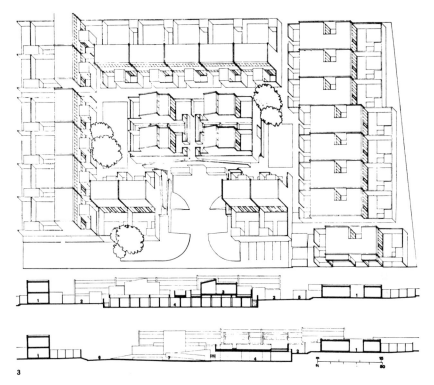

Fig. 10.3 Phippen, Randall and Parkes housing at Crawley (*Architectural Design*)

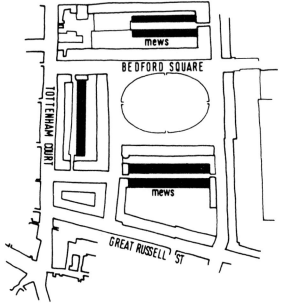

Fig. 10.4 Traditional 'mews' developments around Bedford Square (*from History of Urban Form, Second Edition, by A. E. J. Morris, George Godwin 1979*)

a solution that depended on an understanding of the way in which pedestrians, and particularly playing children, behave. Gone were the soulless garage courts so attractive for ball games, gone were the diagrammatic play areas for different ages of children, gone were the engineer's kerbed and sightlined roads; it was a more mature and sophisticated acceptance of the manner in which ordinary people had demonstrated their mode of living. Halton Brow contained many advances in thinking, which on reflection were all historical regression, in that traditional circumstances, habits and social customs were respected. It represented a kind of slowing down of architectural thought processes, while social ones perhaps caught up, so that the gap between architecture and society might be narrowed and a more modest and gentle domestic environment be the result.

Aesthetically Halton Brow demonstrated a deliberate intention to create a vernacular image. An admitted desire to 'fit in' with Halton village was made by the architects[21] and the result was an apparently random layout of brick, small-windowed, pitched-roof houses of both one and two storeys. But Halton Brow's achievement was not for the development of a kind of domestic vernacular; it was for the integrity of thinking contained in its design principles. The danger was that as with the Unité and Park Hill, the image of its vernacular style might be taken in substitute for its inherent content.

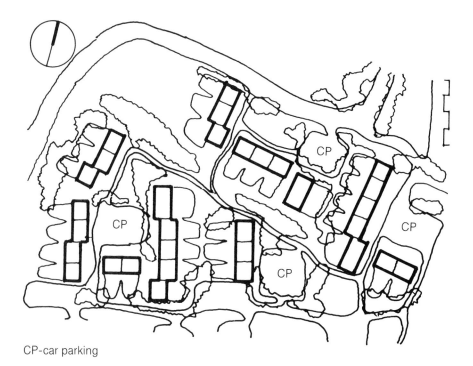

CP-car parking

Fig. 10.5   Part layout of Halton Brow, Runcorn (*E. R. Scoffham – adapted from drawing by Runcorn Development Corporation*)

Fig. 10.6 Vernacular at Palace Fields, Runcorn (*Stewart Johnstone*)

'Absolute clarity of organisation', sought by Peter Rich to prevent built form from 'degenerating into a maze',[22] was at odds with the social objectives that inferred adaptability and change, and the evolution of this vernacular style. The need for control to prevent the anarchy in which the latter might too easily result was a central issue of planning. Yet the events of the post-war years had demonstrated all too clearly the dissatisfaction that resulted from a too dictatorial control – a control that assumed its own right to impose a solution that it believed appropriate for an ignorant society. Society had now found its voice and those whose task it was to decide society's future did so at their own peril. The design and planning professions were at pains to discover the sociological workings of society so that they might produce more appropriate, and less criticised, solutions. The more they discovered, however, the more perverse and fickle society appeared to be, so that a solution was even more difficult to decide upon – a situation easily aggravated by the participation of society in schemes for its future.

It was a situation readily explained by society's condemnation of the products of Le Corbusier's Utopia, products which it was ready to accept, at least to try, at a time shortly after the war when a fresh start and a 'new society' were promises on the horizon. That horizon was now judged to have been reached and in consequence of its shortcomings society preferred the misguided products of a misunderstanding of Howard's earlier Utopia, or failing that, renovations of the industrial revolution Howard had sought to better.

This dilemma had in a sense been anticipated in 1965 by Christopher Alexander in his prize-winning essay *A City is not a Tree*, in which he demolished most of the then sacred tenets of architecture and planning: the neigh-bourhood concept, pedestrian and vehicle segregation, children's playgrounds, the exclusion of industry from residential areas, and almost every town or city plan of the previous 30 years including Patrick Abercrombie's Greater London Plan.[23] Alexander was concerned to see a more full analysis of the inter-relationships in the way people live, of the 'overlap' inherent in the life of any community.

In his condemnation of Abercrombie's London plan he was not alone, for others had taken exception to its proposals, both in 1943 and in subse-quent years, among them Elizabeth Denby and Ruth Glass.[24] But Alexander's basic message, the derivation of a pattern based on the inter-relationships inherent in society, to permit a free association of individuals to evolve at all levels within the community due to increased mobility and developing tech-nology, was apparently heeded in the master plans for Washington and Milton Keynes.[25] The semi-lattice nature of the town advocated by Alexander in his essay was given expression in the directional grid of roads, enclosing approximately 1 kilometre squares (0.6 mile squares), each being a 'village' at Milton Keynes. Acceptance of the motor car and private transportation was a prime feature of the Milton Keynes plan. The individual had a full range of opportunities for social contact both within and outside the town, and as such the neighbourhood as a social focus for his life was no longer valid. The 'village' did, however, break down the size of the town into areas of identity – areas with which the individual could identify while not requiring them for the social sustenance previously found essential.

In order to permit this orientation towards a car-owning society to take place a reduction in density from those of the previous new towns was advocated. Limitation of size to provide for easy walking distances to the town centre, or to neighbourhood centres, as Cumbernauld and Hook had proposed, was no longer valid. Extra space was required in attaching the car to each house in order that the basic car-owning premise could be satisfied. Beyond this, the design of the individual 'village' represented the same kind of historical regression as did the search for a vernacular compromise. Centres of communal activity were located on the boundary roads, and adjacent to the centres of adjoining 'villages', just as Clarence Perry had advocated in the 1920s to accentuate social activity and share facilities.[26] The location of the car within, or on the plot of, each house was an acceptance of the situation that had for years been usual in the private sector; again demonstrating the lowering barrier between public and private sector housing, instanced by Lord Reith in 1946,[27] and now insisted upon through increased affluence.

The merits of suburbia, certainly in physical terms, appeared to be dawning in the public sector. Yet there was architectural reluctance to adopt the suburban semi-detached house advocated by William Cowburn as having the potential of densities up to 78 bedspaces per acre (193/ha).[28] Nevertheless the similarity in detailed layout between Cowburn's suburban arrangement and Foster Associates' scheme for the Bean Hill site was marked, despite the latter's use of terraced single-storey houses.[29] Bean Hill was designed by

Birkin Haward, an associate with Norman Foster, after his participation in the creation of systematic rectangular layouts for Portsdown Hill, for Clark-hill with Associated Architects and Consultants, and for Brookvale, Runcorn.[30] The same strict discipline of organisation inherent in these three schemes, and built at Clarkhill, was evident at Bean Hill. A wide-frontage single-storey family house was devised with an integral car port, and this was arranged on both sides of short culs-de-sac, forming a rectangular pattern of roads within one sector of the town. The ends of culs-de-sac in the centre of the site were terminated by single-storey two-person houses which do not have integral garages, parking for them being at the head of the culs-de-sac. Wide verges border the culs-de-sac and distributor roads; they were partly necessary to provide some form of privacy barrier to front-facing ground-level bedrooms, but they have facilitated the image of verdant suburbia. The density of the scheme was 11 houses to the acre (27/ha), one less than Unwin's town density of 12 to the acre (30/ha)[31] and all but two-thirds of Howard's Utopian 18 to the acre (45/ha)[32]

In terms of its construction Bean Hill was a technological solution. A single-storey timber-frame prefabricated system was used, comprising load-bearing gable, party and partition walls, and these in turn supported a stressed-plywood roof deck. It was a constructional method paralleled by the joint GLC and Timber Research and Development Association (TRADA) venture into the prefabrication of transportable box units which was later developed commercially as *THUS: TRADA Housing Unit System*.[33] In essence the prefabrication of timber panels for floors, walls and roofs to dimensional and design constraints had been suggested in Darbourne and Darke's Brookvale competition entry of 1969, and as a system it saw development throughout the 1970s by a number of timber fabrication firms. Nevertheless the external cladding was profiled aluminium sheet with an

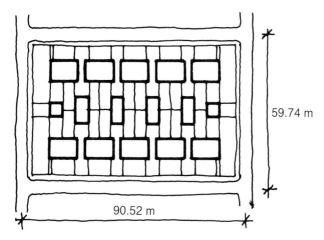

59.74 m

90.52 m

Fig. 10.7 Semi-detached houses arranged in a layout by William Cowburn to a density of 78 persons per acre (*E. R. Scoffham – adapted from drawing by William Cowburn of Cowburn, Bers and Bray*)

Fig. 10.8 Site layout of Foster Associates', Bean Hill, Milton Keynes
(*Architectural Design*)

enamelled finish, and a prefabricated core unit provided kitchen and bathroom with hot and cold water supplies, heating and drainage. This latter
evoked the immediately post-war temporary prefabricated house, while the
aesthetic produced by external materials and basic house shape made no
concession towards a vernacular style. It was as uncompromising as was
Clarkhill by comparison with its neighbour Bishopsfield,[34] and was in
marked contrast to Halton Brow, at Runcorn.[35]

Being a single-storey solution Bean Hill was a scheme that showed signs
of becoming relatively invisible in the landscape, and tree planting was an
essential part of the Milton Keynes plan. Its regularity of layout, by contrast
with the adjacent Netherfields scheme in the grid square immediately to the
north east, seemed almost relaxed. Netherfields was designed by the Development Corporation with Derek Walker as its chief architect,[36] but the team

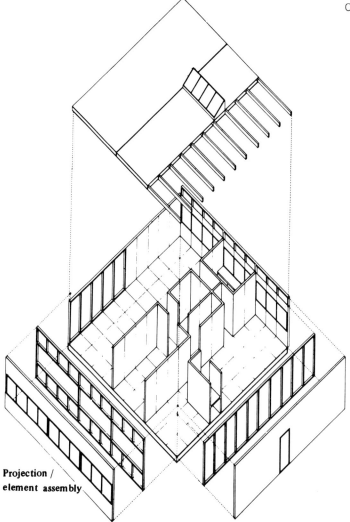

Projection /
element assembly

Fig. 10.9 Constructional assembly at Bean Hill (*Architectural Design*)

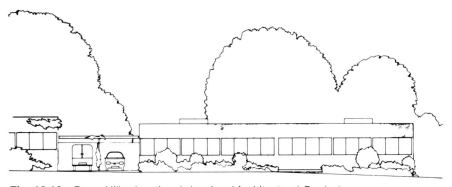

Fig. 10.10 Bean Hill, elevational drawing (*Architectural Design*)

Fig. 10.11 Bean Hill street scene (*Nigel Atkinson and Simon Bee*)

working on the project, notably Christopher Cross, Jeremy Dixon, Michael Gold and Edward Jones, was largely that which had some success in the Brookvale competition to which entry it bore a surprising resemblance.[37]

Parallel rows of two- and three-storey houses were arranged across the site apparently without recognition for natural features, and were fed by a grid of distributor roads and culs-de-sac which brought the car adjacent to each house. In this respect it was similar to Bean Hill, the same regression to, or acceptance of, the traditional road–house situation was apparent. It was also similar in its technological approach to construction and in the lack of any concession to familiarity in its profiled metal cladding and aluminium roof.

The ruthlessness of the Netherfields layout demonstrated the same dogmatic architectural approach evident in the pursuit of a Corbusian Utopia through mixed developments, and 'streets in the air', that had received such criticism. It did, however, support Rich's assertion that 'clarity of organisation' was essential. Such determined order was perhaps acceptable once, within its framework, there was an inbuilt flexibility, adaptability and choice. To some extent both the architects of Bean Hill and Netherfields would argue that this was achieved by an amply dimensioned house shell and a ground-level location. But what they appeared to miss, both in their use of materials and in their aesthetic, was an acceptability to society in social and visual terms. In this respect they were isolated architectural solutions, more thoroughly established in terms of society's user requirements than high rise and the complexities of low rise–high density, but lacking in the essential item that would endear them more readily to society. Society had shown that it was oblivious of architectural motives and identified with the visual result. Surveys at Park Hill demonstrated that its tenants were just as unimpressed by its appearance as they were with the slabs and towers of mixed development;[38] its more appropriate method of access passed them by.

In the essence of suburbia that was Milton Keynes official recognition appeared to have been given to popular housing. But this recognition was only in certain physical attributes, not in totality. Suburbia, or popular housing, depended for its success on individuality and variety, the ability to

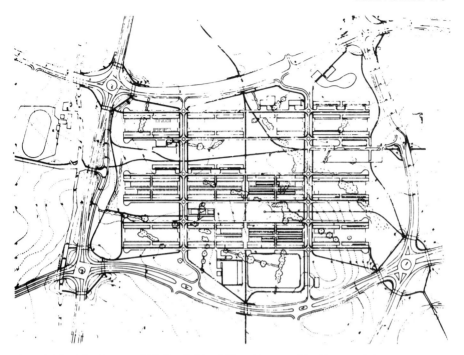

Fig. 10.12 Site layout of Netherfields, Milton Keynes (*Architectural Design*)

Fig. 10.13 Netherfields perspective (*Nigel Atkinson and Simon Bee*)

express oneself in however banal and superficial a manner this might appear to educated taste. Once again architecture appeared to fall into the trap of packaging society into a well intended and thoroughly analysed built form with no attempt to meet its visual and cultural development half-way. It remained to be seen whether the formalism of Bean Hill and Netherfields would be more successful in the public sector, all other things being equal, than the apparently irregular vernacular of Halton Brow. A break away from the physical and psychological straitjacket of controls over the design of roadways and over the spacing of buildings, represented in 1970 by Halton Brow, had been earlier argued for, and achieved with success by Eric Lyons in his work for Span. At Runcorn the management procedures of the development corporation overcame the compartmentalisation of responsibilities that had hindered a more subtle approach elsewhere. For Eric Lyons his unique relationship with Span Developments, where architect and developer had come to a close working arrangement, aided the success of schemes in the 1950s at Blackheath, Ham Common and Cambridge.[39] In 1972 the kind of approach that Lyons had developed through these relatively small projects was adapted to the larger New Ash Green village speculation in Kent, where the merging of traditional builders' motives, evident in suburbia, and the intellectual order of architecture resulted in a vernacular compromise.[40]

Indeed, Eric Lyons was largely responsible for the promotion of competitions based on an architect–developer collaboration, in which competition was through projects to which both architect and developer had jointly committed themselves. Two sites, in the new towns of Redditch and Bracknell, were the subject of such a competition in 1971, and the results indicated an evolving domestic vernacular that a partnership of architect and developer, one tempering the ideals of the other, appeared to produce.[41] Redditch found the venture such a success that it promoted a further similar competition in 1973, in which it was later joined by East Kilbride Development Corporation.

This form of partnership had been devised to overcome some of the criticisms of the competition system – to prevent the selection of architectural solutions that might prove unbuildable or otherwise embarrassing despite their evident merits – which had followed the abortion of Brookvale in 1969. Milton Keynes, and indeed other authorities, used the principle into the 1980s and a Conservative Minister of the Environment concerned about architectural patronage added support in 1981 by promoting national competitions on similar lines.

A domestic vernacular, for want of a better expression, had been developing for some time and with some consistent success as the Good Design Awards of the Ministry of Housing, now Department of the Environment, bore witness. It is well to remember that entries for Good Design Awards represent schemes designed between 3–6 years earlier than the year of the award. In 1964 four of the sixteen awards went to Eric Lyons only 2 years after Park Hill had been awarded a medal. Despite this the private sector made few submissions for awards until well into the 1970s. The high-density category for entries was abolished in 1970 but only a year earlier in 1969 Lillington Gardens had received a medal at 101 dwellings per acre (250/ha.)[42] In 1970 comment on the awards picked out, 'intimate scale, traditional materials, straightforward detailing, uncluttered landscapes, variegated roof-lines' as being 'common to almost all award winners', and grouped them under the heading 'eclectic vernacular'.[43] In 1971 it appeared that architects were coming to terms with 'a new ethos in which size is no longer a virtue, and housing sites are places to be refurbished rather than reformed'. Indeed, it was even remarked that the division between private and public sector housing was becoming increasingly difficult to spot.[44] By 1972 editorial comment in the *Architects' Journal* wondered whether we were 'witnessing declining standards or a necessary consolidation' in view of the 'apparent dullness' of the award-winning schemes.[45]

By 1975 Martin Pawley remarked upon the static image of successful housing over a period of 14 years, 'all that remains is the endless repetition of an increasingly stylised vernacular whose only real virtue – its cheapness and simplicity – is rapidly disappearing under the pressure of rising construction and maintenance costs'. Nevertheless the 'urban village character' of Popham Street, Islington by Andrews Sherlock and Partners, he identified with 'the final development of a layout once widely criticised and extending back into the nineteenth century', and went on to remark on the 'painstaking re-achievement of a traditional pattern of development' and 'the ubiquity of the retreat into the past' of other award-winners in 1974.[46]

An inflationary costs spiral and the professional uncertainty following high rise and industrialisation failures had unquestionably knocked the adventure out of architecture; but awards over the years had also exposed the predilection of architecture with images rather than realities. In 1972 the image of a domestic vernacular was portrayed as almost outworn, as if a new style was required in the face of the consistent success of well-tried and established methods. Thus it was significant that comments on awards in 1971 mentioned that it was becoming increasingly difficult to spot the differences between public and private sector housing. However, these were awards judged by architects for architects, and a vast amount of housing remained elsewhere as a reminder that the gap between educated taste and popular choice was wide. Methods of bridging this culture gap had been suggested by William Cowburn based on 'zones of choice' within which a regulated freedom was permitted,[47] but this was little different from Habraken's argument in substance. It made no real recognition of the need for the two cultural polarities to shift towards one another themselves.

Similar concern with images had been demonstrated from the early 1950s when architecture reacted to initial building in the new towns.[48] The openness and lack of urbanity were found to be unsatisfactory and attempts were made to evoke nostalgic images of Italian townscapes to remedy the matter. Later the same device was used to portray the image of 'Civilia', a varied, tongue-in-cheek, urban and architectural city,[49] and later, too, in a dream of 'sociable housing;'.[50] All of these portraits, admirable though they were in showing a world that might be, became as Utopian as those of Le Corbusier, Archigram and even Ebenezer Howard, whose misplaced reality they set out to condemn. They missed the essential ingredient of the involvement of society at its current state of evolution, in the creation of its own destiny.

But the concern of architects with the creation of urbanity had some impact on those whose responsibility it was to enforce the 'rules' governing development of the built environment. In 1973 Essex County Council produced a guide aimed at securing an improvement in the standard of private-sector housing, that demonstrated how it was possible to achieve the objectives of the dimensional 'rule-book' regarding turning heads, sight-lines, spacing of buildings and so on, while maintaining the kind of townscape evident in the traditional town and village so often quoted as Britain's vernacular style.[51] By introducing an environmentally more acceptable hier-archy of residential roads, Essex planners demonstrated that it was not the 'rules' that had prevented the development of a more urban fabric but a psychological blockage on the part of those submitting plans for approval, and of those whose lot it was to approve or reject them. By careful design and careful consideration it was demonstrated how it was possible to provide a more urban framework within which a variety of styles, built forms, and materials might exist side by side.

Utopias were now of little benefit. In his search for a contemporary vernacular in 1946 J. M. Richards argued that 'we can only progress demo-cratically at a speed which does not outpace the slow growth of the public's understanding, in particular its assimilation of social and technical change'.[52] For 20 or more years architecture had sought to achieve objectives that society did not recognise in a manner that society had now rejected. Now that this rejection had taken place architecture was on its guard, it was on its best behaviour, too, to rediscover a role for itself that society would accept. It had moved perceptibly away from the area of Utopian fantasy, of isolated architectural logic and a dogmatic belief in its own self-righteousness. It had begun to realise that society had much to teach about architecture if only it would listen. Architecture, in Britain at least, showed signs of having stopped 'searching the horizon for the promise of a new vernacular' and having accepted 'for what it is worth the one on our own doorstep'.[53]

As evidence of this good behaviour the GLC in its 1971 design for the large Alsen Road site reinstated as footpaths many of the old roads cleared in 1972, so that the site was grafted back into the communication pattern of the area. Twenty per cent of the dwellings were houses with gardens, in scale with the old houses which existed on the site, and which still surrounded it. Unfortunately, the centre of the site, for what has now become realised as arbitrary reasons of density, was occupied by tall flatted blocks.[54] On the Queensmore Road site small clusters of houses, originally designed for sale but later for rent, each had a garage near the front door, so bringing back the semi-detached idea in a new form.[55]

At Swinbrook Road, what might a few years earlier have been demol-ished and its inhabitants dispersed, was turned into a participatory exercise

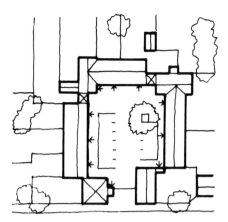

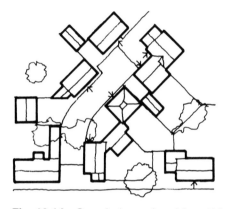

Fig. 10.14 Sample 'mews' and 'court' layouts from Essex County Council design guide (*E. R. Scoffham – adapted drawing from A Design Guide for Residential Areas by Essex Council Council*)

in which 70 per cent of the people indicated they would like to remain in the area as a community. The result was not architectural novelty but a slow change in tune with a developing understanding by the community of what it wanted. It was a closing of the gap between designer and designed-for.[56]

Rehabilitation and improvement work following the 1969 Housing Act accentuated this co-operation. Design work and consultation inevitably took longer, and frustrated many, but appeared to result in a greater social satisfaction among residents. In this context the sites for new buildings that occurred adjacent to older areas, as they must in the conurbations, were being increasingly developed with low buildings in scale, and similarity of aesthetic, with their surroundings. They did not have the ingredients for monumental architecture, and a growing volume of work, integrating old and new, rehabilitating old houses and filling-in the gaps of time and neglect, was becoming evident. In the Barnsbury Mews Area the GLC fitted three-storey maisonettes into an existing street pattern of Georgian houses. At Ewart

Road, a typical south London area of by-law streets, the pattern of roads was interrupted and the existing scale maintained with a variety of two- and three-storey houses and patio dwellings over garages. Ruthin Road, Palace Road and Lilford Road were all similar infill sites respecting surroundings in their design while achieving relatively high densities.[57] London was far from being alone in this respect. At Jericho, Oxford, a pattern of gradual renewal became the showpiece of the Government's current housing policies.[58]

The process of gradual renewal that these projects exemplified was established in a methodical manner by the Housing Renewal Unit of architects Castle Park Hook and Partners. Using the cellular renewal ideas of Robert McKie the practice devised procedural measures whereby various disciplines were co-ordinated to resolve financial and physical factors, and occupants' attitudes were assessed to achieve an integrated yet responsive professional service.[59]

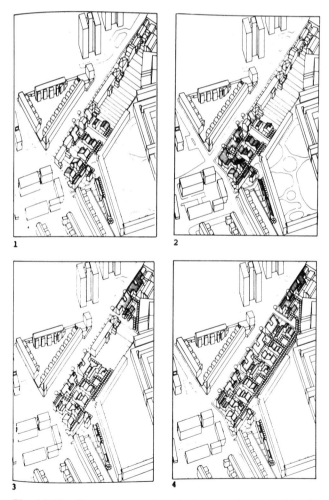

Fig. 10.15   The process of gradual renewal revealed by the Housing Renewal Unit of Castle Park Hook and Partners (*Architectural Design*)

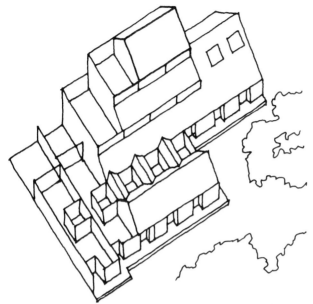

Fig. 10.16 Axonometric of dwelling assembly at Setchell Road, Southwark (*E. R. Scoffham – adapted from drawing by Neylan and Ungless*)

Neyland and Ungless, who had followed the traditional vein of their 1961 Bishopsfield scheme at Harlow throughout their housing work at Linden Grove and Emmanuel Road,[60] continued to elaborate at Setchell Road for Southwark Borough. This was their largest project since Bishopsfield, 8.48 acres (3.43 ha) for 312 dwellings at 103 bedspaces per acre, (255/ha), and it became an amalgamation of their previous work. At first sight it was quite traditional, even ordinary, conveying a cottagey atmosphere, but on analysis demonstrated a logical and uncomplicated design that kept the existing street pattern and existing trees, and achieved a relatively high density with the majority of dwellings on the ground in buildings no higher than three storeys.[61]

On smaller, in the main infill sites, as the GLC recognised[62] it was possible to achieve something nearer to a domestic vernacular style because of an increased desire, and necessity, to fit in with surrounding older buildings. But not all sites were small, nor did they have the freedom from density requirements that inferred housing of a multi-storey or over-complex nature, which inevitably became monumental and less domestic in the size of buildings. For the GLC it was somewhat easier to achieve vernacular objectives in its town expansion schemes where density objectives were lower. Roman Way at Andover, a scheme of 793 dwellings, separated dwellings into groups with large open spaces between them. A house type was designed that enabled a terrace to turn a corner, a device well known to Raymond Unwin at the beginning of the century, thus aiding the enclosure of individual spaces, around which were dwellings with traditionally pitched roofs.[63] At Hastings housing was again broken into small groups of low buildings following the

Fig. 10.17 Roman Way, Andover (*Department of Architecture Slide Library, University of Nottingham*)

contours of the South Downs, and used local brick and pitched roofs to make the visual link with vernacular cottages of the past.[64]

The prevailing background, as far as many architects were concerned, was one of compromise that had resulted in a popular visual mediocrity, and their dismay was not relieved by an inflationary situation that had pared housing standards to the bone. Against this gloom 1975 was heralded as European Architectural Heritage Year, which while hardly dramatic in its immediate effects did prick the conscience to focus attention on matters of preservation, continuity, tradition and ultimately style. The diverse influences of improvement, infill, gradual renewal, familiarity and participation appeared drawn together through an increasing respect for what was already in existence. The unacceptable reality of mediocrity was contrasted with a more favourable past to produce hope for a more favourable future.[65] It was an optimism that provided an image which was social, not in a sentimental nostalgic sense, but one that saw the diversities of culture, tradition, social custom and idiosyncracy as a rich and growing organism – an image that reflected both past and future into the present.

Four housing projects were given Heritage Year awards for exceptional merit: Friary Quay, Norwich by Fielden and Mawson, Pershore Central area housing by Darbourne and Darke, Malt Mill Lane, Alcester by Walter Thomson of Associated Architects, and Lowfellside, Kendal by Frederick Gibberd and Partners.[66] Each of these projects held a uniqueness of response to situation that identified them as part of a continuing heritage. Darbourne and Darke in particular continued to a mature development the theme of traditional materials and identity of dwelling that had been started at Lillington Gardens and had progressed by way of Brookvale and Marquess Road to overturn the council house image in favour of one that suggested slow growth and owner occupancy. Change became important in terms of its frequency and manner. The wide sweeping changes of the post-war years had been too large and too frequent to be assimilated and had resulted in the lack of identity and mediocrity that was the prevailing vernacular compromise – a no-mans-land of uncertainty.

The polarities of educated taste and popular choice became exposed in an ironic manner. Popular choice was seen not to be as limited in its range as was educated taste, particularly that of architects and planners. As Richards had pointed out in 1946, 'it is only the architect's eye that picks out incongruities of style and misleads him into condemning it for its failure in knowledge and taste. But taste has not failed, because taste was never exercised.'[67] The range of styles that architects had submerged under the intellectual rationalism of a brave new world gained in social value. Style, in addition to plan arrangement and size of dwelling, became a matter of choice. Popular choice had been appreciative of a far wider range of styles than had architectural taste throughout the history of post-war rationalism. What it had lacked was educated taste to enable it to realise the style of its choice accurately, not as pastiche but with respect. Professional taste had steered housing up the cul-de-sac of over-cautious ordinariness, as Byker had demonstrated by being so popular and so unordinary. If the professions were not in a position, of their own volition, to enable society to achieve the choice it wanted then society would find others to do the job. So it appeared that non-architects provided the enlightening influence of the value of tradition and of style – in everything from self-sufficiency to real ale. It became fashionable to be individual – to be oneself. Architecture, and particularly housing, followed into a more genuine concern for craftsmanship and for character – a kind of real architecture where it could at last rediscover, and be, itself – what the *Architectural Review* called, 'a genuine marriage between modern facility and traditional feeling'.[68]

The result of this change of attitude in the latter half of the 1970s was an incorporation of traditional layout patterns and of styles as a means of rediscovering and continuing a lost vitality. It meant a rejection of the clinical sterility of brave new world attitudes and a rediscovery of the romance and picturesqueness of what Team 10 had rejected as 'pseudo-vernacular village enclaves'.[69] Now perhaps the pseudo of popular ordinariness could be dropped.

Milton Keynes best demonstrated, in one location, the development of this hypothesis. The 'village' identity structured into a grid of roads has been explained, and it acted as a framework within which the individuality of each 'village' sector could be expressed through the preoccupations of individual architects. After the intellectual ruthlessness of Netherfields and Bean Hill, despite their well-intended and well-organised packaging, later schemes exposed a more romantic desire for traditional identification.

On two sites of rented housing at Great Linford, Martin Richardson attempted to produce what he described with honest banality as 'a nice place'. At Hartley in 1973 he hoped that a direct response to the attractive site would generate an 'enjoyable combination of ordinariness and surprise', through a

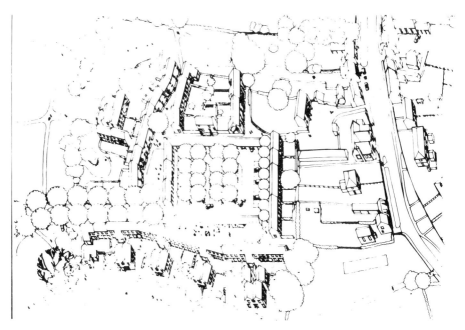

Fig. 10.18   Site axonometric, Hartley, Milton Keynes (*Architectural Design*)

Fig. 10.19   'Ordinariness' at Hartley (*Nigel Atkinson and Simon Bee*)

mixture of spaces and building forms.⁷⁰ At Church Lees and Sandy Close in 1975 he attempted 'an experiment in seeing how ordinary one dare be', by stepping down the contours, by varying the house projections and by not pairing entrances. Hartley has now become one of the most cherished pieces

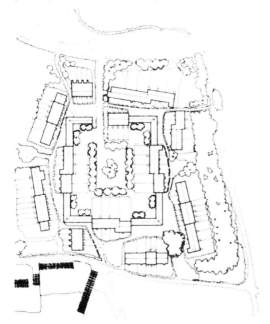

Fig. 10.20   Site plan, Hazelwood, Milton Keynes (*from The Architecture and Planning of Milton Keynes by Derek Walker, Architectural Press 1982*)

Fig. 10.21   Village scale at Hazelwood (*Nigel Atkinson and Simon Bee*)

Fig. 10.22 Sketch of Mews Court at Bradwell Common (*Martin Richardson*)

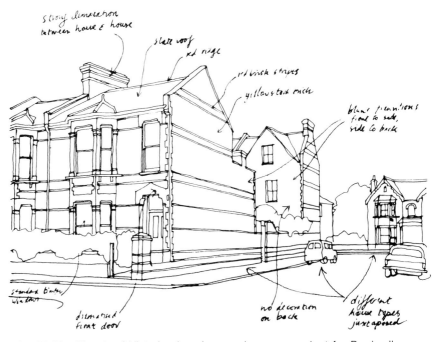

Fig. 10.23 Sketch of Victorian housing used as a precedent for Bradwell Common (*Martin Richardson*)

Fig. 10.24 Mews Court, Bradwell Common (*Nigel Atkinson and Simon Bee*)

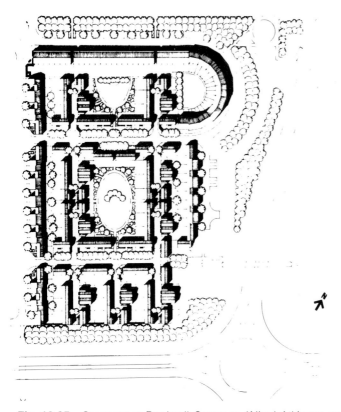

Fig. 10.25 Crescent at Bradwell Common (*Nigel Atkinson and Simon Bee*)

of housing in the city.[71] Later, at Bradwell Common, 175 dwellings for rent were arranged into a layout of distinct parts, and a system of orange, buff and white bands 'individualises and relates' the houses of different groups.[72] To its critic in 1981 the mews courts 'recall updated artisan cottages out of D. H. Lawrence, with a tang of petrol fumes replacing the reek of horse manure, and the glitter of copper pans giving way to the flicker of sleepless TV screens'. Similarly the terrace and crescent 'recalls urbane North Kensington'.

In a project at Hazelwood by the development corporation's architects houses were arranged in two loose concentric rings around vehicle access in the centre, with a traffic-free area between the two rings. Its critic in 1978 eulogised 'strong echoes of traditional village scale, and they are reinforced in the central square by the way cars are parked like agricultural implements under the barn-like tiled car ports'.[73] Almost as a manifestation of the village, occasional ground-floor rooms were projected under tiled roofs to suggest the conversion at some time to a corner shop.

Similar analogous descriptions occurred elsewhere. In comment on Shankland Cox Partnership's housing at Hillingdon, 'a fleeting glimpse of what looks like some old terraces that have been recently painted and have had, perhaps, a few more windows put in – terraces, one might suspect, that were built in the 1840s [and] had fallen into disrepair'; a housing that 'manages to catch the spirit of the past and of the present in one image'.[74] Oliver Cox had been one of the design team members for Alton East at Roehampton, a project that had demonstrated a reluctance to accept the aesthetic rules of the new architecture. The term 'people's detailing' had then been used to describe the approach, as it was now at Hillingdon. In a description of the design method Oliver Cox identified with many of the principles Ralph Erskine had used at Byker and had later developed at Eaglestone, Milton Keynes[75] – though his result was less idiosyncratic in appearance – to aim at 'what might be called the 'non-estate''.[76]

The wholesome 'good life' flavour that permeated these public authority projects reflected the 'non-estate' of Oliver Cox and eliminated the boundaries between public and private estates that Lord Reith had had in mind in 1946. The private sector was similarly engaged in qualitative assessment that had been necessary in order to satisfy the 'guides', not only of Essex County Council, but also of many other planning authorities around the country. The private sector appeared, in many ways, to be in a better position to respond to the pressures for choice, individuality and tradition, than did public authorities, bound as they were by cost yardsticks and mandatory requirements. It is not surprising that some developers were able to offer products that not only optimised upon techniques of construction but offered, in addition to a range of choice of dwelling size and arrangement, a choice of style.

Guildway Ltd employed Martin Richardson to develop a range of house plans based on its prefabricated timber construction methods. The company's 'Lakes' line was the result of this collaboration. The public sector was unable, through its financial procedures, to arrange for extension outside the

Figs. 10.26 and 10.27 Traditional identification at Hazelwood (top) and Eaglestone, Milton Keynes (*Nigel Atkinson and Simon Bee*)

mandatory house shell. Guildway offered a modular package on a 600 mm (23.62 in.) grid and in 2.4 m (2.6 yd) increments within which was a range of plan configuration and a choice of roof pitch from 22.5 to 45 degrees, of roof form whether hipped, gable hipped, half hipped, or a permutation of these, of garage and utility location, of materials and of porch and chimney

Fig. 10.28   Oliver Cox's '*non estate*' at Hillingdon (*Architectural Review, October 1978*)

details.[77] The choice could respond to individual preference for style as well as local planning 'guides'. Participation here became a choice within the financial constraints of the customer, the system and the required style. The Trojan Horse of industrialisation was so well camouflaged that it could now be appreciated for its social and economic worth. It was a return to the definition of industrialisation that had been short-lived at the end of the Second World War, but which had nevertheless been demonstrated in isolation at the end of the First War at Dormanstown.[78]

Dormanstown, as its name implies, was to house workers at Dorman Long's iron and steel works at Coatham to the designs of Adshead, Ramsey and Abercrombie. It was started in 1917 and demonstrates how a steel frame 'Dorlonco' system was used to construct a house that in image was unmistakably neo-Georgian. As Adshead wrote in the *Town Planning Review* of 1915–16, 'There will be scope for embodying in the standard cottage some of the character which we associate with good tradition, and which depends so much upon obtaining characteristic proportions.'[79]

In analysis of Guildway's illustrations there appeared many similarities to Richardson's earlier work for the Yorkshire Development Group (YDG). His YDG assembly drawings were remarkably similar in approach to the house form and style drawings of Guildway. As he wrote in 1977,[80] 'I saw YDG Mark I as a sort of contemporary vernacular',[81] and continued, '. . . [from] the constructional and economic breakpoint at which variety and economy meet, the point on the curve where returns for greater repetition diminishes. The visual objective would be to create greater interest, surprise, intricacy.'

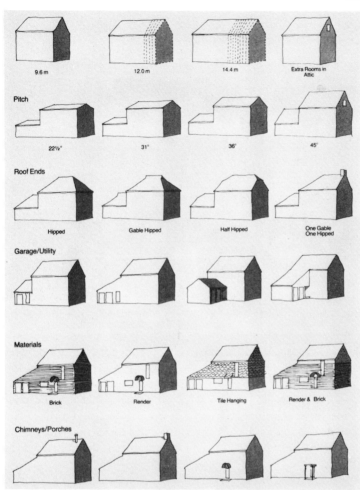

Fig. 10.29 Shape and style options by Guildway Ltd (*Guildway Ltd*)

Technology had now, it seemed, found its appropriate level, one where it could be appreciated without being seen, and when seen appreciated for its familiarity. It was no longer the plaything of professionals and administrators but the plaything of society. While secure within the image of tradition for which it had fought, society sought, during increased leisure time and unemployment, to avail itself of the sophisticated technology that had generated both the leisure and the unemployment. Through the gadgetry of kitchen, video and computer, society occupied this time with games of technological fantasy whose image it had rejected; 'when you look out of the window you do not want to be reminded by the appearance of neighbours' houses that you live in a world of change, though within your four walls you want to enjoy all the benefits of progress that you can'.[82]

The choice now offered, at all levels, had broken a number of barriers. The 1974 Act that had encouraged greater flexibility by 'widening the choice'

Fig. 10.30 Martin Richardson's style variations for Guildway Ltd (*RIBA Journal, June 1969*)

appeared to have achieved its purpose. Yet the public sector was still held to constraints of cost and standards that seemed to hinder full attainment of this ideal, until in 1981 the Conservatives abolished the Parker Morris standards they had recommended in 1961, and the cost yardsticks to which these standards had been inextricably bound since 1969. Each scheme was to be assessed on its merits, as once had been the case.

REFERENCES

1. See Chapter 5 and 6.
2. Greater London Council, *85 Years of LCC and GLC Housing*, 1973.
3. 'Stirling gold', *Architectural Design*, July–Aug. 1980, pp. 16–19.

4. See Ch. 7.
5. Greater London Council, op. cit.
6. See Ch. 3.
7. Sir G. Parker-Morris, *Homes for Today and Tomorrow* (Parker-Morris Report), 1961.
8. C. Buchanan, *Traffic in Towns* (Crowther and Buchanan Reports), 1963.
9. New Towns Act, 1946.
10. See *Housing Manual*, 1949, for a hangover in attitude from prewar days.
11. W. Cowburn, 'A defence of popular housing', *Arena*, Sept.–Oct. 1966, pp. 76–81.
12. J. M. Richards, *The Castles on the Ground*, 1946.
13. Greater London Council, op. cit.
14. Ibid.
15. *Architectural Review*, Apr. 1971, pp. 209–12.
16. See Ch. 11.
17. Greater London Council, op. cit.
18. *Architectural Review*, Apr. 1971, pp. 216–20.
19. Ibid., pp. 213–15.
20. *Architects' Journal*, 14 Oct. 1970, pp. 889 ff.
21. Ibid.
22. P. M. Rich, 'Notes on low rise–high density housing', *Arena*, Mar. 1966, pp. 242 ff.
23. C. Alexander, *A City is not a Tree*, Kaufmann International Design Awards 1965. Originally published in *Architectural Forum* and reprinted in *Design*, Feb. 1966.
24. See Ch. 7.
25. Llewelyn-Davis, Weeks, Forestier-Walker and Bor: *Washington New Town Master Plan and Report*, 1966; *Milton Keynes – Interim Report*, 1968.
26. See Ch. 3.
27. New Towns Act, 1946.
28. *Architects' Journal*, 25 Sept. 1968, pp. 638–9.
29. *Architects' Journal*, 9 May 1973, pp. 1136–7, and *Architectural Design*, Nov. 1972.
30. See Ch. 7.
31. R. Unwin, *Nothing Gained by Overcrowding*, 1912.
32. E. Howard, *Garden Cities of Tomorrow*, 1945 edn.
33. 'Housing; THUS timber box units', *Architects' Journal*, 26 Feb. 1975, pp. 467–8.
34. See Ch. 7.
35. See Ch. 9.
36. *Architectural Review*, Jan. 1973, p. 32.
37. *Architects' Journal*, 30 Apr. 1969, *RIBA Journal*, June 1969.
38. I. Reynolds and C. Nicholson, 'Living off the ground', *Architects' Journal*, 20 Aug. 1969, pp. 459–70.
39. R. F. Jordan, 'Span', *Architectural Review*, Feb. 1959.
40. *Architects' Journal*, 4 July 1973, pp. 21 ff. (See also 'Rus in Urbe', *Architects' Journal*, 9 July 1975, pp. 52–4).
41. *Architects' Journal*, 9 Feb. 1972, pp. 284–7.
42. Martin Pawley, 'DoE housing awards scheme', *Architects' Journal*, 30 Apr. 1975.
43. *Architects' Journal*, 16 Dec. 1970, pp. 1423 ff.
44. *Architects' Journal*, 1 Dec. 1971, pp. 1225 ff.

45. *Architects' Journal*, 24 Jan. 1973, pp. 197 ff, and 31 Jan. 1973, pp. 259 ff.
46. Martin Pawley, op. cit.
47. W. Cowburn, 'Choice and design', *Baumeister*, June 1968.
48. See Ch. 2.
49. *Architectural Review*, June 1971.
50. *Architectural Review*, Oct. 1973.
51. Essex County Council, *A Design Guide for Residential Areas*, 1973.
52. J. M. Richards, op cit. p. 15.
53. Ibid, p. 16.
54. Greater London Council, op. cit.
55. Ibid.
56. Ibid.
57. Ibid.
58. *Architects' Journal*, 5 Feb. 1975, pp. 275–9. (See also, Michael Fleetwood, 'What gradual renewal means', *Architects' Journal*, 5 Feb. 1975, pp. 283–4.)
59. Tom Woolley, 'Housing renewal unit', *Architectural Design*, Aug. 1976, pp. 465–7.
60. See Ch. 9.
61. *Architects' Journal*, 9 May 1973, pp. 1117–18.
62. Greater London Council, op. cit.
63. Ibid.
64. Ibid.
65. 'Old lamps for new', *Architectural Review*, **158** (945), Nov. 1975, p. 258.
66. '1975 Heritage Year Awards', *Architects' Journal*, 25 June 1975, pp. 1300–4.
67. J. M. Richards, op. cit. pp. 33–4.
68. 'Heritage motives', *Architectural Review*, **158** (945), Nov. 1975, p. 282.
69. See *Architectural Design*, Sept.–Oct. 1977, p. 723.
70. Ibid., p. 716.
71. Alastair Best in *Architectural Review*, Oct. 1981, pp. 232–6.
72. *Architectural Review*, Jan. 1980, p. 27.
73. John Penton in *Architectural Review*, Oct. 1978, pp. 244–6.
74. Stephen Gardiner in *Architectural Review*, Oct. 1978, pp. 248–50.
75. *Architectural Design*, Dec. 1975.
76. Oliver Cox in *Architectural Review*, Oct. 1978, pp. 251–4.
77. *Guildway Catalogue*, 1982; *RIBA Journal*, Mar. 1981, p. 34.
78. Simon Pepper and Mark Swenarton, 'Neo-Georgian maison-type', *Architectural Review*, Aug. 1980, pp. 87–92.
79. Adshead, 'The Standard Cottage', *Town Planning Review*, vol. VI, 1915–16, p. 248, and reported in Pepper and Swenarton, op. cit.
80. Martin Richardson in *Architectural Design*, Sept.–Oct. 1977, p. 708.
81. *Yorkshire Architect*, Nov. 1970.
82. Adrian Forty and Henry Moss, 'Pseudo-vernacular', *Architectural Review*, Feb. 1980, pp. 73–8.

11 BASIC SHAPES

The perennial conflict of approach between those who sought a rational functional arrangement of dwellings and those who realised the virtue of patterns rooted in a picturesque tradition was now exposed. The conflict was particularly marked at Milton Keynes where the two approaches could be seen almost on adjacent sites – Netherfield and Bean Hill versus Great Linford and Eaglestone. It was a conflict that had been perpetuated in post-war housing since the two Alton estates at Roehampton in the 1950s.

Ever since public intervention had moved the environmental professions perceptibly away from a belief in their own self-righteousness and into the ordinariness of a vernacular comprise little movement had been possible in the derivation of alternative layouts and shapes for housing. Netherfields and Bean Hill had ruthlessly answered a functional problem in their layouts and had matched this with similar ruthlessness of aesthetic. It was thus with an element of caution that a bold application of rationality was repeated, unless such rationality could be seen to be founded in worthwhile familiarity and tradition.

At Milton Keynes, and indeed in general elsewhere in the 1970s, density requirements had not inferred the complexities that were the order of the day when high densities had been sought. To an extent car ownership and its desired proximity to dwelling had been the cause of this. But the assumption that a low density was inevitable in order to arrive at a built form solution appropriate to current physical requirements had had its objectors throughout the post-war years. They ranged from those to whom low density meant 'prairie' sprawl, who evoked remedial images of urbanity and who incorrectly tabulated the land take should the nation's then increasing population be so accommodated,[1] to those who attempted to arrive at a better understanding of density by a study of built form alternatives. This last group was represented by the comparisons of density and built form in some of London's eighteenth-century residential squares by Elizabeth Denby, and by an exposure of the fallacies of overcrowding on which early post-war density and built form solutions had been based by Ruth Glass.[2] Their arguments had been reinforced by others throughout the post-war period to little avail for events were never such as to make them relevant. However, the disillusionment with high rise and complex forms lent fresh emphasis to their work, and more recent events appeared to support the rational scientific nature of an approach which postulated that density in itself was of little importance unless it was related to built form.

J. M. Richards had made just this point in his arguments on the virtues of suburbia in 1946 though in somewhat less than scientific phrase: ' . . . by-laws which place a limit on the number of houses to the acre, though beloved by the garden-suburb sentimentalists, are the most fatal to the true suburban spirit. It is an essential part of its character that the suburb should constitute a world in itself, susceptible of delimitation. Above all things it needs to be compact. Space as such is not an asset, and a low density only dilutes the rich suburban landscape.'[3]

In fact the suburban density was largely that established by Raymond Unwin in 1919 at 12 houses to the acre (30/ha), reducing to 8 per acre (20/ha) in rural areas. Ebenezer Howard had said little on the question of density; it was Lewis Mumford who had calculated Howard's density to be 17–18 houses to the acre (42–45/ha) from the figures given in *Garden Cities of Tomorrow*.[4] Nevertheless, Walter Segal took up the spirit of Richard's argument in his calculations of the densities that were possible by using low-rise forms of courtyard houses.[5] In the context of what was to follow, his argument, in 1947, for the use of the square in residential planning was appropriate.[6] Using sunlight criteria for the spacing of blocks he recommended the layout of dwellings in a square surrounding a central green space, similar in retrospect to the indigenous tradition of Georgian squares that Elizabeth Denby was later to praise in terms of density.

A perhaps unwitting demonstration of the virtue of the square as a means of achieving high density while providing ample open space was provided by David Gregory-Jones's entry for the Golden Lane Competition.[7] The conditions had specifically asked for the exclusion of outside environmental

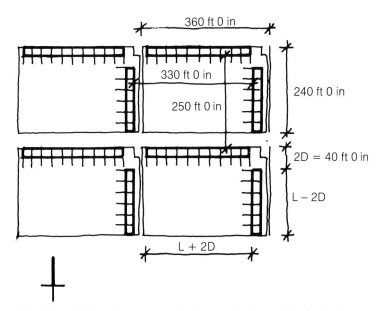

Fig. 11.1 Walter Segal's courtyard layout of 1947 (*E. R. Scoffham – adapted from drawing by Walter Segal*)

influences and for the provision of open space, lacking in the area as a whole, within the scheme. His solution was almost a too-literal interpretation of this brief for he arranged dwelling blocks around the periphery of the site, so achieving a large central square for recreational use. As a solution it answered the density requirement of the brief, 200 persons per acre (494/ha), by buildings lower in terms of height than any of the other premiated competitors. But in 1952 the provision of enclosed squares was too near in concept to the grim reality of introverted five-storey flatted blocks for this solution to be successful.

Nevertheless, when David Gregory-Jones was later working in the LCC Architects Department on development of the scissors, or cross-over maisonette with Colin Jones, a similar theme was revealed in 1962 when details of the block type were released.[8] The block was devised to achieve high densities and in the layout examples illustrating its potential it was shown that 200 persons per acre (494/ha) could be achieved using a six-storey block around squares 200 by 180 feet (61 by 55 m) in size; and 140 persons per acre (346/ha) was attained by surrounding a square the size of Bedford Square in London, including the accommodation of 184 cars within the six-storey blocks – as many as the normal daytime car population parked in the square. Unfortunately the block was never used in this manner; almost all its built derivations were in conventional mixed developments.

Other comparisons using a similar six-storey block, this time adopting the then current 'streets in the air' theme, were made by the Taylor Woodrow

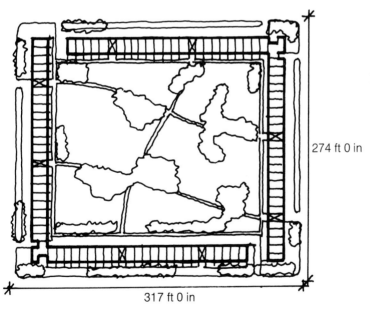

274 ft 0 in

317 ft 0 in

Fig. 11.2 Scissors maisonette block arranged around a space the size of Bedford Square, to a density, including the open space, of 140 persons per acre, and including 184 cars. (*E. R. Scoffham – adapted from drawing by London County Council*)

Group in a study of Fulham undertaken for the Ministry of Housing.[9] The continuous six-storey block was used in comparative layouts at densities of 136, 200 and 250 persons per acre (336, 494 and 618/ha) and the results in terms of built form were compared favourably with four-storey Georgian terraces in Bloomsbury. But as with the work at the LCC on square layouts it remained a theoretical study.

These studies did, however, herald a mathematical approach to residential planning by the Centre for Land Use and Built Form Studies (LUBFS) at Cambridge University under Professor Sir Leslie Martin and Lionel March.[10] What LUBFS proved was that the courtyard layout had a higher land use intensity or plot ratio than other built forms, and they suggested linear ribbons of housing enclosing courtyards, or squares, to achieve optimum density conditions. Most of the then traditional concepts of different built forms for different densities were demolished. In an example quoted to the 1967 Royal Institute of British Architects Conference[11] Lionel March cited the Hook plan which had allowed 16 acres (6.48 ha) of open space for every 1,000 people, and which, by interpolation, meant that 20 acres (8.09 ha) would be the space requirement for 1,280 people. March revealed that this could be done using a ribbon of three-storey houses, each with a small garden, surrounding the necessary open space and to a resultant density of 200

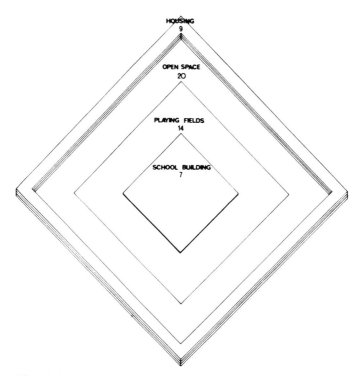

Fig. 11.3 *Land Use and Built Form Studies*: Distribution of land use (*from Urban Space and Structures by Martin and March, CUP*)

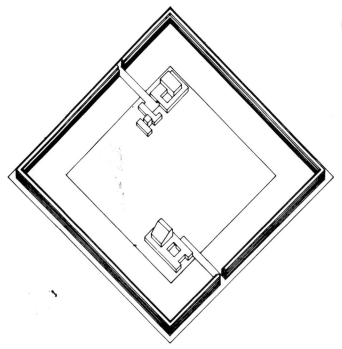

Fig. 11.4 *Land Use and Built Form Studies*: Configuration around square (*from Urban Space and Structures by Martin and March, CUP*)

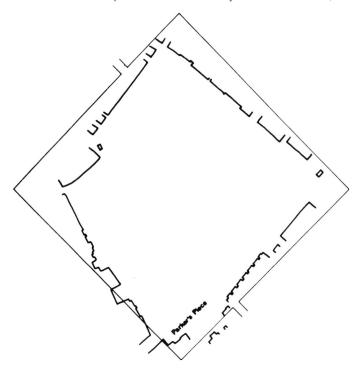

Fig. 11.5 *Land Use and Built Form Studies*: Comparison of space with Parker's Piece, Cambridge (*from Urban Space and Structures by Martin and March, CUP*)

persons per acre (494/ha). The built form would be similar in effect to Parker's Piece in Cambridge by using terrace housing similar to that of Howell and Amis overlooking Hampstead Heath in 1956,[12] and the access road would be as in any simple terrace development.

Mathematical evidence was supplied in the form of the fresnel square[13] in which successive rings of the same area get narrower in proportion to the square of their distance from the centre. To this a typical land use distribution in urban housing areas was applied by arranging the open space in the centre of the square, followed by gardens, then by houses, and on the outside by access roads and car accommodation. The resulting spaciousness between the houses was remarkable, becoming even more pronounced once major open space was located within the square.

Initial demonstrations of the validity of these theoretical studies came in the form of two housing schemes designed by the London Borough of Merton under P. J. Whittle, who was later succeeded by Bernard Ward. The design team used the perimeter idea to develop the Pollards Hill site near Mitcham Common,[14] where they managed to achieve an exchange of land so that recreational uses could be placed in the centre of the site so allowing unhindered perimeter development to take place. The form of the perimeter was a series of alternating P-shapes, one accommodating a short vehicle cul-de-sac and the other amenity open space between the housing blocks. The blocks themselves were three-storeys high, arranged as a continuous terrace forming interlocking P-shapes, thereby achieving a greater length by convolution, and hence a density of 116 bedspaces per acre (286/ha). Each house had its own integral garage and private garden and had immediate access to the amenity open space from which opened the central public space. The corner junctions were made up of two-person walk-up flats. Merton's second scheme, by the same design team, was at Eastfields, Mitcham and used the same peripheral idea but with less convolution of the continuous terrace.[15] In consequence the density was lower, 96 persons per acre (237/ha), but the same advantages in terms of car access and ground-level conditions remained as the house types were identical.

Seen against the bulk of post-war housing, much of which achieved lower densities by either higher blocks or a greater complexity of interlocking, these schemes were remarkable. The 116 persons per acre (286/ha) of Pollards Hill roughly equated with 100 persons per acre (247/ha) at the LCC's Roehampton estates, where two-, four-, eight- and eleven-storey blocks and slabs had been used, none had integral garages and few had ground-level access or a private garden. 'Relaxed simplicity' was the phrase Lionel March used to describe the results of the Cambridge work.[16] It demonstrated the historically retrogressive trend that was appearing in housing at a number of different levels.

The implications of the Cambridge research were far-reaching. Their advocacy for setting down facts, 'before rushing into producing exciting physical answers to non-existent problems', stood to alter the nature of housing architecture; to prevent the kind of 'intellectual pleasure that is

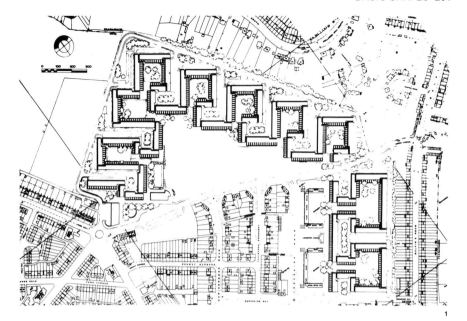

Fig. 11.6 Site layout of Pollards Hill showing central open space (*Architectural Design*)

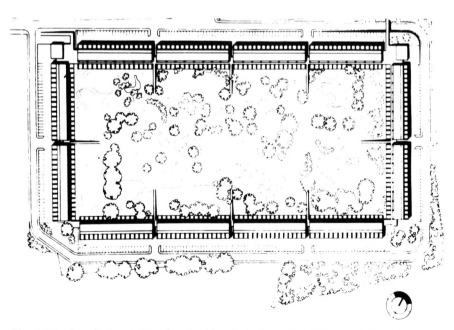

Fig. 11.7 Acacia Avenue project by Merton Borough (*Architectural Design*)

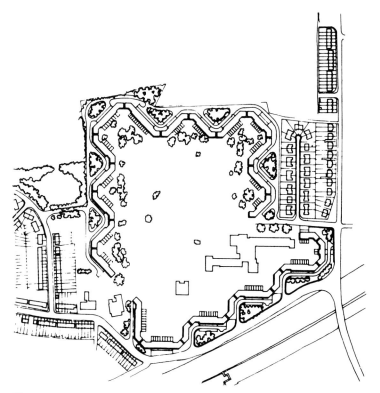

Fig. 11.8   Eastfields, Merton, as originally planned with school inside perimeter housing (*Architectural Design*)

derived from a clever arrangement of inadequate space'. It remained to be seen whether architecture could accept the apparently retrogressive position that should naturally follow. Here the architects of Pollards Hill and East-fields were open to question, for they had produced housing of an aesthetic that was arguable not of the 'relaxed simplicity' that March advocated. Both schemes were built in Wimpey's 'no fines' concrete system, clad in white stove enamelled steel panels, and rough cast at ground-floor level. To its architectural critic[17] the Pollards Hill panelling was highly successful and sophisticated, simple and obvious. Yet it demonstrated the same perversity in architects to pursue personal technical and aesthetic logic that occurred in Bean Hill and Netherfields at Milton Keynes. While the historical regression, or relaxed simplicity in terms of layout, that was apparent in these schemes, was for architecture a considerable achievement in progressive thinking after the complexities of the post-war years, it appeared that on a visual level architecture was as arrogant as ever. A merging of the two approaches inherent in the evolution both of a domestic tradition and of a framework for future built form had not yet been tackled in any meaningful way.

Richard McCormac, a team member for the two schemes at Merton, was the first to come near to making the link. In his winning scheme for the

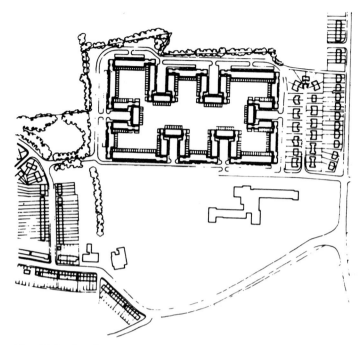

Fig. 11.9 Eastfields as built with housing alongside school and to an increased intensity of block configuration (*Architectural Design*)

Huddersfield Building Society's competition in 1971,[18] he adopted the perimeter theory yet combined it with ideas of change and adaptability in a visually familiar manner that was necessary in private housing for sale. Huddersfield was an ideas competition and it was never intended to build; but McCormac's motives in providing a house that would grow and adapt to the changing patterns of family life over the years saw expression in a small private development of eight houses at Woughton Green in Milton Keynes.[19] Here in 1973 McCormac and Jamieson arranged two groups of four houses around the edges of gravelled vehicle courts, while in each L-shaped prefabricated timber-framed and brick-clad house a flexible room arrangement offered multiple variations of living relationships.

The ideas of Pollards Hill were extended at a larger scale in 1974 when McCormac and Jamieson won a limited competition, as a member of a consortium of professional firms, for 977 dwellings at Duffryn, Newport, Gwent. The intention at Pollards Hill had been to obtain the highest possible density using the perimeter theme with a minimum house frontage. At Duffryn the density was prescribed at 70.8 persons per acre (175/ha), about two-thirds that of Pollards Hill, and this enabled house frontages to be 24.61 feet (7.5 m) wide, double those of Pollards Hill, giving each living-room a view of the garden. The 90 degree convolution angle of Pollards Hill was relaxed to 45 degrees so facilitating a corner plan that enabled a flexing of the ribbon of building to accommodate the shape of the site.[20] In the architects' words, 'the form is subordinate to the situation, and the internal logic of the courtyard idea, which informs most of our work, tends to make buildings which are receptacles of space rather than objects standing in space'. The criticism of the Pollards Hill scheme in terms of its unfamiliar aesthetic was to an extent answered: 'we, like others, are concerned that our work should be accessible, but the extent to which we are prepared to absorb vernacular or popular elements depends upon what they offer as an internal discipline'.[21] It was possible to incorporate a school within the perimeter wall of housing at Duffryn and the centre of the site as a result became a huge green, traffic-free area incorporating all the recreational land of the scheme.

In his criticism of Duffryn Peter Davey expressed the ability of perimeter planning 'to extend to the working-class the benefits of living in individual houses with close contact with nature', and after praising the virtues of 'the British bourgeois suburb' he continued, 'these are the kind of middle-class freedoms that Duffryn offers to its working-class tenants'. Nevertheless, he did criticise the ruthless uniformity of the continuous block which was only relieved by three changes of brick facings to the prefabricated timber-frame construction that reflected the three sections implemented by three different architects to McCormac and Jamieson's designs, and he wondered why the

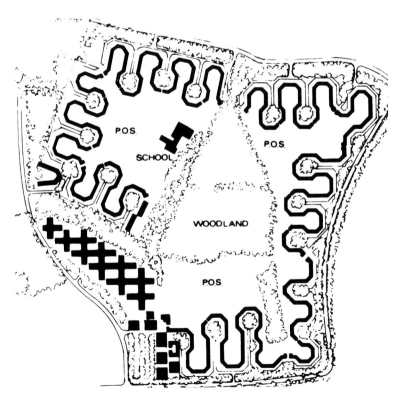

Fig. 11.10 Site layout of Duffryn, Gwent, including central open space, woodland and school (*Architectural Design*)

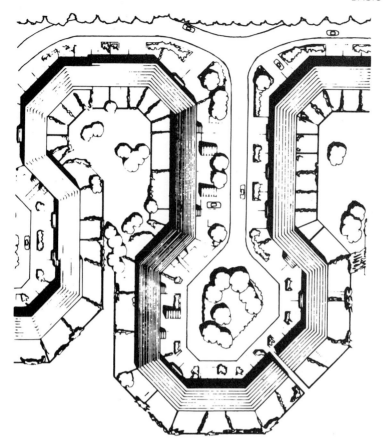

Fig. 11.11   Part of building 'ribbon' at Duffryn showing corner junctions
(*Architectural Design*)

nearby Welsh tradition of brick detailing had not been used to enliven the
uniformity.[22]

Back at Merton, a further scheme at Watermeads reflected the aesthetic
of Pollards Hill and Eastfields in a block configuration similar to that of
Duffryn; and the perimeter idea was adapted to insert new housing into a
relatively dense urban fabric at All Saints, South Wimbledon.

The problem of providing around 9,000 houses in the central area of
Milton Keynes to a coherent plan was resolved by dividing the housing area
into 590 by 426 feet (180 by 130 m) sectors, each accommodating about 500
people depending on density. The intention at Milton Keynes was not that
of density but a conscious attempt to create street-orientated town housing
while providing the full benefits of car access and pedestrian movement. To
satisfy this brief a perimeter development was used around the edges of each
rectangular sector, with flats in the corners and family houses along the sides,
while at each corner opportunity was provided for town facilities: surgery,
club, library, shop or office. The perimeter buildings enclosed a public open

Fig. 11.12 Watermeads, Merton, reflecting the aesthetic of Pollards Hill and Eastfields (*from A Broken Wave by Lionel Esher, Penguin Books 1983*)

space 328 by 164 feet (100 by 50 m) which had access from individual gardens – a space that was intended to be protected and safe, and provide a sense of identity for the surrounding families.

Within this framework the houses could be varied in frontage, height and type to achieve the required dwelling mix which included a high proportion of small dwellings for the city centre. Consistency was to be maintained by uniformity of detailing and a predominantly brick façade urban scene. The first phase of the town-centre housing was commenced at Fishermead in 1974 and consisted of a perimeter of three-storey terraces and three-storey corner units of flats and a shop. The external finishes were cream facing bricks, cream enamelled asbestos sheets on timber wall panels and brown acrylic-finished horizontal sliding aluminium windows. Conniburrow was a further extension in Fishermead style, while Downs Barn, an outer sector, was mainly two-storey but included some three-storey houses and provided all the houses on larger plots.[23]

The scale and cohesion of the housing at central Milton Keynes must be recognised, but seen against the pattern of history where towns grew gradually, constantly changing to fresh pressures, being added to and renewed in phases, these wilful intentions were open to criticism. To an extent this was answered in the ability of the framework to accommodate different housing requirements in different locations. The determined aesthetic and rigid geometrical order defeated the attainment of a familiarity through social intervention that might have given visual variety within a sustained framework – a mutual respect that has been the achievement of those towns in history to survive social and economic pressures intact. The notion that this was city centre housing suggested that it should provide a framework that offered a more classical order than the irregularity of village or suburb. Here the contrast with central area housing in Edinburgh, Bath or Bloomsbury was pertinent. The visual sterility of the modern movement must be judged to be responsible for providing a background of inability to respond to these ideals – ideals that Nash, Craig and the Woods had achieved so successfully.

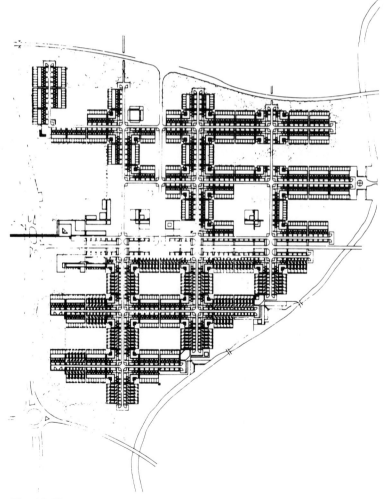

Fig. 11.13   Springfield section of central area housing at Milton Keynes

Fig. 11.14   Perspective of Fishermead housing as intended (*Architectural Design*)

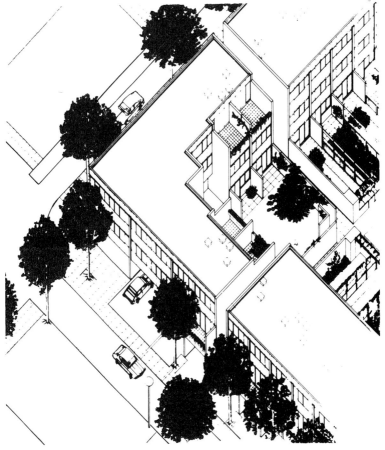

Fig. 11.15   Axonometric of three-storey corner junction, Fishermead (*Architectural Design*)

In plan and organisation the form was certainly classical, almost ruthlessly so, but in appearance it was classless – 'low profile' was the term used by Milton Keynes Development Corporation – a reflection of the state of British housing now that the barriers of working class and middle class, public and private had been felled.

The framework that had been derived out of the work of LUBFS at Cambridge appeared to answer long-term objectives of adaptation and change without any disruption of the original intent. At what stage that adaptation or change may occur will depend to large measure on how successfully the present housing accommodates it. The simplicity of the house plans, certainly the wider-frontage ones, would seem to answer the need for an amply-dimensioned shell that permits renovation and adaptation to occur. The aesthetic might not so easily adapt; but the precedent is there in history for façades to be remodelled to accommodate changes in taste and style. Whether Milton Keynes planners are so adaptable remains to be seen. While

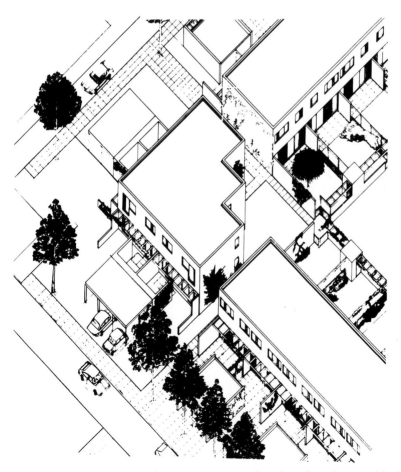

Fig. 11.16 Axonometric of two-storey corner junction, Conniburrow (*Architectural Design*)

Fig. 11.17 Conniburrow (*Nigel Atkinson and Simon Bee*)

flexibility and adaptability have been prime motives in the planning framework they have been translated at the level of physical provision, not as part of a developing social system – a pattern that will continue to develop while the physical framework remains the same.

Another central area housing project at Southgate, Runcorn, by James Stirling and Partner in 1976, had similar classical reminders in its square planning, but it also contained the dilemma that its appearance was unendearing. In its write-up Southgate was described: ' . . . the height of terraces relative to the size of a typical square, 300 feet by 300 feet, (91.4 m) of similar proportion to eighteenth century squares in Bath, Edinburgh, etc.' Whereas the Georgian square had houses fronting on to it, at Runcorn the organisation was in the form of L-shapes with two fronts and two backs facing into each square. The unendearing aspect of the scheme was provided by an industrialised system of construction with diagonally ribbed external concrete units, and plastic panels against the walkways[24] – a surprising contradiction in 1976 in view of the then well-known means of achieving social satisfaction and the much publicised criticism of industrialised building.

In attempting to resolve the tight brief restrictions of fixed density, height, garage and playspace provision on a site at Ascot Road, London, Douglas Stephen and Partners adopted a courtyard plan with related infill terraces among adjacent Victorian houses. The garages were located underneath the blocks and the raised central courtyard gave entry to the dwellings above while acting as a tree-surrounded playspace. The layout of the scheme confirmed the existing street pattern and the open central space made an analogy with the Victorian back square while acting at the same time as a front to the houses.[25]

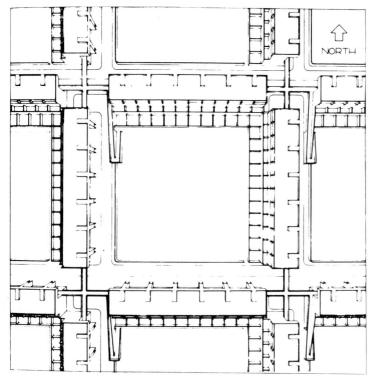

Fig. 11.18 Axonometric of typical square at Southgate, Runcorn (*Architectural Review, November 1976*)

Fig. 11.19 Southgate, looking towards town centre (*Stewart Johnstone*)

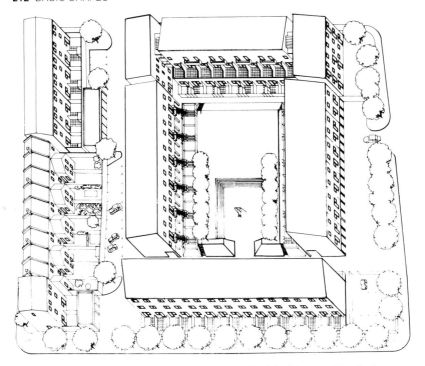

Fig. 11.20 Axonometric of Ascot Road housing (*Architectural Design*)

The search for, and apparent acceptance of basic shapes that was inherent in these projects had a sense of inevitability about it that the Cambridge work had mathematically underlined. It was becoming clear that before the so-called rationality of the new architecture had blinkered the professions, an arrangement of land and buildings had been taking place with an almost automatic correctness – a subconscious awareness of how to optimise on natural resources.

It is easy now to look back at the post-war years and to condemn them for the shortsightedness of those whose task it was to direct the pattern of housing. These people were working in a different climate, where inno-vation, technological development and social change were pursued almost fanatically. Now that events had demonstrated the futility of that approach a more relaxed look at what might have been could be undertaken in the hope that the necessary corrections to the legacy of built fabric that existed from these idealist days, and from earlier ones, might be made, and the future pattern of housing be more sane. Martin and March had demonstrated that the quest for higher densities by technological and ever more complex design solutions was, 'a game of professional acrobatics based on a false premiss. It generated more problems than it actually solved, and had the sole benefit of creating more jobs requiring solution.'[26] The false premiss was that density was bound up with notions of height. Evidence was provided that built form and land use were inter-related functions and that the range of densities commonly found in housing, even the three densities of 100, 136 and 200 persons per acre (247, 336 and 494/ha) that Abercrombie categorically associated with different building forms, could be achieved by using two- and three-storey housing with gardens, once an arrangement of land use had been made to optimise on the size and shape of housing sites. In connection with this last point, they demonstrated that the commonly assumed data regulating size of housing areas suffered from the same false precision as did conceptions of density. Assumptions involving walking distances, size of neighbourhood and length of cul-de-sac adversely affected built form solutions through their too-rigid adherence. A small change in the distances inferred by these assumptions induced a significantly larger change in area and hence in density.[27]

A return to this apparently basic order was demonstrated through an ideas competition for views on 'places fit to live in and how to create them', significantly sponsored by the Letchworth Garden City Corporation in 1976. David Dennis' successful entry dealt with urban restructuring taking advantage of the declining population of British cities. He located a central open space corresponding 'to the existing parks and commons that we find throughout London'. Around this were residential squares, each of 426 people, beyond them employment and shopping with the public transport route running down its centre. Dennis was careful to point out that his rigid 'square' was a diagram only and in application would respond to site conditions. Both employment and public transport would be within 5 minutes walk of all the housing. He suggested that the 'employment zone and major roads could be gradually built up around the existing high streets that already form the backbone to London today'. Green 'corridors' containing schools and playing fields threaded their way through both housing and employment and formed the pedestrian routes. In order to appease possible density critics he pointed out that resettlement of the whole of the population of England and Wales at the proposed density of 12 persons per acre (30/ha), allowing for a 10 per cent increase in numbers, would take up 12.5 per cent of the land

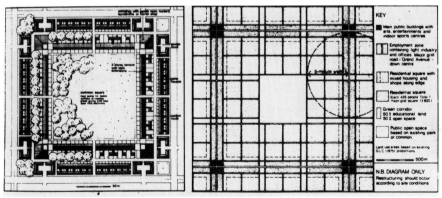

Fig. 11.21 David Dennis' restructuring diagram for the Letchworth competition in 1976 (*Architectural Design*)

of England and Wales as urban development compared with the 8 per cent at present.[28] At the densities shown to be possible using perimeter planning the figure could be much less.

This optimisation of resources was to an extent precipitated by an energy crisis in the mid 1970s following an OPEC oil price review. It was a short-lived crisis but it acted as a catalyst of ideas for the optimisation not only of energy in the fuel sense, but of all resources in a search for autonomy. Letchworth's suggestions seen in this light were appropriately low-key, and they pointed in the direction of a future pattern of urban development being modelled on a framework that already existed from earlier days – a framework with which society might identify by familiarity and understanding. It suggested a slow change, not of growth, but of optimisation.

A similar approach was also adopted in 1976 by John Seed in an attempt to model the 'possible spatial characteristics of an urban structure capable of remaining habitable, workable, convenient and attractive, in a context of increased energy constraint'.[29] Note the 'attractive'. Using Milton Keynes as a case study he offered a pattern of interactive neighbourhoods – city villages similar in concept to those of Nicholas Taylor[30] – each being relatively self-contained with a virtually complete spectrum of urban facilities. In application to Milton Keynes he adopted the grid principle of its planning, and supported the perimeter concept for it 'not only has the capacity to accommodate increases in numbers of dwellings in each city square, but each square could also support, in addition to housing, all the necessary local facilities such as schools, recreation space, market garden allotments and other land, including some light industry'. It was a return to the village – a need for defensive environments that were not restrictive – a notion that seemed increasingly necessary, even if the predicted serious energy deficiency of the 1990s was not to come about.

John Turner's advocacy was for a rearrangement of the knowledge we already have to 'formulate practical performance standards for environmental design that would generate social and economic as well as physical harmony'. He quoted the new town plantations of Edward I in the Middle Ages, where a progressive development by individuals had been allowed within an ordained framework. It was a framework that had often survived while the contents had changed with the passing of time – a framework that encouraged progressive development according to the 'will of autonomously organised people and communities'. In shape that framework was a loose grid around which perimeter development took place.[31]

Indeed, Patrick Abercrombie, despite his other failings on the question of density zoning noted that the grid plan was 'immeasurably superior to no plan haphazard', and it served as the framework for his own 'precinct' development of Bloomsbury in the County of London Plan of 1943.[32] After the geometrical complexities of so-called rational housing layouts it seemed that the perimeter development of a loose grid had returned to serve us today, and according to Gerald Dix 'should never have been overlooked'.[33]

To accommodate this sort of comprehensive three-dimensional thinking into our vocabulary of urban planning and architecture a different attitude appeared to be needed. The kind of basic understanding that had been inferred in these later optimisation examples, and appeared to be natural in the past, had been destroyed about the time architecture and planning became professionalised. In Leslie Martin's words;[34]

'the use of a mathematical formulation in the attempt to describe the ordering structure that lies behind a building or a city can be seen as another aspect of that texture of relationships through which we try to understand the complexity of an urban area. In developing such a study, the specialised division between

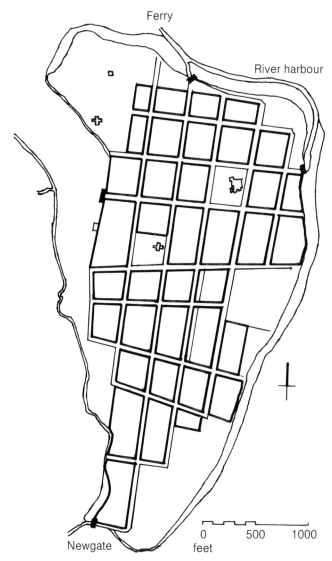

Fig. 11.22   Layout of Winchelsea in 1292 (*E. R. Scoffham – adapted from drawing by M. W. Beresford*)

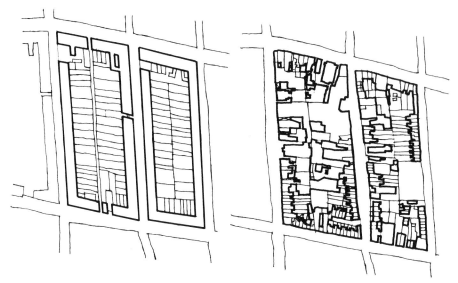

Fig. 11.23 Salisbury, two chequers in 1751 and 1954 indicating original perimeter development and subsequent 'growth' (*E. R. Scoffham – adapted from drawing by M. W. Beresford*)

architecture and planning has no particular significance and the developing language would take a form which others, notably the geographers and economists, are already using'.

The control of size over an unknown time-scale that Howard was concerned with at the turn of the century is somewhat less of an issue in Britain today now that a slow growth rate and a decline of technological progress are evident. Growth is now a social phenomenon, not a technological one, and the innate resourcefulness of Dennis and Seed provided directions for an alternative route to Howard's 'real reform'. Size in itself is, however, still an issue but one that some basic shapes would appear to contain in a comprehensible form. Cambridge denounced arbitrary sizing based on ill-defined notions and provoked a stopping of a conceptual clock in favour of an understanding of these basic truths. A turning back, too, of the professional clock appears to be necessary to cope with this inter-relationship of time and size in any meaningful way – to a professional situation that could create a Bath, an Edinburgh new town, even a Salisbury or a Winchelsea, for our classless individuality. In the words of Aldo van Eyck, 'think about that and you'll know why the thought process in planning can't be divided on the basis of part–whole, small–large, few–many; that is into architecture and planning'.[35]

REFERENCES

1. *Architectural Review*, Oct. 1973.
2. See Ch. 7.

3. J. M. Richards, *The Castles on the Ground*, 1946.
4. See Ch. 1.
5. See Ch. 7, and W. Segal, *Home and Environment*, 1948.
6. W. Segal, 'An argument for the use of the square in residential planning', *Architect and Building News*, 18 July 1947.
7. *Architects' Journal*, 6 Mar. 1952.
8. *Architects' Journal*, 28 Feb. 1962, pp. 453–60.
9. J. Tetlow and A. Goss, *Homes, Towns and Traffic*, 1965, p. 171.
10. Sir L. Martin and L. March, *Land Use and Built Form*, Cambridge Research, 1966.
11. L. March, 'Homes beyond the fringe', *Architects' Journal*, 19 July 1967.
12. See Ch. 9.
13. Sir L. Martin and L. March, *Urban Space and Structures*, 1972.
14. *Architectural Review*, Apr. 1971, pp. 204–6, and *Architectural Design*, Oct. 1971, pp. 613–18.
15. *Architects' Journal*, 23 Jan. 1974, pp. 177–9.
16. L. March, 'An examination of layouts', *Built Environment*, Sept. 1972, pp. 374–8.
17. *Architectural Review*, Apr. 1971, pp. 211–12.
18. *Architects' Journal*, 27 Oct. 1971, pp. 912–14, and 3 Nov. 1971, pp. 972–3.
19. See *Architectural Design*, Sept.–Oct. 1977, p. 696.
20. Ibid., pp. 691–3 and 701.
21. Ibid., p. 693.
22. Peter Davey in *Architectural Review*, Apr. 1980, pp. 207–20. (See also *Architects' Journal*, 13 Feb. 1980.)
23. 'Central Area Housing', *Architectural Design*, Aug. 1974, pp. 515–26; 'Milton Keynes Feedback', *Architectural Design*, **160** (954), Oct. 1974, pp. 660–5.
24. 'Work of Stirling at Runcorn', *Architectural Review*, Aug. 1976, pp. 282–8.
25. *Architectural Design*, Sept.–Oct. 1977, pp. 640–2.
26. L. March, 'An Examination of Layout', op. cit.
27. Sir L. Martin and L. March, *Urban Space and Structures*.
28. Andrew Rabeneck, 'Two comps.', *Architectural Design*, June 1976, pp. 364–5.
29. John Seed, 'Sustainable urban structure', *Architectural Design*, Sept. 1976, pp. 564–6.
30. Nicholas Taylor, *The Village in the City*, 1973.
31. J. F. C. Turner, 'Principles for housing', *Architectural Design*, Feb. 1976, p. 101. For a full explanation see M. W. Beresford, *New Towns of the Middle Ages*, 1967.
32. See Gerald Dix, 'Patrick Abercrombie: pioneer of planning', *Architectural Review*, Aug. 1979, pp. 130–2.
33. Ibid., p. 132.
34. Sir L. Martin and L. March, *Urban Space and Structures*, p. 54.
35. Aldo van Eyck, 1959; quoted in A. Smithson (ed.), *Team 10 Primer*, 1960, p. 5.

12 XENOPHOBIA

It is the individual who has emerged again in Britain to carry his point of view after the events of almost three decades of utilitarian authority that purportedly had society in mind. That the individual has emerged and not society is a peculiarly British conundrum which foreigners attribute to a high degree of social responsibility – a measure of the respect that British society is prepared to show towards the individual. British housing can now be seen to be unique, 'reflecting the image of a distinct form of civilisation and which can in no way be compared to the boundless barbarism of continental tenement blocks'.[1] So wrote Austrian Roland Rainer in 1947 as a warning, before the advent of tower and slab, that the kind of dwellings contained in them were anathema to the individuality of British society. They were a foreign import that had little to do with the British context of housing. They came after a barbaric war, and they came with support from, primarily, architects who demanded a change and who followed the example of *émigré* Continental architects to provide a different image to that of inter-war suburbia and barracks-like flatted blocks. They seemed to come for just that visual reason, without any analysis of their appropriateness to British life. But there was analysis, false though it is now seen in retrospect, to demonstrate how decentralisation and decongestion of the London metropolis could be achieved by new towns and a planned rebuilding policy to a pyramidal density zoning system that presupposed the inclusion of that foreign import.[2] Analysis there was too, to merge the opposing differences of town and country[3] – differences so apparent to Ebenezer Howard in 1898 yet so misunderstood in a quest for urbanity without overcrowding and openness without loss of density, which resulted in the contempt in which society now holds those responsible for the provision of housing.

Except for the Scottish tradition of urban tenement living and the apartment dwellings of relatively wealthy Londoners the British tradition was never that of high blocks. In the rest of the world high living has never been so denounced. 'But whether this explains the foreignness of foreigners, or shows their greater tolerance and adaptability, or demonstrates the high expectations of the British in assuming that two-storey detached housing is their due, can only be conjectured,' according to Colin Boyne.[4]

The derivation of a British solution to the problem of British housing was, in a sense, demonstrated by those who argued the social virtues of 'streets in the air' from the homogeneity of the by-law street and the writing of Young and Wilmott.[5] Alas their product was as foreign to the individual as were tower and slab. Only on the upsurge of a move towards lower-rise solutions did housing more peculiarly British at last begin to find recognition among the environmental professions. Even in the new towns architects longed to satisfy their desires to design visually exciting, high-density flats, however invaluable was their more mundane work on two-storey housing,[6] and in the private sector little occurred to excite architects other than Eric Lyons. Yet on the reintroduction of low rise–high density forms it was a foreign import, the courtyard house from Europe that provided the impetus to a dense fabric of building – an 'alien casbah' which in name evoked something entirely opposed to an expectancy of British housing.[7]

Architects appeared to prefer all except that which was British. It was largely the private sector and public authority officials who seemed strangely perplexed and unmotivated by this new architecture; who continued the provision of ground-level houses with gardens, so boring and featureless to architects, yet so successful among the British. However, it seemed that at Runcorn, Merton and Milton Keynes, the magic virtues of the British house, Howard's marriage of town and country in house and garden, had found a place in architecture. The individuality of British housing – the ability to express oneself within a set of common standards of which society approved, appeared at last. But it emerged cautiously, in embryo as it were, for architecture was reluctant to release its controlling hand, as well it might, for society was not judged ready to understand those common controls within which its individuals should operate. Excessive control had been a packaging, an arrogance, and an imposition of taste that society had rightly rejected; yet the stage when it could, with confidence, be trusted to make individual choice that credibly would not result in anarchy seemed a long way off. The process of merging had to be a gradual one, one that developed a mutual trust of society for architecture, and vice versa, so that architecture might reach its former position as a servant of society and of the individual, rather than an expensive luxury or a perverted art form.

John Turner had advocated 'legislative planning' in an analogy with the new towns of Edward I, which was in essence a setting out of the limits of what individuals were free to do rather than the imposition of standard procedures to which they must adhere.[8]

This position begged a turning back of the clock – an historical regression. Since the end of the Second World War events in Britain had been changing fast – too fast for society to assimilate, and to willingly accept, not just in architecture but in the whole area of technological progress. Technology had governed change, not society itself; technological solutions had been proposed to solve ever more technical problems without the first premiss – to what end – being questioned. The means had justified the end. Industrialisation could never solve the housing problem no matter how many units it could produce unless its product was that which society had demonstrated its willingness to accept. The individuality of British housing confounded an industrialised solution, until the day when society and industrialised technology, like the architect, had gained for each other a mutual trust. Hence a slowing down of technological change and of architectural extrovertism so that society might, in a sense, catch up and decide in which direction architecture and technology could best be used for its own ends. Only then could the innovating role of the designer assume a proper usefulness, one where the rate of innovation was governed by society itself.

The evolution of a traditional vernacular, the establishment of a framework of choice and change in which the individual might participate, and the derivation of apparently simplistic built forms related to broader land use concepts were all parts of this historical regression. In the evolution of a vernacular gone was technological wizardry, aesthetic fancy and visual tour-de-force on the part of the architect, and a substitution made of traditional materials and orthodox shapes – a familiarity with which society could identify by understanding.

A framework for choice and change evoked the random nature in which the traditional town and village had grown over a period of time with a resultant consistency of appearance. A simplicity of approach to built form, density and land use created arrangements suggesting Georgian streets and squares, collegiate quadrangles and medieval planned towns of comparable or even better densities and land use patterns than those latter-day solutions based on technical innovation and geometrical sorcery. To quote Alexander, 'It is more and more widely recognised today that there is some essential ingredient missing from artificial cities. When compared with ancient cities that have acquired the patina of life, our modern attempts to create cities artificially, are, from a human point of view, entirely unsuccessful.'[9] The rate of technological change had prevented acquisition of that 'patina of life'; what was invented in the morning seemed almost absolute after lunch.

Taking these indications of an historical regression further involved their relationship to time and to size. Those disasters which exposed the weakness of housing out of tune with British peculiarities had helped to emphasise the virtues of housing from earlier times as being more able to provide for these peculiarities by a better understanding of British society and the wishes of the individual. Despite its drawbacks, particularly those seen at the end of the war and in the 1950s for which a new broom was devised in the shape of slum clearance,[10] the nineteenth-century terrace house had advantages that were seen to be sadly lacking in more contrived solutions: a house–entrance–road situation, sometimes a garden, however small, an understandable, familiar appearance and arrangement of rooms, a robust construction and, perhaps above all, an appropriate shape. These virtues, exploited by 1969 Housing Act improvement and conversion schemes, highlight the faults of post-war replacements, not just in terms of their present-day usefulness but more in terms of their potential for similar improvement and conversion at a future date. Ample size had facilitated adaptation, but more than this so had a dimensional basis of space and shape, and an adequate structural module and safety factor. It was often argued that minimum space requirements[11] in the public sector prevented such a loose-fit and hence longer-life approach;[12] but though Parker-Morris areas may have been smaller than nineteenth-century equivalents, it was the arrangement of that space to a size and shape within a structural discipline that permitted flexibility and change, in both short and long terms. In a reappraisal of late Victorian and Edwardian terrace housing Stefan Muthesius declared that, 'to foreign observers, especially from those countries where most people live in flats, this type always seemed peculiarly English and in most aspects a "vastly superior" way of living'.[13]

At the level of urban framework similar arguments of time and size were appropriate. The relative ease with which rectangular, admittedly repetitious nineteenth-century street plans had been adapted to accommodate changes

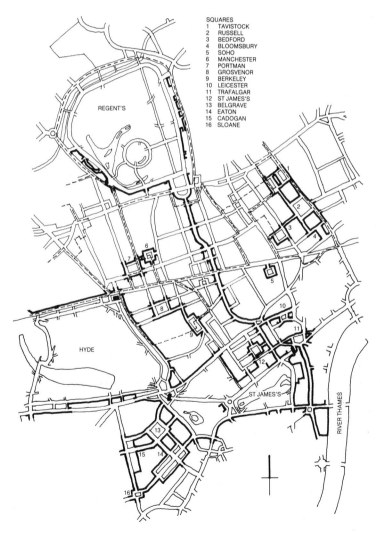

SQUARES
1   TAVISTOCK
2   RUSSELL
3   BEDFORD
4   BLOOMSBURY
5   SOHO
6   MANCHESTER
7   PORTMAN
8   GROSVENOR
9   BERKELEY
10 LEICESTER
11 TRAFALGAR
12 ST JAMES'S
13 BELGRAVE
14 EATON
15 CADOGAN
16 SLOANE

Fig. 12.1   Parks and squares of central London (*E. R. Scoffham*)

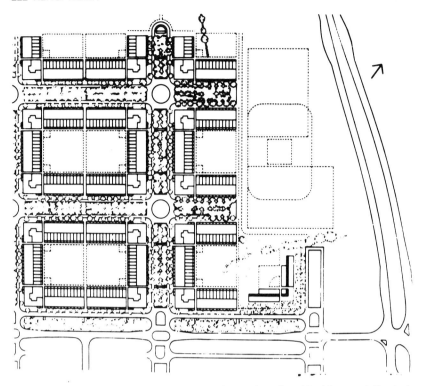

Fig. 12.2 Plan of Milton Keynes central area housing (*Architectural Design*)

in land use, increased car ownership, children's play-spaces, planting and so on, exposed fears that geometrical inter-war layouts and certainly post-war high rise–high density estates might not accommodate change so easily. The almost unplanned simplicity of earlier layouts inherently assumed a land use and built form arrangement that in the long term had proved beneficial. Cambridge provided the lead for a return to these arrangements and to earlier courtyard patterns that had a built-in potential for future change of land use and of function.[14]

In translation of the Cambridge research into built reality, certainly in its central area, Milton Keynes was to Steen Eiler Rasmussen, 'an utterly English phenomenon'. To him it represented 'a continuation and a perfection of the special London patterns of the seventeenth and eighteenth centuries that was so different from all continental city planning of that period'.[15] The basic requirement of English housing was for close contact with the countryside, and the opportunity this offered for attractive surroundings in which to enjoy openness, air and a view. The result at Milton Keynes was thus not new but the continuation of a tradition of built form management that was reminiscent of the initial building and growth of the West End of London, where the grid of roads – like Milton Keynes about 1 km (0.6 mile) apart – controlled the development of housing between them, introducing squares and access to the English landscaped hunting parks of St James's, Hyde and Regent's to a comprehendable plan.

As a framework it offered the opportunity for the implementation of speculative 'pattern book' housing – styles of common consent that had provided, within John Turner's 'legislative planning' framework,[16] a basis for the development of not only London, but also other Continental cities such as Amsterdam. It was a pattern that 'confirms a satisfactory achievement of social equilibrium. So the need for individual expression in housing may be inverse to the acceptability of the overall image', according to Richard McCormac.[17]

Milton Keynes offered the same opportunity for implementation of the speculative 'pattern books' of a Guildway, and so the attainment of that 'social equilibrium'; but this has not happened. The 'acceptability of the overall image' in the city centre and indeed elsewhere in Milton Keynes represented a continuation of Rainer's 'boundless barbarism' that was to the English entirely foreign – an arian purity – the built realisation of the sterility of nowhere. Utopia may, in fact, be the achievement of British housing and planning in accurately representing the social state of negotiated classless conformity into which post-war utilitarian authority had steered it.

Despite its sterility central Milton Keynes represented a renewed interest in urbanism – a curiosity about how to make towns, or at least central areas as opposed to suburbia and the village. This renewal of interest brought a

Fig. 12.3 Covent Garden as originally planned (*Professor S. E. Rasmussen*)

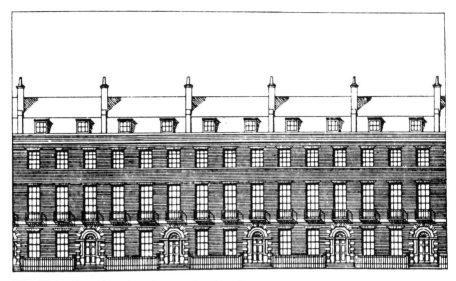

Fig. 12.4 Georgian elevations to Bedford Square; '*a satisfactory achievement of social equilibrium.*' (*Professor S. E. Rasmussen*)

fresh influence from Europe in the work of the Krier brothers, Rossi, Culot and Bofill. Again it seemed that architects might be looking abroad for ideas to satiate their visual appetites, but with a difference. The essential peculiarities of British, or at least English, urbanism were being spotted by critics such as Bob Allies and, it appeared, by Jeremy Dixon whose work he was then criticising. Allies' disclosure was that 'the Englishman's concern for the privacy of his own dwelling is constituent with a relative disaffection for the public realm. Unlike his fellow Europeans the Englishman does not revel in the opportunity provided by the great public space to congregate and promenade', and it was a necessary reminder.[18] The origins of this essential difference, from the early political stability of England by comparison with its Continental neighbours, led to patterns that, while rooted in European ideas, were uniquely English. They were not formal urban redevelopments but suburban speculations on sites between the urban centre and the countryside. They contained garden squares that identified them in terms of the English town and country compromise. Jeremy Dixon saw in London, 'a weak tradition of true urbanism but a sophisticated and rich tradition of suburbanism',[19] and it was this tradition that he expressed in his housing at St Mark's Road, Kensington.

In combining several minimal–area dwellings into a larger whole he identified with an English tradition of maintaining the identity of the house while serving a more general urban or street function. He introduced devices that were reminiscent of the garden architecture of Gertrude Jekyll; the fronts were ornamented street façades while the backs, in the convention of London, were plain; the raised entrance above a basement area, the gateposts and bay windows evoked the late Victorian and Edwardian street scene, to

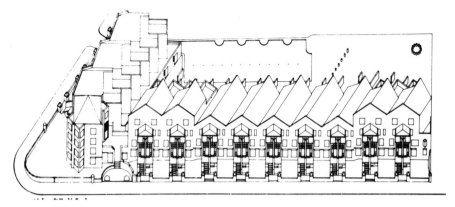

Fig. 12.5   Street architecture at St Mark's Road, Kensington (*Jeremy Dixon*)

the inclusion of net curtains – 'the system was developed in the eighteenth century; it is understood by both inhabitants and the passer-by. It is what makes the English street work' wrote Jeremy Dixon.[20]

This rediscovery of the English street and continuation of the English residential tradition had been lacking from the urban thinking of central Milton Keynes. It depended on historical elements to create a façade – suggestions of both the decoration and the philosophy of the English house in an English setting that pre-dated the rationalism of the 'new architecture'. 'Streets in the air' had now rooted themselves in the ground of 'England's green and pleasant land'. But whether the manner in which Jeremy Dixon had stylistically reproduced the net-curtained English street would be familiar to the net-curtained English had yet to be revealed. The rigorous architectural intellect that could produce, at the same time, the sterility of central Milton Keynes and a revalidation of the urban street was perhaps that same rigorous intellect that had produced the sophisticated new architecture of Alton West, the methodical social structuring of Park Hill and the industrialised variety of Thamesmead. While the images of public and private housing had appeared to merge in the acceptance of tradition, while the English virtue of house and garden and the tradition of built form and land use had been revalued, the gap between popular choice and educated taste remained. Mass housing, when in architect's hands, at least on the evidence at Milton Keynes, Merton and St Mark's Road, appeared to be the province of technological innovation and aesthetic licence – a pursuit of the same vicarious pleasures that typified the social disasters of the post-war years.

These vicarious pleasures were still evident at various levels despite acknowledgement of the uniqueness of English housing. Style could become a matter of choice for society through the likes of Guildway 'pattern books', and for the architect through his intellectual and visual curiosity. In an attempt to make buildings that were, to use Piers Gough's word 'pretty', he described his Phillips West Two building: 'the front is "Spanish" and inside on the first floor courtyard it's kind of "Roman" '. Guildways 'pattern books' were unmistakably English to suite popular choice; the architect seemed to prefer anything but English in a conscious desire to be liked.[21] Piers Gough thus represented a contradiction, and a negation of architecture. The rationalism of the language of the modern movement seemed incapable of responding to the reality of the British housing scene – the need for a national housing that was liked by the British. Architecture was responding to its inability in an erratic manner displaying all the withdrawal symptoms of a post-mortem architecture – what Charles Jencks called post-modern – in an attempt to discover the cause of its failure.

Architecture's vicarious pleasures: its invention of descriptions to justify its actions, its obsessions and abstractions, its intellectual constructivism, failed to recognise, by yet more 'rational' argument, the basic principles upon which it might achieve a worthwhile role in housing. In its search for moral justification architecture had violated tradition, particularly the localised traditions of Britain, and it had lost sight of what it was trying to represent. Too often it was trying to represent its own personal motives – its own myths. But what it should have been doing was representing the myths of society, the nationalistic and regionalised traditions of British people, or even, once the ability to have ultimate choice had been won, to represent the myths of the individual concerned. In a discussion on Houses, Housing and the City in 1981 Bob Stern advised,

If she wants to commission a country house and she's in the mood for columns, that's one image system, and she could develop an argument for it. If she wants it to look like a Cotswold cottage, that's another system, and so forth. I don't think there is a crisis. The only crisis is that architects set up the barrier.

'Or as James Gowan said in the same discussion.'

'All architects are projecting their ideas as high as this, there is little chance of any member of the public understanding what we do and very little chance of redeeming the situation.'[22]

Figures quoted by Simon Pepper would seem to support the fact that the public had understood little of what architecture had to offer throughout the post-war period, and that architecture had had but a minor impact on housing. Between 1952 and 1976 something over 8 million dwellings were built in Britain. In terms of their shape about a quarter were terraced, a quarter detached and over one-third semi-detached. Those dwellings built as flats, mainly by public authorities, comprised about 20 per cent of the total, and in fact nearly 60 per cent of the output of flats by local authorities in the mid-1960s was in low blocks of four-storeys or less. The impact of the diverse story of built form alternatives had been insignificant in terms of numbers.

In the construction and appearance of housing the figures reflect a similar pattern. Eighty-five per cent of post-war housing had pitched roofs, 93 per cent was built using normal cavity brickwork. While industrialisation did make a significant contribution to housing output in the late-1960s – about 40 per cent – it was the low technology systems that made the most impact. Wimpey's 'no-fines' system, developed since the 1920s, made up almost a quarter of the industrialised housing units of 1969. It was a very ordinary scene, and a depressing one for architecture.[23]

To add to the depression an analysis of the housing problem in 1979 by Jane and Roy Darke exposed five areas for attention: the homeless including squatters, council tenants and especially those in high flats or on 'dump' estates, tenants in private rented accommodation, owners trapped in declining districts, and the long-term occupants of institutions.[24] At least two of these categories had been aggravated directly by the environmental professions' inability to offer a satisfactory and long-lasting product. The progressive replacement of post-war embarrassments and the renewal of outworn areas to alleviate some of the Darkes' housing problems, to the same statistical breakdown that had been achieved by 1976, would indicate an increase of ordinariness. But if the figures revealed the majority of this ordinary housing to be satisfactory and free from stress then architecture needed to look at what it had missed. The lasting products of housing provision had been the amply dimensioned late-Victorian and Edwardian house, and the more generously laid-out of the 4 million houses with gardens that had been such a great leap forward in housing standards during the inter-war years. Those products of the post-war period that conformed to the ideals of these two groups – and

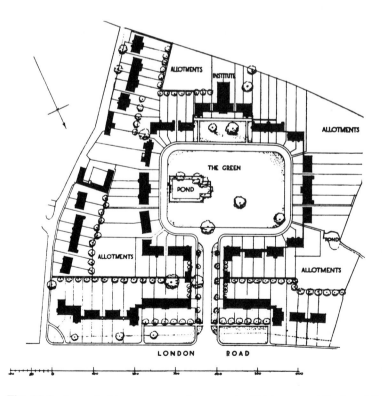

Fig. 12.6   Layout of houses around a green by Crickmer and Foxley at East Grinstead in 1923 (*Country Life Books, Hamlyn Group Picture Library*)

the figures indicated a fair proportion – would seem to be equally lasting. That lasting quality can now be seen to be their Britishness.

In order to discover the uniqueness of a national housing expectancy the roots of housing and planning in Britain become exposed. These roots are fixed in the desire to mitigate the appalling squalor that nineteenth-century industrial urbanism had created. The town-hating, non-urban attitude that epitomised late-Victorian, Edwardian and inter-war housing had been a continuation of the same tradition that had created the Georgian 'suburbs'. The virtues of British housing were rooted in a lineage of Utopian literature that went back in history to before the industrial revolution and the Renaissance.

Fig. 12.7 Uplands Estate, Southampton; Georgian inspired speculation from 1921 (*John Ford*)

Howard had restated the British housing argument, and it must not be forgotten that the argument was based on planned new communities, not the suburban extension that was perpetuated in its name. Garden city was a British phenomenon that was copied throughout the world because foreigners saw in it something infinitely better than they had themselves. Parker and Unwin had translated Howard in social and visual terms that vowed never to reproduce the dreariness and uniformity of the by-law street. At Letchworth and Hampstead, in the words of Percy Thomas when presenting the Royal Institute of British Architects Gold Medal to Unwin in 1937 he, 'materialised the Englishman's ideal conception of house as a unit of house and garden combined'.[25] The quotation could now be extended to read: 'housing as a unit of houses and open space combined'.

This renewed interest in national identity was lent fresh emphasis by a German, Hermann Muthesius, in his book *The English House*, originally published in Berlin in 1904–5 and not translated into English until 1979.[26] His study of housing in England between 1860 and 1914 sprang out of an

Fig. 12.8 Raymond Unwin drawing from *Town Planning in Practice* to illustrate a varied manner of turning a regular corner (*from Town Planning in Practice by R. Unwin, Benjamin Blom Inc*)

interest in craft traditions and the uniqueness of the English country house. He revealed what he thought the British took for granted, that the domestic architecture of the past was original and innovative, and managed to achieve the picturesque and rural romantic ideals of a national identity. The English house of the period established a pattern of middle-class house-building that has remained as the ideal to the present. The suburbs that saw expression of the rural romantic ideal were to Muthesius a reflection that the Anglo-Saxon race did not possess the gift of building cities. Nevertheless, he recognised the English problem of lifeless city centres if everyone was to live in the suburbs, and concluded that the only remedy for the English was to remove them all into open country.

Unwin almost saw this achieved after the First World War through the 1919 Housing Act which implemented the model of housing he had started with his partner Barry Parker at Letchworth and Hampstead. The roots of their ideas were very largely stated in *Town Planning in Practice*,[27] and they are, like those of Muthesius, lessons for today. The manner in which the book reveals ways of grouping houses around squares and along streets, as well as most of Parker and Unwin's built examples, seem simple, relaxed and familiar by comparison with the intellectually rationalised solutions of recent years. Paradoxically one of Unwin's main visual sources was Camillo Sitte's organic town building study of German towns in 1889.[28]

After the technological events of post-war housing and the avoidance of craftsmanship, virtually at all costs, the relatively modest yet visually rich and

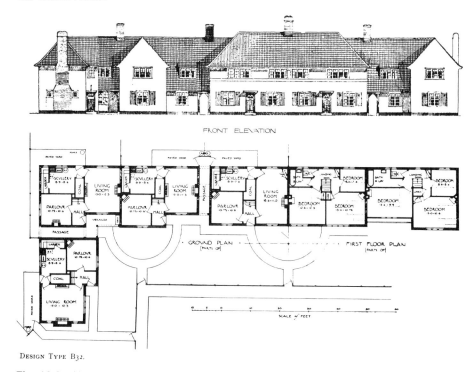

FRONT ELEVATION

DESIGN TYPE B32.

Fig. 12.9 Nottingham City's house type B32 by Cecil Howitt (*Cecil Howitt and Partners*)

Fig. 12.10 Housing around a green on the Lenton Abbey Estate, Nottingham, 1926–28 (*E. R. Scoffham*)

traditionally familiar houses of the inter-war years, when built at their best in controlled groups, are worthy examples. They are examples that often display local characteristics and regional idiosyncracies that reflect, just as had Port Sunlight, Saltaire, Bourneville and New Earswick, a natural local vernacular. Even the most unco-ordinated examples reflect a uniqueness of style that was conventionally nationalistic. As Duncan Simpson wrote, 'the Englishman's mock-Tudor house is not his castle; it's his homely country cottage, his piece of Old England, conveniently brought up to Croydon for him'.[29]

The message for housing in Britain today would appear to be concealed at the point where the modern movement took leave of its roots in the arts and crafts movement, at the point where the nationalistic traditions of its origins were abandoned in favour of things foreign. That point is surely the taking-off point for housing again. The so-called 'English disease' of industrial strife is perhaps a too-selfconscious awareness that towns and technology are not English, that the values of technology are doubtful ones in the light of mounting unemployment and declining growth.

The socialism of towns and technology have, for Britain, no place in the kind of housing to which it nationally and naturally aspires. The democratic visions of semi-autonomous villages, arts and crafts skills, and home-based electronic communications may be nearer to our national identity – an identity to which a pattern of housing, land use and built form can respond through a deep-rooted understanding – a pattern that has been in existence for a considerable period of time but which has been forgotten by the march of progress.

Foreigners have perennially provided Britain with ideas, from the unfamiliar ones that gave birth to the barbarism of modern movement rationality, to the gentle scholarly reminders that Britain should be itself and exploit what they have always regarded as its strengths, but which Britain has been unable to see because they were too familiar.[30]

British housing architects must welcome the clarity of foreign comment with a measure of philoxenia – love of strangers – that may enable them to provide for Britain a tradition of xenophobic housing – a fear of things foreign to its individuality.

Ironically British architects working abroad have traditionally been careful in their response to local expectations, from the heady days of Empire to the oil wealth of the Gulf States. Indeed, the products of 'the colonial master' are now seen in many parts of the world to impart an identifiable local tradition to those developing countries keen to establish their identity by buildings that exhibit almost universally the same sterile internationalism. The lesson of post-war British housing is the same as that of *The English House*, that for every identifiable region or country the only true progress is through the development of indigenous vernacular traditions within, and in parallel with, the development of indigenous traditions of built form.

REFERENCES

1. R. Rainer, *Die Behausungsfrage*, 1947, Vienna, p. 33.
2. J. R. Forshaw and P. Abercrombie, *County of London Plan*, 1943.
3. See Chapter 5.
4. D. A. C. A. Boyne, 'Making a good point', *Architectural Review*, July 1979, p. 7.
5. See Ch. 6.
6. J. B. Duff, *British New Towns*, 1963, p. 56.
7. See Ch. 7.
8. J. F. C. Turner, 'Principles for housing', *Architectural Design*, Feb. 1976, p. 101.
9. C. Alexander, *A City is Not a Tree*, 1965.
10. See Chapter 6.
11. Circular 36/37, 1967.
12. A. Gordon, 'Architects and resource conservation', *RIBA Journal*, Jan. 1974.
13. S. Muthesius, 'A re-appraisal of late Victorian and Edwardian housing', *Architectural Review*, Aug. 1979, p. 93. Muthesius quoted R. Eberstadt, 1908, from *Technische Gemeindeblatt*, vol. XI, pp. 6–8.
14. See Ch. 11.
15. S. E. Rasmussen, 'Open-plan city', *Architectural Review*, Sept. 1980, p. 141.
16. J. F. C. Turner, op. cit.
17. R. McCormac, 'Housing and the dilemma of style', *Architectural Review*, Apr. 1978, p. 205.
18. R. Allies, 'Housing, North Kensington, London', *Architectural Review*, Dec. 1980, p. 344.
19. In ibid., p. 345.
20. Ibid., p. 346.
21. P. Gough in 'Six British architects', *Architectural Design*, Dec. 1981, pp. 106–7.
22. In ibid., p. 110.
23. Taken from S. Pepper 'The people's house', *Architectural Review*, Aug. 1977, p. 270.
24. J. and R. Darke, *Who Needs Housing?* 1979, p. 143.
25. *RIBA Journal*, 24 Apr. 1937; quoted by D. Hawkes in 'The architectural partnership of Barry Parker and Raymond Unwin', *Architectural Review*, June 1978, p. 330.
26. H. Muthesius, *The English House*, 1979.
27. R. Unwin, *Town Planning in Practice*, 1909.
28. C. Sitte, *Der stadte-bau nach seinen künstlerischen Grundsätzen*, 1889.
29. D. Simpson, 'Beautiful Tudor', *Architectural Review*, Aug. 1977, p. 31.
30. The latest advice was provided by the outgoing head of the London School of Economics, Rolf Dahrendorf, in a series on BBC TV, 1982–83.

REFERENCES

This list provides fuller details of the references supplied at the end of each chapter.

Abercrombie, P., *Greater London Plan*, HMSO, 1944.

Adshead, S., 'The standard cottage', *Town Planning Review*, **VI**, 1915–16.

Alexander, C., *A City is Not a Tree*, Kaufmann International Design Award, 1965. Originally published in *Architectural Forum* and reprinted in *Design*, Feb. 1966.

Allies, R., 'Housing, North Kensington, London', *Architectural Review*, **168**, Dec. 1980.

Ashworth, H., *Housing in Great Britain*, London: Skinner, 1957.

Atkinson, G. A., 'Radburn layouts in Britain, a user study', *Official Architecture and Planning*, 29 Mar. 1966.

Barlow, Sir M. (chairman), *Royal Commission on the Geographical Distribution of the Industrial Population*, Cmnd 6153, HMSO, 1940.

Barr, A. W. C., *Public Authority Housing*, Batsford, 1958.

Bell, C. & R., *City Fathers*, Barrie & Rockliff, The Cresset Press, 1969.

Beresford, M. W., *New Towns of the Middle Ages*, Lutterworth Press, 1967.

Boyne, D. A. C. A., 'Making a good point', *Architectural Review*, **166**, July 1979.

Brett, L., 'Post-war planning estates', *Architectural Review*, **110**, July 1951.

Brooke, H. Lord (chairman), *Living in Flats*, HMSO, 1952.

Browne, K., 'Straightjacket', *Architectural Review*, **131**, May 1962.

Bruckmann, H. & Lewis, D. L., *New Housing in Great Britain*, New York: Universe Books, 1960.

Buchanan, C., *Traffic in Towns*, HMSO, 1963.

Buchanan, P., 'Byker, the spaces between', *Architectural Review*, **168**, Dec. 1980.

Burt, Sir. G. (chairman), *Post War Building Studies, No. 1; House Construction*: HMSO, 1944.

Campbell, K., 'Home Sweet Home', *Building*, **225**, 31 Aug. 1973.

Chermayeff, S. & Alexander, C., *Community and Privacy*, New York: Doubleday, 1963; Harmondsworth: Penguin Books, 1966.

Collins, G. R. & C. C., *Camillo Sitte and the Birth of Planning*, London: Phaidon Press, 1965, New York: Random House, 1965.

Cook, P., *Archigram*, **1–5**, 1961–64.

Cook, P., 'The suburban ethic', *Architectural Design*, **154**, Sept. 1974.

Cowburn, W., 'A defence of popular housing', *Arena*, **81**, Sept.–Oct., 1966.

Cowburn, W., 'Choice and Design', *Baumeister*, **65**, June 1968.

Craig, J., 'London planning in retrospect', *Official Architecture & Planning*, **28**, May 1965.

Cullen, G., 'Prairie planning', *Architectural Review*, **114**, July 1953.

Culpin, E. G., *The Garden City Movement up to Date*, The Garden Cities & Town Planning Association, 1914.

Darke, J. & R., *Who Needs Housing?* Macmillan, 1979.

de Wolfe, I., 'Civilia', *Architectural Review*, **149**, June 1971.

de Wolfe, I., 'Sociable housing', *Architectural Review*, **154**, Oct. 1973.

Denby, E., 'Oversprawl', *Architectural Review*, **120**, Dec. 1956.

Denington, E. (chairman), *Our Older Homes: a call for action*, HMSO; 1966.

Dix, G., 'Patrick Abercrombie: pioneer of planning', *Architectural Review*, **166**, Aug. 1979.

Dudley, W. H. E. (chairman), *The Design of Dwellings*, HMSO, 1944.

Duff, J. B., *British New Towns*, Pall Mall Press, 1963.

Edwards, A. T., *A Hundred New Towns for Britain*, Hundred New Towns Association, 1934.

Essex County Council, *A Design Guide for Residential Areas*, Chelmsford, Essex, 1973.

Fleetwood, M., 'What gradual renewal means', *Architects' Journal*, **161**, 5 Feb. 1975.

Forshaw, J. R. & Abercrombie, P., *County of London Plan*, Macmillan, 1943.

Forty, A & Moss, H., 'Pseudo-vernacular', *Architectural Review*, **167**, Feb. 1980.

Frank, D., 'Habraken in Hackney', *Architects' Journal*, **154**, 15 Sept. 1971.

Frank, D., 'The greatest happiness', *Architects' Journal*, **151**, 27 May 1970.

Fry, R. M., *Fine Building*, Faber & Faber, 1944.

Glass, R., 'Higher or lower', *Architectural Review*, **114**, Dec. 1953.

Glass, R., 'Social determinants of housing design', *Official Architecture & Planning*, **28**, May 1965.

Gordon, A., 'Architects and resource conservation', *RIBA Journal*, **81**, Jan. 1974.

Greater London Council, *85 years of Housing by LCC and GLC Architects*, 1973. Subsequently published as *Home Sweet Home*, London, Academy Editions, 1976.

Habraken, N. J., *De Dragers en de Mensen*, Amsterdam: Scheltema and Holkema, 1961.

Habraken, N. J., *Supports: an alternative to mass housing*, Architectural Press, 1972.

Habraken, N. J., 'Supports responsibilities and possibilities', *Architectural Association Quarterly*, **1**, Winter 1968–69.

Hamdi, N. & Wilkinson, N., 'Public and private possibilities in housing', *Architectural Association Quarterly*, **2**, July 1970.

Hoffman, H., *One Family Housing in Groups*, Thames & Hudson, 1967.

Hook, M., 'New homes for old', *Architects' Journal*, **151**, 10 June 1970 and **152**, 1 July 1970.

Howard, E., *Garden Cities of Tomorrow*, Faber, 1945. First published as *Tomorrow: a peaceful path to real reform*, Swan Sonnenschein, 1898.

Jones, D., 'The role of the courthouse in urban renewal', *Keystone*, Summer 1961.

Jordan, R. F., 'Span', *Architectural Review*, **125**, Feb. 1959.

Kelly, B., *Prefabrication of Houses*, New York: Wiley, 1951.

Le Corbusier, *Oeuvre Complete, 1910–1965*, 7 vols, Zurich: Editions d'Architectures, 1937–65.

Le Corbusier, *Plan Voisin de Paris*, 1925.

Le Corbusier, *Une Ville Contemporaine de 3 millions d'Habitants*, 1922.

Le Corbusier, *Urbanisme*, Paris: Cres, 1925.

Le Corbusier, *Vers une Architecture*, Paris: Cres, 1923.

Le Corbusier, *Ville Radieuse*, 1933. Published in England as *The Radiant City*, Faber & Faber, 1967.

Ling, A., *Runcorn New Town Master Plan*, Runcorn Development Corporation, 1967.

Llewelyn-Davies, Weeks, Forestier-Walker & Bor, *Milton Keynes – Interim Report*, London, 1968.

Llewelyn-Davies, Weeks and Partners, *Washington New Town Master Plan & Report*, Washington (Co. Durham), Washington Development Corporation, 1966.

London County Council, *The Planning of a New Town*, 1961.

Lynch, K., 'The form of cities', *Scientific American*, **190**, Apr. 1954.

McAllister, G. & E. G., *Town and Country Planning*, Faber & Faber, 1941.

Macintosh, D., *The Modern Courtyard House*, Lund Humphries, 1971.

McCormac, R., 'Housing and the dilemma of style', *Architectural Review*, **163**, Apr. 1978.

McKean, J. M., 'Self-build housing', *Architectural Design*, **46**, Aug. 1976.

McKean, J. M., 'Walter Segal', *Architectural Design*, **46**, May 1976.

Manthorpe, W., 'The machinery of sprawl', *Architectural Review*, **120**, Dec. 1956.

March, L., 'An examination of layouts', *Built Environment*, **1**, Sept. 1972.

March, L., 'Homes beyond the fringe', *Architects' Journal*, **146**, 19 July 1967.

Marley, Mr Justice (chairman), *Report of the Departmental Committee on Garden Cities and Satellite Towns*, HMSO, 1935.

Martin, Sir L. & March, L., *Land Use and Built Form*, Cambridge Research, Apr. 1966.

Martin, Sir L. & March L., *Urban Space and Structures*, Cambridge University Press, 1972.

Mellor, T., 'The persistent suburb', *Town Planning Review*, **26**, Jan. 1955.

Miller, A., 'Radburn, its validity today: part 1', *Architect and Building News*, **2**, 13 Mar. 1969.

Miller, A., 'Radburn, its validity today: part 2', *Architect and Building News*, **2**, 27 Mar. 1969.

Miller, A., 'Radburn planning, an American experiment', *Offical Architecture and Planning*, **29**, Mar. 1966.

Miller, A. & Cook, J. A., 'Radburn estates revisited', *Architects' Journal*, **146**, 1 Nov. 1967.

Mumford, L., *Culture of Cities*, L. Hill, 1938.

Muthesius, H., *The English House*, Crosby Lockwood Staples, 1979. Translated by J. Seligman and edited by D. Sharp from the original *Das Englishe Haus*, Berlin: Wasmuth, 1904–5.

Muthesius, S., 'A Re-appraisal of late Victorian and Edwardian housing', *Architectural Review*, **166**, Aug. 1979.

Nairn, I., 'Counter attack', *Architectural Review*, **120**, Dec. 1956.

Nairn, I., 'Subtopia', *Architectural Review*, **118**, June 1955.

National Building Agency, *Generic House Plans, Two and Three Storey Houses*, London, 1965.

National Building Agency, *Metric House Shells, Two Storey Houses*, London, 1968.

National Council of Social Service, *The Size and Social Structure of a Town*, Allen & Unwin, 1943.

National Garden Cities Committee, *A National Housing Policy*, 1919.

National Playing Fields Association, *Playgrounds for Blocks of Flats*, 1952.

Osborn, F. J., *New Towns After the War*, Dent, 1942.

Osborn, F. J., Taylor, W. G., & Purdom, C. B., *New Towns After the War*, Dent, 1918.

Padovan, R., 'Housing in Southwark', *Architects' Journal*, **157**, 25 Apr. 1973.

Parker-Morris, Sir G. (chairman), *Homes for Today and Tomorrow*, HMSO, 1961.

Pawley, M., 'DoE housing awards scheme', *Architects' Journal*, **161**, 30 Apr. 1975.

Pawley, M., 'Mass Housing', *Architectural Design*, **40**, Jan. 1970.

Pepper, S., 'The people's house', *Architectural Review*, **162**, Aug. 1977.

Pepper, S. & Swenarton, M., 'Neo-Georgian maison-type', *Architectural Review*, **168**, Aug. 1980.

Perry, C. A., 'The neighbourhood unit in neighbourhood and community planning' (*Regional Survey of New York and its Environs*, vol. 7), New York, Regional Plan of New York, 1929.

Pevsner, N., 'Roehampton, LCC housing and the picturesque tradition', *Architectural Review*, **126**, July 1959.

Purdom, C. B., *The Building of Satellite Towns*, Dent, 1949.

Rabeneck, A., 'The new PSSHAK', *Architectural Design*, **45**, Oct. 1975.

Rabeneck, A., 'Two comps.', *Architectural Design*, **46**, June 1976.

Rainer, R., *Die Behausungsfrage*, Vienna: Gallus-Verlag, 1947.

Rasmussen, S. E., 'Open-plan city', *Architectural Review*, **168**, Sept. 1980.

Reith, Lord (chairman), *First Interim Report of the New Towns Committee*, Cmnd 6759, HMSO, 1946.

Reith, Lord (chairman), *Second Interim Report of the New Towns Committee*, Cmnd 6794, HMSO, 1946.

Reith, Lord (chairman), *Final Report of the New Towns Committee*, Cmnd 6878, HMSO, 1946.

Reynolds, I. & Nicholson, C., 'Living off the ground', *Architects' Journal*, **150**, 20 Aug. 1969.

Rich, P. M., 'Notes on low rise – high density housing', *Arena*, **81**, Mar. 1966.

Richards, J. M., *An Introduction to Modern Architecture*, Harmondsworth, Penguin, 1956.

Richards, J. M., 'Failure of the new towns', *Architectural Review*, **114**, July 1953.

Richards, J. M., *The Castles on the Ground*, Architectural Press, 1946.

Schaffer, F., *The New Town Story*, Paladin, 1972.

Scott, Mr Justice (chairman), *Report of the Committee on Land Utilisation in Rural Areas*, Cmnd. 6378, HMSO, 1942.

Seed, J., 'Sustainable urban structure', *Architectural Design*, **46**, Sept. 1976.

Segal, W., 'An argument for the use of the square in residential planning', *Architect and Building News*, **191**, 18 July 1947.

Segal, W., 'Changing trends in site layout', *Arena*, **81**, Mar. 1966.

Segal, W., *Home and Environment*, L. Hill, 1948.

Sert, J. L., *Can Our Cities Survive*? Cambridge, Mass.: Harvard University Press; London: Oxford University Press, 1942.

Shankland, C. G. L., 'Barbican and the Elephant', *Architectural Design*, **29**, Oct. 1959.

Sheppard, R., *Prefabrication in Building*, Architectural Press, 1946.

Simpson, D., 'Beautiful Tudor', *Architectural Review*, **162**, Aug. 1977.

Sitte, C., *Der stadte-bau nach seinen künstlerischen Grundsätzen*, Vienna: Graeser, 1889.

Skeffington, Sir A. (chairman), *People and Planning*, HMSO, 1969.

Smithson, A. (ed.), *Team 10 Primer*, MIT Press, 1960.

Smithson, A. & P., 'Golden Lane project', *Architects' Year Book*, **5**, 1953.

Smithson, A. & P., *Ordinariness and Light*, Faber & Faber, 1970.

Smithson, A. & P., 'Scatter', *Architectural Design*, **29**, Apr. 1959.

Smithson, A. & P., *Urban Structuring*, Studio Vista, 1967.

Spurrier, R., 'The architectural implications of the Buchanan Report', *Architectural Review*, **135**, May 1964.

Stein, C. S., *Towards New Towns for America*, Amsterdam: Reinhold, 1958.

Stephenson, G., 'The planning of residential areas', *RIBA Journal*, **53**, Feb. 1946.

Stephenson, G., 'The Wrexham experiment', *Town Planning Review*, **25**, Jan. 1954.

Tarn, J. N., *Working Class Housing in Nineteenth Century Britain*, Lund Humphries, 1971.

Taylor, N., *The Village in the City*, Temple Smith, 1973.

Tetlow, J. & Goss A., *Homes, Towns and Traffic*, Faber & Faber, 1965.

Thompson, R. L., *Site Planning in Practice*, Frowde and Hodder & Stoughton, 1923.

Tindale, P., 'Component development in the public sector', *Architectural Association Quarterly*, **2**, Jan. 1970.

Turin, D., 'The seamy side', *Architects' Journal*, **140**, 23 Sept. 1964.

Turner, J. F. C. & Fichter, R., *Freedom to Build*, Collier–Macmillan, 1973.

Turner, J. F. C., 'Housing the people 7: the practice of housing', *Architectural Design*, **46**, Mar. 1976.

Turner, J. F. C., 'Principles for housing', *Architectural Design*, **46**, 1976.

Tweddell, N., 'The new town village,' *Architectural Review*, **127**, Sept. 1960.

United Nations, A Report on the Human Habitat; *How Do You Want to Live?*, 1972.

Unwin, R., *Nothing Gained by Overcrowding*, P. S. King, for Garden Cities and Town Planning Association, 1912.

Unwin, R., *Town Planning in Practice*, London: T. F. Unwin, 1909.

Unwin, R., & Parker, B., *The Art of Building a Home*, Longmans, 1901.

Uthwatt, Lord Justice (chairman), *Report of the Expert Committee on Compensation and Betterment*, Cmnd 6386, HMSO, 1942.

Voelcker, J., 'What happened to CIAM', *Architectural Design*, **30**, May 1960.

Walker, M., 'Flats, their numbers, types and distribution', *Architects' Journal*, **105**, 6 Feb. 1947.

Walters, Sir J. T. (chairman), *The Provision of Dwellings for the Working Classes*, Cmnd 9191, HMSO, 1918.

Wharton, K., 'Sad storeys for children', *Architect and Building News*, **7**, 1 Oct. 1970.

White, R. B., 'Prefabrication, past, present and potential', *RIBA Journal*, **69**, Sept. 1962.

Willis, M., *Environment and the Home*, 1954.

Willis, M., *Private Balconies*, 1956.

Willmott, P. & Young, M., *Family and Class in a London Suburb*, New English Library, 1957.

Womersley, J. L., 'Some housing experiments on Radburn principles', *Town Planning Review*, **25**, Oct. 1954.

Woolley, T., 'Housing improvement', *Architectural Design*, **46**, Aug. 1976.

Woolley, T., 'Housing renewal unit', *Architectural Design*, **46**, Aug. 1976.

Official publications

(Other than those included in alphabetical list of references under name of author or of committee chairman)

Appearance of Housing Estates, The, 1948.

Better Homes, the Next Priorities, Cmnd 5339, 1973.

Circular 36/67; Housing Standards, Costs and Subsidies, 1967.

Deeplish Study, The, 1966.

Density of Residential Areas, The, 1952.

Design Bulletin, No. 6, *Space in the Home*, 1963 and 1968.

Design Bulletin, No. 7, *Housing Cost Yardsticks*, 1963.

Design Bulletin, No. 16, *Metric Dimensional Framework*, 1968.

Design Bulletin, No. 25, *The Estate Outside the Dwelling*, 1972.

Flats and Houses, 1958.

Houses 1952, Second Supplement to the *Housing Manual*, 1949, 1952.

Houses 1953, Third Supplement to the *Housing Manual*, 1949, 1953.

Houses, the Next Step, 1953.

Housing Act, 1919.

Housing Act, 1921.

Housing Act, 1949.

Housing Act, 1969.

Housing and Planning Act, 1974.

Housing (Financial and Miscellaneous Provisions) Act, 1946.

Housing Manual, 1944.

Housing Manual, 1949.

Housing (Repairs and Rents) Act, 1954.

Housing Statistics Great Britain, No. 24, February 1972.

Housing Subsidies Act, 1956.

Housing Subsidies Act, 1967.

Housing (Temporary Provisions) Act, 1944.

National Parks Act, 1948.

New Towns Act, 1946.

Old Houses into New Homes, Cmnd 3602, 1968.

Report of the Inquiry into the Collapse of Flats at Ronan Point, Canning Town, 1968.

Rents and Subsidies Act, 1975.

Roads in Urban Areas, 1966.

Town and Country Planning Act, 1947.

Widening the Choice: the next steps in housing, 1973.

BIBLIOGRAPHY

Abercrombie, Sir P., *Town and Country Planning*, Oxford University Press, 1959.

Aebeli, P., 'Eclecticism', *Architectural Review*, **166**, Oct. 1979.

Alexander, C., 'Major changes in environmental form required by social and psychological demands' in *Papers and Proceedings of the Second International Symposium on Regional Development*, Tokyo: Japan Center for Area Development Research, Sept. 1968.

Alexander, C., *A Pattern Language*, Oxford University Press, 1977.

Ashworth, W., *The Genesis of Modern British Town Planning*, Routledge & Kegan Paul, 1954.

Baillie Scott, M. H., *Houses and Gardens*, Newnes, 1906.

Black, S., *Man and Motor Cars*, Secker & Warburg, 1966.

Bowley, M., *Housing and the State, 1919–1944*, Allen & Unwin, 1945.

Brett, L., *Landscape in Distress*, Architectural Press, 1965.

Brett, L., *Parameters and Images*, Weidenfeld & Nicolson, 1970.

Broady, M., *Planning for People*, National Council for Social Services, 1971.

Buchanan, C. D., *Mixed Blessing: the motor car in Britain* L. Hill, 1958.

Burnett, J. B., *A Social History of Housing 1815–1970*, David & Charles, 1978.

Creese, W. L., *The Search for Environment*, Yale University Press, 1971.

Cullingworth, J. B., *Housing and Local Government in England and Wales*, Allen & Unwin, 1966.

Cullingworth, J. B., *Town and Country Planning in England and Wales*, Allen & Unwin, 1965.

Dale, R. W., 'The garden versus farm controversy', *Journal of the Town Planning Institute*, **40**, Dec. 1953.

Daly, J., 'The myth of quantifiability', *Architects' Journal*, **148**, 21 Aug. 1968.

Davey, P., *Arts and Crafts Architecture*, Architectural Press, 1980.

Donnison, D. V., *The Government of Housing*, Penguin Books, 1967.

Dusart, E., 'Order for change, flexibility and urban geometry', *Architectural Association Quarterly*, **1**, Oct. 1969.

Dyos, H. J., (ed.), *The Study of Urban History*, Edward Arnold, 1968.

Glass, R., 'Urban sociology', *Current Sociology*, no. 4, 1955.

Goodman, R., *After the Planners*, Penguin, 1972.

Greene, D., & Webb, M., 'Drive-in housing', *Architects' Year Book*, **12**, 1968.

Gropius, W., *The Scope of Total Architecture*, London: Allen & Unwin, 1956; New York: Harper & Row, 1955.

Hall, P., *London 2000*, Faber & Faber, 1964.

Hix, J., 'Maximum house space', *Architectural Design*, **40**, Mar. 1970.

Jacobx, J., *The Death and Life of Great American Cities*, London: Cape, 1962; New York: Random House, 1961.

Jacobs, J., 'The self generating growth of cities', *RIBA Journal*, **74**, Mar. 1967.

James, J. R., 'Residential densities and housing layout', *Town & Country Planning*, **35**, Dec. 1967.

Jones, F. M., 'A study in obsolescence', *Town Planning Review*, **38**, Oct. 1967.

Leach, E., 'A runaway world', *Reith Lectures 1967*, Oxford University Press, 1968.

Le Corbusier, *The Marseilles Block*, London: Harvill Press, 1953.

Lipman, A., 'The architectural belief system and social behaviour', *British Journal of Sociology*, **19**, 1968.

Lyall, S., *The State of British Architecture*, Architectural Press, 1980.

Lyons, E., 'New village image', *Architects' Journal*, **150**, 23 July 1969.

Madge, J., *Tomorrow's Houses*, London: Pilot Press, 1946.

March, L., 'Towards a garden of cities', *The Listener*, 21 Mar. 1968.

Medhurst, F. & Lewis, D. P., *Urban Decay*, Macmillan, 1969.

Mercer, E., *English Vernacular Houses*, (RCHM England), HMSO, 1976.

Merrett, S., *State Housing in Britain*, Routledge & Kegan Paul, 1979.

Mumford, L., *The City in History*, Secker & Warburg, 1961.

Mumford, L., 'The neighbourhood and neighbourhood unit', *Town Planning Review*, **25**, Jan. 1954.

Needleman, L., *The Economics of Housing*, London: Staples Press, 1965.

Newby, H., *Green and Pleasant Land?* Hutchinson, 1979.

Nicholson, J. H., *New Communities in Britain*, National Council of Social Service, 1961.

Noble, J., 'Appraisal of user requirements in mass housing', *Architects' Journal*, **144**, 24 Aug. 1966.

Osborn, F. J., *Green Belt Cities*, Faber & Faber.

Osborn, F. J., 'Housing density in England', *Town and Country Planning*, **22**, Dec. 1954.

Osborn, F. J. & Whittick, A., *The New Towns*, L. Hill, 1963.

Papageorgiou, A., *Continuity and Change*, Pall Mall, 1971.

Pawley, M., *Architecture Versus Housing*, Studio Vista, 1971.

Pepper, S., 'The garden city legacy', *Architectural Review*, **163**, June 1978.

Pike, A., 'Failure of industrialised building in housing programme', *Architectural Design*, **37**, Nov. 1967.

Rapoport, A., 'Designing for complexity', *Architectural Association Quarterly*, **2**, Winter 1970.

Rapoport, A., 'The personal element in housing', *RIBA Journal*, **75**, July 1968.

Rasmussen, S. E., *London, The Unique City*, Penguin Books, 1960.

Rich, P. M. (ed.), 'Housing primer – low and medium rise', *Architectural Design*, **37**, Sept. 1967.

Richards, J. M., 'Style was a dirty word', *Architectural Review*, **166**, Nov. 1979.

Ritter, P., *Planning for Man and Motor*, Pergamon, 1964.

Rodwin, L., *The British New Towns Policy*, Cambridge Mass.: Harvard University Press, 1965.

Roskill, O. W., *Housing in Britain*, a survey commissioned by the Town and Country Planning Association, 1964.

Saarinen, E., *The City; its Growth, its Decay, its Future*, New York: Reinhold, 1943.

Segal, W., 'Patio houses', *Architect and Building News*, **173**, 2 Feb. 1943.

Senior, D., 'Gardens and food production', *Town and Country Planning*, **23**, Mar. 1955.

Sennett, R., *The Uses of Disorder*, New York: Knopf, 1970.

Sharp, T., *Town Planning*, Penguin, 1940.

Sheffield Corporation, *Ten Years of Housing Policy*, Sheffield, City Architect's Department, 1962.

Sheppard, R., *Building for the People*, Allen & Unwin, 1948.

Smithson, A. & P., *Without Rhetoric – an Architectural Aesthetic, 1955–1972*, Latimer, 1973.

Stamp, G., 'The rise and fall and rise of Edwin Lutyens', *Architectural Review*, **170**, Nov. 1981.

Tetlow, J. D., 'Sources of the neighbourhood idea', *Journal of Town Planning Institute*, **46**, Apr. 1959.

Tripp, H. A., *Road Traffic and its Control*, E. Arnold, 1938.

Weaver, Sir. L., *Cottages: their planning, design and materials*, Country Life, 1926.

Williams, R., *The Country and the City*, Paladin, 1975.

Willmott, P., *The Evolution of a Community*, Routledge & Kegan Paul, 1963.

Womersley, J. L., 'Housing the motor car', *Journal of Town Planning Institute*, **48**, Oct. 1961.

INDEX

Page numbers shown in *italic* type indicate illustrations.

Aalto, A., 105
Abbey Farm, Thetford, 165–6
Abercrombie, Professor (Sir) P., 12–14, 56, 100–1, 170, 213–14
access, 18, 34–6, 38, 47, 62, 81, 85, 91–2, 109, 174, 188
  balcony, 53, 55, 70, 72, 85, 89
  central corridor, 70, 72
  deck, 79–96, 117, 121, 147
  dual, 35, 43–4
  footpath, 39
  loop, 43, 45
  road, 43
  staircase, 55, 70, 85
Ackroyden Estate, Wimbledon, 60, 64, 66, 75, 90, 126, 163
Adams, T., 5
adaptability, 144–57, 169, 174, 203, 218, 220
Adelaide Road, London, 150, 154
Adshead Ramsey and Abercrombie, 190
agriculturalists, 100
aircraft industry, 19, 129–30, 134
Aix-en-Provence CIAM, 81–3
Albertslund, Denmark, 119
Alexander, C., 169–70, 220
Alexandra Drive, Lambeth, 112
Algiers project, 79–80, 157
Allies, W., 224
All Saints, South Wimbledon, 205
Alsen Road, London, 178
Alton East, Roehampton, 64–8, 70, *65*, 120, 163, 188, 195
Alton West, Roehampton, 65–70, *67*, *82*, 90, 95, 120, 131–2, 163, 195, 225
Aluminium Bungalow, 129
Amis, S., 66
  and Howell, W., 101, 200
Amsterdam, 103, 223
Andrews Sherlock and Partners, 177
Anglo-Saxon, 229
Angrave Street, Shoreditch, 106–7, *106*, 111
Archigram, 143–4, 148
Architectural
  Association, 120
  Press, 147
  Review, 183
Architects'
  Collaborative, 112
  Journal, 177

Arcon Bungalow, 129
Ardler Development, Dundee, 109
arts and crafts, 231
Arup, O., 54
Ascot Road, London, 210, *212*
ASSIST project, Glasgow, 155
Associated Architects, 182
  and Consultants, 120, 171
'association', 84
Atelier 5, 111
Atkinson, R., 52
atrium, 105
Attlee, C., 13
autonomy, 214
Aylesbury Development, Southwark, 138–9

Backström and Reinius, 55
Baily, M., 112
balconies, 60, 63, 72, 80, 84
Baldwin Hills Village, Los Angeles, 37–8, *38*, 43
Balency system, 95, 133–4
Banner Estate, 70–1
Barbican, 75, *75*
Barlow, Sir M., 12
  report, 12–13
Barnett, Dame H., 7
Barnsbury Mews Area, London, 179–80
Barr, A. W. C., 64
Basildon, 43, 166
Bath, 207, 210, 216
bathrooms, 8, 66, 72, 104, 172
Battersea, 56
Baudouin and Lods, 51
Bauhaus, Ulm, 52, 103
Baxter Clark and Paul, 109
Bean Hill, Milton Keynes, 48, *48*, 170–6, *172–4*, 183, 195, 202
Beaver's Farm, 120–1, 134, 164
Becontree Estate, 9
Bedford Square, London, 197, *197*, *224*
Bellamy, E., 4
Bentham Road, Hackney, 65, 68, 76, 80, 89, 95, 126
Beresford, M. W., 215–16
Bergpolder flats, Rotterdam, 51
Berlin, 103–5, 228
'beton brut', 65
Bessemer Park, Spennymoor, 121

Bing, A., 35
Birmingham, 54
Bishopsfield, Harlow, 106–9, *107–8*, 114, 116, 120, 126, 163, 172, 181
Blackheath, 176
Black Road, Macclesfield, 154
blitz, 12, 51
Bloomsbury, 207, 214
Bofill, R., 224
Bor, W., 59
Bourneville, 4, 231
box-frame, 54
Boyne, D. A. C. A., 218
Bracknell, 22, 176
Bradwell Common, Milton, Keynes, 185–7, 188
Brandon Estate, 75–6, 77, 152
Brawne, M., Gold, M., Jones, E. and Simpson, P., 117
Bredsdorff, 119
Brenner, A., 103–4
Brentwood, 114, *114*
Breuer, M., 52
Broadclyst Village, 117, *118*
Bromley, 155
Brooke, Lord, 62–4
Brooklands Park, Blackheath, 70
Brookvale, Runcorn, 124–6, *124–6*, 135–6, *137*, 145, 171, 174, 176, 183
Browne, K., 111
Brussels CIAM, 104
Buchanan, C., 39, 46–8, 109
 report, 165
Buchanan, P., 158
Buckingham, J. S., 4
Burghley Road, Camden, 123
Burnham Place, Radburn, *37*
Burt committee, 17
Byker, Newcastle upon Tyne, 156–9, *157–9*, 183, 188
by-law street, 12, 84, 89, 118, 120, 180, 218, 228
 control, 101

Cadbury, G., 4
California, 112
Camberwell, 70, 81, *82*, 89–90, 143
Cambridge, 166, 176
 University, 222
Campbell, K., 66, 149–50
Canada Estate, 73–4, 87, 95, 142
Carbrain, Cumbernauld, *44*, 101
Cartlidge, T., 92
Carysfort Road, London, 148, *149*
Castle Park Hook and Partners, 180
Cedars Road, Clapham Common, 144, 164
Central Housing Advisory Committee, 18–19, 62
Chamberlain, N., 12
Chamberlin Powell and Bon, 75, 105
charitable trusts, 51

Chatham Village, Pittsburgh, 37
Chermayeff, S., 52, 112
 and Alexander, C., 112, 118
Chicago, 27
China Walk, London, 54
Christensen, E., 109
Churchill Gardens, 56, *56–7*, 59–60, 90
Church Lees and Sandy Close, Milton, Keynes, 184–8, *185*
CIAM, 51–2, 76, 79, 81–5
civic design, 142
'Civilia', 177–8
Claredale Street, Bethnal Green, 87, 142
Clarkhill, Harlow, *119*, 120–1, 123, 125–6, 134, 163, 171–2
Cleaver Square, Lambeth, *24*
Clements Lane, Haverhill, 114
cluster, 86–7
coalition government, 13
Cockaigne Housing Group, 112
Code of Practice, 63
Collerton, A., Barnett, W. and Smith N., 90–2
Collins, C. J., 112–13
Collins, H., 11
Commission of Housing and Regional Planning, 35
Committee for the Industrial and Scientific Provision of Housing, 130
community, 27, 84, 91, 114
compartmentalisation, 112
compensation, 14
competitions, 5, 27, 56, 90, 103, 104–5, 106, 109, 111, 117, 124–6, 176, 203, 213
components, 132, 134–7, 139, 145, 147–8, 154
Comprehensive Town and Country Planning Act, 9
Concrete Ltd., 134
Conniburrow, Milton Keynes, 206–7, *209–10*
conservative, 21, 176, 192
consortia, 134–5, 138
construction, 17–18, 104, 116, 121, 131, 226
convolution, 200–4
co-operative housing, 112, 146, 148, 154
Cooperative Planning Ltd., 92
Copenhagen, 109
corridor, 84, 89–90, 143, 213
cost yardsticks, 121–2, 133–5, 156, 188, 192
County of London Plan, 13, 54, 214
courtyard, 103–9, 111–14, 120–1, 196, 204, 219, 222
Covent Garden, London, *223*
Coventry, 41–2
Cowburn, W., 165, 170, 177
Cox, O., 64, 92, 117, 188, 190
Craig, 207
Crawley, 22, 166
Cricketer's Way, Andover, 124
Crickmer and Foxley, 227
Cross, C. and Dixon, J., 125–6

Gold, M. and Jones, E., 174
Crowther Steering Group, 46
cul-de-sac, 7, 23, 33–4, 36, 38–9, 42, 45, 48,
    120, 171, 174, 213
Cullen, G., 20, 22
Culot, 224
Culpin, C., 110
Cumbernauld, 30–1, 43–5, 101–3, 107, 165,
    170

Dacres Estate Lewisham, 74
Daniel Willink Plein, Amsterdam, 51
Danviksklippen, Sweden, 55
Darbourne, J., 90–1, 109, 144
    and Darke, 124–6, 135–6, 145, 171, 182–3
Darke, G. and van Assendelft, R.B., 106, 109
Darke, J. and R., 227
Dartmouth, Lady, 112
Davey, P., 204
Davis, J. M., 39
Dawson's Heights, Southwark, 95
daylighting, 72, 111
decentralisation, 10, 12–14, 23, 54, 56, 99
Deeplish Study, Rochdale, 152
de Jong, F., 148
Denby, E., 23, 52, 100, 170, 195–6
Denington, E., 152
Dennis, D., 213–16
density, 6, 8, 10, 12, 17, 19, 22–3, 29, 47–8,
    64, 72, 79, 100, 105, 118, 166, 181, 195–206
    zoning, 23, 54, 56, 100, 218
Department of the Environment, 155–6
Design Bulletins, 137
Dessau Torten, 103
dimensional, 119, 139, 153, 174, 209, 220–1
    coordination, 137, 146, 154
Dix, G. B., 214
Dixon, J., 224–5
'Dorlonco' system, 190
Dormanstown, Coatham, 190
Doorn CIAM, 83
Downs Barn, Milton Keynes, 207
Dubrovnik CIAM, 81–3, 86
Dudley, W. H. E. (Lord), 18, 59
    report, 18, 29–30, 39, 59

Eaglestone, Milton Keynes, 188, 195
Eastfields
    Mitcham, 200–3, *202–3*
    Northampton, *41*
East Grinstead, *227*
East Kilbride Development Corporation, 176
Edinburgh, 207, 210, 216
    University, 108–9
Edith Avenue, Washington, *93*
Edward 1, 214, 219
Edwardian, 224, 227–8
Edwards, T., 9
eighteenth century, 166, 195, 210, 222
Eindhoven Technical University, 147
Ellenborough, Maryport, 166

Emmanuel Road, London, 181
environmental areas, 39, 47, *47*
Erith Marshes, 94
Erskine, R., 156–7, 188
Essex County Council, 178, 188
E-type house, 103–5
Eugenia Road, 68
Europe, 102–3, 224
European Architectural Heritage Year, 182–3
Ewart Road, London, 179–80

Fairlawn, New Jersey, 35
Fawcett, C. B., 29
Fayland Estate, 70
Ferrier Estate, Kidbrook Green, 76, 95
Festival of Britain, 60, 75
Fielden and Mawson, 182
fire
    brigade, 118
    escape, 60–1
    resistance, 131
Fishermead, Milton Keynes, 206–7, *207–8*
Fitzhugh Estate, Wandsworth, 70
Five Fields, Massachusetts, 112
Flats and Houses 1958, 72
flexibility, 150–7, 174
Forestdale, Aldington, 148
Forest Estate, 70
Forshaw, J. R., 20, 59
    and Abercrombie, P., 13, 54
Fort Leith, Edinburgh, 105
Foster Associates, 48, 170–1
Fredensborg, 105
Friary Quay, Norwich, 182
Fry, M., 52, 130
Fulham, 116

Galley, J.R., 66
Galloway, D., 121
garage, 39, 41–5, 101, 109–10
    courts, 38, 44, 117, 121, 124, 165–8
garden, 4, 9, 10, 23, 56, 62, 68, 81, 101, 114,
    198–200, 224
    cities, 4–14, 18, 23, 27, 33, 35–6, 48, 51, 60,
        79, 81, 99, 104, 126, 228
    City Association, 5, 7, 8–9
    private, 35–6, 38, 42, 44, 102, 116
    suburb, 5, 9, 18, 196
Gateshead, *73*
General Improvement Area (GIA), 152
generic house plans, 137
gentrification, 153–4
George, H., 4
German Trades Union School, Bernau, 103
Gibberd, F., 60, 163
    and Partners, 182
Giedion, S., 104
Gillinson Barnett and Partners, 92, 121
Glass, R., 170, 195
Gleadless Estate, Sheffield, 72
Gloucester Road, Sheffield, 136

Golden Lane, London, 61–2, *61*, 64, 75, 83, *83–6*, 87, 90, 94, 142, 196
Good Design Awards, 176–7
Goodman, Lord, 112
Gough, P., 225–6
Gowan, J., 226
Gracie, V., 157
gradual renewal, 180, 182–3
grain, 86
Greater London Plan, 13–14, 100, 170
Great Linford, Milton Keynes, 184–8, 195
green
  belts, 13, 22, 36
  common, 105, 107, 120
  landscaped, 34
  private, 34, 42
  spaces, 38, 118
Greenbelt, Maryland, 37
Greendale, Wisconsin, 37
Greenhill-Bradway Estate, Sheffield, 41
Green Hills, Ohio, 37
Greenwood, Anthony, 149
Greenwood, Arthur, 9
Gregory-Jones, D., 196–7
grid, 31, 33, 35, 81, 118, 214–16
Gropius, W., 52, 56, 79, 104
  and Fry, 52, 68
Growing House, 103–5
Guildway Ltd., 188–91, *191–2*, 223, 225
Gulf States, 231

Habitat, Montreal, 148
Habraken, Professor J., 146–50, 154, 156, 177
Hackney, R., 154
Halton, Runcorn
  Brook, 166
  Brow, 166–8, *168*, 172, 176
  Village, 168
Ham Common, 176
Hamdi, N., Wilkinson, N. and Evans, J., 149
Hampstead, 5–9, 33, 35, 101, 200, 228–9
Harehills, Hillingdon, 154–6, *155*
Haring, H., 103–5
Harlow, 31, 43, 111
Harrison, H. P., 64
Harrison, R. L. E., 166
Hartley, Milton Keynes, 184–8, *184*
Harvard, 112
Hastings, 181
Hatfield, 22
Haward, B., 171
  Haxworth, M. and Rich, P., 117, 120
  in association with Johns Slater and Haward, 125–6
Hayes, F. O., 70, 81, 90, 95, 143
Hazelwood, Milton Keynes, 188, *189*
Heathrow Airport, 121, 134
Helsingfors, 105
Hemel Hempstead, 22, 43
Herron, R., 143–4
Higgins Ney and Partners, 116

high, 55–7, 70, 123
  building, 10, 73, 92, 95, 218
  flats, 54, 61, 64–76, 85, 87, 227
  rise, 79, 81, 99, 101, 104, 111, 123, 133, 137, 142, 152–3, 163, 177, 195
Highpoint, 52
Hilberseimer, L., 103–5, 114
Hillingdon, 188, *190*
Hillside Homes, New York, 37
Hinchingbrooke, Viscount, 14
Hollamby, E., 112
Holland, 51, 103, 147
Hook, 31, 45, 107, 170, 198–200
Horndean Close, Roehampton, 101
House of the Future, 106
Houses 1952, 21
Housing
  Action Areas, 154
  Action Kits, 155
  Act 1919, 8, 229
  (Additional Powers) Act 1919, 9
  Act 1946, 20, 64
  Act 1949, 20, 64
  Act 1954, 21, 64
  (Repairs and Rents) Act 1956, 21, 24, 64
  (Subsidies) Act 1967, 123
  Act 1969, 152, 179–80, 220
  and Planning Act 1974, 112, 146, 152–3, 191–2
  (Rents and Subsidies), Act 1975, 154
  Corporation, The, 146, 152, 154
  Development Directorate, 154
  Manual 1944, 18, 59
  Manual 1949, 18–19, 39, 41, 60, 62, 131, 165
  Renewal Unit, 180
Howard, E., 2, 4–6, 8, 12–13, 22, 27, 35, 51, 68, 72, 79, 142, 158, 169, 216, 218–19, 228
Howell, W., 66
Howitt, C. and Partners, 10–11, 230
Huddersfield Building Society, 203
Hull, 92, 134
Hyacinth Road, Roehampton, 134, 164
Hyde Park
  London, 223
  Sheffield, 89

Ideal Home
  Exhibition, 106, 149
  magazine, 111
identity, 84, 183, 206, 224
image, 95, 99, 140, 143–4, 157–9, 177–8, 182–3, 191, 225
improvement, 152–7, 179–80, 182–3, 220
industrialisation, 20, 129–40, 147–8, 154, 164, 177, 190, 226–7
industrialised building, 92, 95, 120, 124–5, 129–40, 153, 210, 219–20, 225
Italian townscape, 177–8
Isokon flats, 52

Jacob, C. E., 166

James, C. H., 52
Janet Square, Byker, 157
Jekyll, G., 224
Jencks, C., 226
Jericho, Oxford, 180
Jespersen system, 92
Jones, C., 197
Johnson-Marshall, P., 59–60

Kelly, B., 130
Kensal House, Ladbroke Grove, 52, *53*
Kiefhoek, Rotterdam, 103
Kildrum, Cumbernauld, 101
Killick, J., 66
Killingworth, Newcastle upon Tyne, 156, *156*
King Arthur's Way, Andover, 166
Kingswood Estate, Corby, 121, *122*
Krier brothers, 224
Kvarnholm, Stockholm, 51

Labour
  government, 12, 20, 21, 132
  party, 10, 13
Ladbroke Grove, London, 45, *46*, 166
Laindon 5, Basildon, 121, *123*
Laings, 92, 139
Lambeth Borough Council, 112
La Muette, Drancy, 51
Land Use and Built Form Studies, Centre for
  (LUBFS), 198–200, 209
Lane, L., 64
Lanes, The, Rotherham, 121
Lansbury, London, 60, 62, 75
Larsen-Nielsen system, 132–3, 138
Lasdun, D., 86–7, 142
Lawn, The, Harlow, 60, 163
Lawrence, D.H., 188
Le Corbusier, 2, 51–2, 57–8, 59, 63, 68, 72,
  79, 87, 126, 131, 142, 148, 157, 163, 169,
  178
Leek Street, Leeds, 92, 134
'legislative planning', 219, 223
Le Modulor, 65
Lenton Abbey Estate, Nottingham, *11*, *230*
Leppla, 103
Letchworth, 5–6, 9, 13–14, 17, 22, 28,
  213–14, 228–9
Lever, W. H., 4
Lewis, D., 68
Lewis, W., 59, 64
L-house, 103–5
lifts, 60, 64, 81, 123, 147
Lilford Road, London, 180
Lillington Street (Gardens), Pimlico, 90–2,
  94–5, 109, 120, 125–6, 134, 144, 163, 177,
  183
Linden Grove, Peckham Rye, 114–16, *115*,
  181
Lindos, Rhodes, 119
Linear patio house, 112–13, 146
Ling, A., 39, 41–2, 59, 69

Liverpool, 9
  University, 39
Llewellyn-Davies Weeks Forestier-Walker and
  Bor, 31
local authorities, 13, 20, 152, 155, 165, 226
Lock, M. and Partners, 92
Logie, G., 59
London
  City of, 61
  County Council (LCC), 9–10, 13, 20, 31,
    53, 59–60, 64–6, 87, 92, 106–7, 111, 114,
    120, 132–3, 143, 152, 163, 165–6, 197
  Greater, Council (GLC), 23, 100, 106, 114,
    120, 133, 148–9, 155, 163, 165–6, 171,
    181–2
  metropolis, 218
  Regional Planning Committee, 9
  University, 39, 100
Loughborough Road Estate, 65–6, 76, 80, 89,
  95
Lowfellside, Kendal, 182
low rise–high density, 99–126, 133, 144,
  163–5, 219
Lubetkin, B., 52, 54
Lucas, C., 66
Luftwaffe, 111
Lynch, K., 86
Lynn, J., 87, 143, 147
Lyons, E., 101, 176, 219

Maakssen Broek, Amsterdam, 148
Macmillan, H., 21–2, 131
maisonettes, 63–72, 86, 116
Majorca, 105
Malt Mill Lane, Alcester, 182
management, 112, 117, 124, 130–40, 154, 160
Manchester, 9, 54
Marley, Lord, 9–10
Marquess Road, London, 183
Martin, Professor Sir L., 66, 215–16
  and March, L., 166, 198–200, 212
Massachusetts Institute of Technology, 39
mathematical, 166
Matthew, R., 59
Mayer, H., 103–4
McCormac, R., 202–4, 223
  and Jamieson, 203–5
McKeen, J. M., 154
Mendelsohn, E., 52
Merton, London Borough of, 200–3, 219, 225
mews, 166, *167*, 188
Middle Ages, 214
middle class, 17, 29, 165, 204, 209, 229
Milton Keynes, 31, 48, 166, 170–1, 183–8,
  195, 205–10, 214, 219, 222–5
Milton Road, Haringey, 166
Ministry
  of Health, 6, 9, 13
  of Housing (and Local Government), 21, 45,
    71–2, 91–2, 95, 121, 147, 153, 176–7, 198
  of Town and Country Planning, 13–14, 39

of Works (and Buildings), 12, 129
Mitchell, Sir M. E., 54
mixed development, 59, 64–76, 79, 90, 92, 94, 99, 101, 103, 105, 111, 117, 133, 135, 142, 163, 174, 197
Model By-Laws, 72
modern movement, 51–3, 207, 226, 231
Mogelvang and Utzon, 105
Moore Park Road, Hammersmith, 117
Moorish, 119
Morris Walk, 132–4
Moscow, reply to, 81
Mumford, L., 6, 39, 196
Muthesius, H., 228–9
Muthesius, S., 221
Muuratsalo, 105

Nagel, C., 112
Napper, J. H. and Partners, 92, 121
  Errington Collerton Barnett, 166
narrow-frontage, 19, 21, 44, 64, 66, 72
Nash, 207
National
  Building Agency (NBA), 104, 112, 136–7, 147, 153
  Council of Social Service, 29, 63
  Garden Cities Committee, 8–9
  Housing and Town Planning Council, 54
  Playing Fields Association, 63–4
  Trust, 117
nationalisation, 14
Neel, E., Thomas, R., Squire, R. and Gear, A. M., 129
neighbourhood, 17, 36, 84, 94–5, 124, 213
  cluster, 31
  concept, 30, 170
  unit, 27–32
neighbourliness, 22–3
Netherfields, Milton Keynes, 172–6, *175*, 183, 195, 202
Nevill, R. (Mr Justice), 5
'new architecture', 51, 63, 89, 163, 212, 219, 225
New Ash Green, Kent, 176
New Earswick, 5, 33, 231
New Haven, Connecticut, 112
new towns, 13–14, 21–2, 29–30, 99, 102, 130, 142, 218
  Committee, 14
  Act, 17, 20, 79, 100
  Committee, 14
  Development Corporations, 14, 44
  and Ungless, W., 181
Neyland, M., 106–7, 114–16, 120, 163
Nicklin, E., 87
nineteenth century, 2, 13, 22, 23, 35, 85, 99, 101, 111, 120, 152, 166, 177, 220–1, 228
'no-fines' concrete, 131, 202, 226
'non-estate', 188, 190
Northampton, 41
North Kensington, 188

Nottingham, 92, 134, 230
Notting Hill, London, 34

Oaklands, London, 53
Ocean flats, London, 55
OPEC, 214
openness, 19, 22, 35, 79, 99, 218, 222
open space, 17, 29, 52, 61–2, 85, 107, 119, 121, 166, 198–200, 206, 228
Order in Council 1955, 64
Otterlo CIAM, 83
Oud, J. J. P., 103
overcrowding, 6, 22, 100, 195, 218
overspill, 14
Owen, R., 4

Packington Street, Islington, 92
Palace Road, London, 180
Parker, B., 28
  and Unwin, R., 5, 79, 228–9
Parker Morris, Sir G., 12
  report, 92, 117, 122, 124, 131, 137, 153, 165, 192
Parkers' Piece, Cambridge, 200
Park Hill, Sheffield, 87–92, *88*, 94–5, 111, 120–1, 126, 134, 143, 147, 163, 168, 174, 225
Parkleys, Ham Common, *102*
participation, 126, 146–60, 182–3, 190–2
Partridge, J., 66
'pattern book', 223, 225
Paulton's Square, Chelsea, *24*
Pawley, M., 177
Payne, M., 112
Pelican Yard, Camberwell, 90
Pembury Estate, London, 53
'people's detailing', 163, 188
Pepper, S., 226
Pepys Estate, Deptford, 75, *76*, 152, 163
perimeter, 35, 120, 197–216
Perry, C., 27–8, 30–2, 170
Perry, F., 105
Pershore Central Area Development, 182–3
Pevsner, N., 55, 65
Phillips West Two Building, 225
Phippen, P., 112, 145–6, 148
  Randall and Parkes, 166
Phipps Garden Apartments, New Jersey, 37
'pilotti', 59, 66
planning
  Acts, 13, 20
  'prairie', 20
  profession, 22–3
  system, 13, 152–3
Plan Voisin, 51, 80
playgrounds, 27, 39, 53, 62–3, 114, 118, 168, 170, 210
Pleasant Vale, Southampton, 92
point block, 59–61, 64, 66, 68, 70, 94, 121, 131, 133, 142
Pollards Hill, Mitcham Common, 200–5, *201*

Popham Street, Islington, 177
population, 14, 57, 195
Porchester Square, 152
Portsdown Hill, Portsmouth, 117, 125, 171
Port Sunlight, 4, 231
Powell, G., 61, 83, 90
Powell, M., 59, 64, 66
Powell, P. and Moya, H., 56, 59
precinct, 39, 61
prefabrication, 19–20, 129–40, 145, 148, 172, 188–90, 203
preservation, 182
Preston, 163
Prestonpans, 108–9, *110*, 119
privacy, 19, 38, 53, 62, 100, 102, 109, 111–12, 114
private
  developer, 20
  enterprise, 17, 21, 111, 142
  sector, 1, 20, 148, 156, 170, 177–8, 188, 219
PSSHAK, 149, *150*, 153–6

Quadrant Estate, Highbury, 70, *71*
Queensmore Road, London, 178
Queen's Park, Wrexham, 39–42, *40*

Radburn
  New Jersey, 28, *28*, 34, 39, 43, 48, 109
  planning, 41–3, 121, 166
Rainer, R., 218, 223
Rasmussen, S. E., 222
reconstruction, 12
Redditch, 176
refuse
  chutes, 63
  collection, 119
  disposal, 19, 60, 63
Regent's Park, London, 223
regulations, 23, 101, 154
rehabilitation, 152–4, 179–80
Reimersholm, Sweden, 55
Reith, Lord, 12–14, 17, 20, 29, 79, 165, 170, 188
Renaissance, 228
Reporton Road, Hammersmith, 116–17, *116–17*, 123
Research and Development Group, 92, 117, 136–7
Ricardo, H. and Lethaby, Professor W. R., 5
Richards, J. M. (Sir), 22, 23, 25, 158–9, 165–78, 183, 196
Richardson, M., 92, 134–5, 184–8, 190
Richmond, I., 87
Richmond Park, 66
Rich, P., 118, 169, 174
Robin Hood Gardens, Tower Hamlets, 95, *96*
Roche, F.L., 166
Roman Way, Andover, 181, *182*
Ronan Point, Canning Town, 76, 95, 126, 137–8
Rosenthal, H. W. in association with Evans,

E., Gailey, D. and Shalev, D., 117
Rossi, A., 224
Rowntrees, 5
Royal
  Commission, 12
  Institute of British Architects, 111, 198, 228
Runcorn, 31, *32*, 219
Ruskin, J., 4
Ruthin Road, London, 180
Ryde, The, Hatfield, 112, *113*, 145–6, 148

Safdie, M., 148
Saint Martins, Tulse Hill, 70
St Anne's Rotherham, 92, 124
St Bernard's Estate, Croydon, 111
St James's Park, London, 223
St John's Close, Mildenhall, 166
St Leonard's Hill, Windsor, 52, 68
St Mark's Road, Kensington, 224–5, *225*
St Mary's, Oldham, 92, 136
Salisbury, 216
Saltaire, 4, 231
Salt, T., 4
satellite towns, 9, 13
Scandinavia, 105, 163
Sceaux Gardens, Camberwell, 90, 95
Schlaffenberg, B., 59
science fiction, 144
'scissors block', 70, 72
Scotland, 105
Scotswood Road, Newcastle upon Tyne, 72
Scottish, 102, 218
Scott, Lord Justice, 13
Seed, J., 214–16
Segal, W., 105–6, 154, 196
segregation, 28, 32–5, 38, 45, 101–2, 107, 163–6, 170
Seidlung Halen, Bern, 111, 117, 119
self-containment, 22, 81, 214
semi-detached, 19, 20, 36, 38, 170, 178, 226
Sert, J. L., 51, 76
Setchell Road, Southwark, 181
seventeenth century, 222
Shankland, G., 59
  Cox Partnership, 188
Sharp, T., 39
Sheaf Valley, 89
Sheffield, 41, 72, 92, 134
  University, 87
'sheltered' accommodation, 114
Sherwood Estate, Nottingham, *10*
Siemensstädt, 52, 56
Silkin, L., 14
Silverwood Estate, 68
Simon, E. D. (Lord Simon of Wythenshawe), 9
Simpson, D., 231
single aspect, 103–5, 118
Sitte, C., 6, 33, 229
Skeffington, Sir A., 153
Skelmersdale, 30–1

slab, 56, 59, 66, 68, 70, 131
slum, 10, 20, 23, 51, 53–4, 75, 220
Smithson, A. and P., 83–6, 89, 94–5, 100–1,
  105–6, 142–3, 147
Smith, A. V., 87
Smith, I., 87, 143
social
  amenities, 22, 27
  aspects, 1–2, 7, 27, 57, 89, 139–40, 142, 147,
    165, 169, 182–3
  focus, 19
  intervention, 207
  studies, 23, 95, 174
Somerford Estate, Hackney, 60
South America, 150
Southgate, Runcorn, 210, *211*
South Kensington, London, 34
South Lambeth Estate, 53
Spa Green, Finsbury, 54–5
Span, 101, 176
Speculation, 10–11, 13, 101, 165, 176
Speke, 9
'spine', 94–5, 114, 117, 121, 135, 144
squares, 196–200, 213–14, 229
  garden, 101
  Georgian, 23, 100, 210, 220
  of London, 68, 195
  Victorian, 23, 100, 210
Staal, J. F., 51
Stamford Hill, London, 149–50
standardisation, 19, 140, 150
standards, 5, 8, 13, 17–18, 22, 122, 132, 150,
  156, 182, 192, 219
  amenity, 18, 153
  space, 18–19, 122, 156
Stedman, J., 121
Stein, C., 42, 47
  and Wright, H., 28–33, 35, 43
Stephen, D. and Partners, 210
Stephenson, G., 34, 39
Stern, R., 226
Stevenage, 14, 22, 43
Stirling, J., 163
  and Gowan, 163
  and Partner, 210
Stjernstedt, R., 64
Stout, R., 66
'streets in the air', 79–96, 116, 142, 157, 163,
  197–8, 218, 225
Stichting Architecten Research (SAR), 147–9
Studlands Park, Newmarket, 156
style, 177–8, 182–3, 188–90, 209, 225–6
subsidy, 21, 48, 53, 64, 123, 165
suburb, 7, 9–10, 22, 54, 56, 70, 99, 204, 207,
  228–9
suburbia, 23, 25, 48, 52, 72, 142, 158–9, 165,
  170–1, 174–6, 196, 218, 223
Sunnyside Gardens, New York, 35, *36*
'superblock', 31, 35–9, 42
Sweden, 51, 55, 66, 79, 149
Swedenborg Square, 75–6

Swinbrook Road, London, 178–9
Switzerland, 111
systems, 130–40, 154, 190–2

Talavera Lines, Aldershot, 106
Tarran Bungalow, 129
Taylor, N., 214
Taylor-Woodrow
  Anglian Ltd., 138
  Group, 197–8
Team 10, 83, 157, 163, 183
technique, 19, 129–40
technology, 68, 81, 120, 126, 144, 153, 163–5,
  170–1, 191, 212, 216, 219–20, 225, 229–30
Tecton, 52, 54
temporary house programme, 19, 129, 172
tenements, 51, 155, 218
Tetlow, J. and Goss, A., 43
Thames, 56
Thamesmead, 94–5, 121, 133–4, 136, 140,
  144, *145–6*, 164, 225
Theakston and Duell, 117
Thomas, P., 228
Thomson, W., 182
Thunström, O., 51
timber frame, 171–2, 203
Timber Research and Development
  Association (TRADA), 148, 171
Tor Gardens, Kensington, 70
town and country planning
  Act 1932, 9
  Act 1947, 9, 14
town Planning, 13–14
Town Planning Review, 190
Traffic in Towns, 46–8
transport, 7, 31, 33, 43, 99, 101, 165–6
Tripp, Sir A., 39, 47
Tudor-Walters Report, 7–8, 18, 33–4, 109
Turner, J., 150, 154, 156, 214, 219, 223

Ungless, W., 114
Uni-seco Bungalow, 129
Unité d' Habitation, 57, 59, 64, 66, 79–81, *82*,
  84, 87, 89, 94–5, 111, 126, 131, 142, 163, 168
United Nations Stockholm conference, 112
United States of America, 27, 32–3, 111–12
Unwin, R., 2, 5–7, 9, 23, 27, 33–5, 100, 126,
  171, 181, 196, 228–9
Uplands Estate, Southampton, *11*, *228*
urban
  renewal, 51, 99, 112
  structure, 144, 213–14
urbanity, 17, 23, 81, 89, 100, 111, 178, 195,
  218, 223–4
Usk Street, Bethnal Green, 86–7, 142
Uthwatt, Mr Justice, 12, 14
Utopia, 2, 66, 68, 72, 126, 146–8, 153, 169,
  171, 178, 223, 228

van der Rohe, M., 105
van Eyck, A., 216

van Tijen Brinckmann and van der Flugt, 51
Vers une Architecture, 51
Victoria, 4
Victorian, 116, 118, 224, 227–8
Vienna, 104
'vill', 29
Villa Savoie, 52
Ville Contemporaire, 51
Ville Radieuse, 79–81, *80*, 87, 94, 126, 143, 147

Walker, D., 172
Walker, M., 57
Wall, J. N., 64
Wall, The, Byker, 157–8
Walters, R., 106
Ward, B., 200
War Office, 106
Warwick Estate, Westminster, 70
Washington, Co Durham, 31, 91–2, 170
Watermeads, Merton, 205
Wates Ltd., 111, 148
Wedgewood House, London, 54
Wellbank, M., 117
Welles Coates, 52
Welsh, 205
Welwyn Garden City, 9, 13–14, 17, 22, 28, 34, *34*

Werkbundsiedlung Lainz, Austria, 103
West End of London, 222–3, *221*
West Ham, 117
Westminster City Council, 56, 90
White City, London, 53
White, R. B., 131–2, 134
Whittle, P. J., 200
wide frontage, 19, 44, 48, 171, 209
Willenhall Wood, Coventry, 42–4
Willis, M., 23
Wilson, H. (Sir), 30–1, 101
  and Womersley, 92
Wimpey, 131, 202, 226
Winchelsea, *215*, 216
Womersley, L., 41, 72, 87
Woodberry Down, London, 55, *55*
Woods, The, 207
Working class, 8, 10, 17, 18, 20, 29, 89, 204, 209
Wornum, G., 52
Woughton Green, Milton Keynes, 203
Wythenshawe, 9, 28

Yorke, F. R. S., 52
Yorkshire Development Group (YDG), 92, 134–6, *135*, 190
Young and Wilmott, 23, 100, 153, 218